D0298057

IN SEARCH OF PIRATES

To Joe

IN SEARCH OF PIRATES

A MODERN-DAY ODYSSEY IN THE SOUTH CHINA SEA

Robert Stuart

MAINSTREAM
PUBLISHING

EDINBURGH AND LONDON

Copyright © Robert Stuart, 2002
All rights reserved
The moral right of the author has been asserted

First published in Great Britain in 2002 by
MAINSTREAM PUBLISHING (EDINBURGH) LTD
7 Albany Street
Edinburgh EH1 3UG

ISBN 1 84018 569 4

No part of this book may be reproduced or transmitted in any form or by any
other means without permission in writing from the publisher, except by a
reviewer who wishes to quote brief passages in connection with a review
written for insertion in a magazine, newspaper or broadcast.

Copyright permissions cleared by author. The author has tried to trace all
copyright details but where this has not been possible and amendments are
required, the publisher will be pleased to make any necessary arrangements at
the earliest opportunity.

A catalogue record for this book is available from the British Library

Typeset in Caslon

Printed in Great Britain by
Butler & Tanner Ltd, Frome and London

– PREFACE –

THIS book is dedicated to Joe, but it is insufficient as an expression of my gratitude to him. Without his help and commitment to the story, and most of all his friendship, this book could never have been written. Not only did Joe help with my research, he also encouraged me to understand the culture and life of Indonesia. I end the book with a quote from Joe: 'Piracy is not a big story in Indonesia. It is just a way of life.' Part of my story is about coming to understand that way of life.

I began researching and writing this book with a preconceived idea of piracy – that the pirates responsible for the world's highest rate of sea piracy (in the South China Sea) were, by any other name, criminals. Over the almost three years I spent looking into the subject and visiting and living in Batam – one of the Indonesian islands most associated with piracy – I came to a very different conclusion. As Ishmael (or 'Kelin', his pirate codename) said: 'Is it a crime to wish not to be poor?' Indonesia, a potentially rich and prosperous country, is beset by endemic poverty. Ishmael, like others there, turned to piracy to escape poverty. Having witnessed that poverty, I would have done the same in his position.

– CHAPTER ONE –

BEFORE the MV *Cheung Son* (a small cargo ship) went missing in the South China Sea, the captain had reported its last position as latitude 22 degrees and 20 minutes north, longitude 118 degrees 49 minutes east. This detail, amongst others, appeared on an alert sent out by the International Maritime Bureau in Kuala Lumpur, Malaysia, when contact with the ship was suddenly lost on 16 November 1998. It had left Shanghai port several days earlier and was bound for Malaysia carrying a cargo of furnace slag.

Other details on the alert about the *Cheung Son* were largely prosaic, confined in most part to the ship's markings, colours, type, flag and provenance. More significant was the portentous paragraph: 'The vessel could have changed her name, particulars, colour and flag. The name may have been changed to *Hiti* or *Marztzmeyoy* or any other name . . .' The tone is unmistakably one of resigned acceptance that the ship had been pirated.

The alert ended on a perfunctory, plaintive note: 'Any person, port authority, customs, trades with information about the vessel are requested to urgently contact ICC-International Maritime Bureau . . .'

By the time the alert was issued, the crew of the MV *Cheung Son* were most certainly dead, their bound and weighted bodies riddled with bullets or mutilated by *parangs* and dumped in the sea.

(What follows is a fictionalised account of the hijacking by pirates of the MV *Cheung Son* in November 1998 and the brutal massacre of its twenty-three crew members.)

Three days into the *Cheung Son*'s relatively short voyage, the captain had noticed on the vessel's radar a fast-moving vessel heading in his direction. Most probably, he assumed, it was a Chinese Navy launch on routine patrol randomly selecting ships for inspection for contraband (smuggling is rife in the South China Sea). Taking up his binoculars he scanned the horizon in the direction of the blip on his radar screen. Eventually spotting it, and convinced it was indeed a Navy launch and headed in his direction, he cursed. An onboard inspection would lose him valuable time. Maybe the patrol would just circle his ship, note its registration, make routine radio contact and then move on. It was a vain hope.

As the launch approached, the captain noticed the gunner on the launch's heavy machine-gun manoeuvring the gun's barrel in the direction of his ship. A series of sharp klaxon bursts followed as the launch sped into the ship's wake and steered towards its port bow. Curious, the *Cheung Son*'s crew peered over the side, expecting at any moment an order to drop boarding ladders. But the captain was suspicious. With his binoculars now trained on the launch's crew, he noticed their motley, ill-fitting uniforms, and how they slouched, smoking cigarettes, their weapons (old AK 47s) slung casually over their shoulders. They lacked the taut official demeanour of military discipline. As for their seamanship, the way they steered the launch, banking it perilously on turns and over-revving the engine, made them appear like delinquent nautical joyriders.

Tempted as he must have been at this point to send out an urgent SOS, the captain resisted, knowing that the ship's radio and navigation systems were probably being monitored by the launch's radio operator. At the first sign of a message going out, all the ship's communications would have been shot to bits. He considered making a run for it, but this would have been equally futile, since it would have taken him over a kilometre to get up full steam, during which time the *Cheung Son* would have come under a sustained barrage of gunfire. The captain was now in no doubt that he was under attack from pirates.

As the launch drew alongside, a loudhailer blared: 'Chinese Navy customs. You are ordered to stop for boarding . . .' The captain reluctantly complied and threw the ship's engines into idle, then ordered boarding ladders to be prepared. A perilous climb followed for the twenty-three Chinese crew as they scrambled up the side of the *Cheung Son*, now listing heavily in the swell. Having delivered its boarding party, the launch then put a safe distance between itself and the ship, the launch's machine-gun all the time swivelling menacingly from side to side as the gunner covered the ship's deck.

Once on board, the charade abruptly ended when the leader of the pirates fired a withering volley over the heads of the *Cheung Son*'s crew and started shouting orders. As the frightened crew immediately prostrated themselves on the deck, small groups of pirates were detailed to search the ship. If they had appeared at first an ill-disciplined bunch, they now acted with impressive military efficiency. Courageously, the *Cheung Son*'s captain protested, only to be beaten unconscious by the pirates' leader. Screaming at the cowering crew, he warned them that any attempt at resistance would result in death. The ship was now in his control.

While the crew sat on the hot deck under guard, the ship was systematically pillaged. The captain's safe was opened and thousands of dollars were taken along with other valuables – watches, cameras, CD players, the crew's personal effects. The galley was also plundered and, much to the delight of the pirates, crates of Chinese beer and spirits were discovered.

Meanwhile, on the deck the pirates' leader spoke anxiously into a cellular phone, impatiently walking up and down. Finally stopping, he marched over to the ship's captain, recovering from his beating, though an angry gash on his head was bleeding profusely. Roughly shaking him, the pirate ordered him to give the ship's position into the phone. The captain obliged, realising what was happening – he was speaking to the pirates' 'mother' ship. This confirmed without a doubt that the ship was to be stolen. More ominously, it also confirmed the *Cheung Son*'s crew's death sentence. The pirates had boarded the ship unmasked, which meant, of course, that if they were arrested, the *Cheung Son*'s crew would be able to identify them. No amount of pleading by the captain would save him and his crew now. All he and his crew had left was the faint hope that a passing ship might recognise the *Cheung Son* and report back to the Maritime Bureau.

But that was a faint hope indeed. Once the ship was steered out of the shipping lane, it was as good as lost.

Down in the engine room, the engineers were ordered to maintain an idling speed. The captain, now back on the bridge and badly concussed, was ordered to maintain the ship's position. Only the pirates' leader was with him, and, though armed, was distracted by the horizon as he scanned it for the 'mother' ship. The captain seized his chance to tackle the pirate. Lunging at him, he grasped the pirate's rifle and both fell struggling to the floor. But at the point of almost overpowering the leader, another pirate entered and slammed the butt of his gun into the captain's back. The captain reeled over in agony. The pirate leader got to his feet unsteadily. Had it not been for the fact that he needed the captain until their support ship arrived, he would no doubt have killed him immediately.

As dusk approached, huge anvil-shaped clouds massed on the horizon. The sea and sky were transformed into the silken colours of antiquity – crimsons, mauves, salty blue. Though still very humid, the heat of the day had cooled, much to the relief of the crew, who now sat cross-legged with their hands bound on the for'ard deck. Denied food and water ever since the pirates had boarded the *Cheung Son* early that morning, they had become restless, some coughing and moaning, some with a glazed, sickly expression, the first sign of dehydration. Their captors, meanwhile, sat around talking and laughing, drinking the beer they had stolen from the galley. When their leader arrived, still shaken from his scuffle with the captain, they listened intently to what he had to say. Their support ship was due to arrive, so they should ready the *Cheung Son*'s crew in preparation for the docking. They immediately set about roughly untying the crew and getting them to their feet. Assuming they were about to be executed, some of the crew pleaded for mercy; those who tried to resist were kicked and punched.

Within minutes, the pirates' support ship arrived. A cargo ship of similar size to the *Cheung Son*, its for'ard deck was laden with netted pallets and stacked with gallon cans and other materials. The captain knew exactly what those cans contained – paint. His ship was to be 'phantomed' – repainted, re-registered, and either used to steal cargoes from unsuspecting shipping companies or sold on.

With his cellular phone to his ear, the pirates' leader barked orders at his men to get the crew ready on the bow and stern hawsers. Approaching from the stern, the support ship threw its engines into reverse to slow it for docking. A perilous manoeuvre followed as the support ship came alongside. The swell between the two ships created a vacuum that brought them into inevitable collision. The grinding and smashing of their steel hulls as the manoeuvre was completed rent the air and sent piercing vibrations through the decks of both ships.

Locked finally by the hawsers, the derricks (cranes) went into action, precariously swinging the palleted cargoes on to the *Cheung Son*'s deck. Around ten minutes later, the unloading had finished. Stacks of paint cans and brushes lay alongside provisions on the deck. Meanwhile, with a couple of sharp klaxon bursts, the support ship slew away.

Repainting a yacht or cabin cruiser can be a big enough challenge, but a cargo ship of over 16,000 tons is a different proposition altogether, especially at sea. Working off planked stages on a constantly listing hull would not only be considerably dangerous, but the mere practicalities of keeping steady large cans of paint and preventing them from falling into the sea was no mean task in itself. Despite that, the crew were set to work. And they were made to work virtually non-stop until the job was finished. Casualties would be inevitable, but the urgent imperative was to obliterate totally any of the ship's markings that might give rise to suspicions in the event that a passing ship spotted them. Those of the crew detailed to repaint the vessel's housing and funnel were the lucky ones; those on the hull would hang on for the little life they had left. With each brushstroke, they were literally painting out their lives. Hope must be a terrible thing when there isn't any. Now the *Cheung Son* had been set on a course well outside the shipping lanes, and had all but disappeared.

Harassed and threatened constantly by their captors, as well as the arduousness of the job, it must have been an unbearably harrowing experience for the crew. Fed on meagre rations with infrequent short breaks, and working in temperatures of over 30 degrees Celcius, their strength and spirits must have been quickly sapped. But they were dispensable. On one occasion, this proved horrifically true.

Deciding to take his chances with the sea rather than accept certain death at the hands of the pirates, a young Chinese boy, who had worked in the galley, leapt from his painting plank into the sea. Seeing this, the pirate guard raised the alarm by calling to his comrades. At last they had some entertainment to break the monotony of the long day. As the young boy swam through the large bow waves of the ship, watching his futile bid for freedom, those pirates that had guns prepared to fire at him, arguing at the same time how to get the maximum amount of sport from this poor, desperate boy. The first volley encircled him like a cage of lethal steel. Undeterred, the boy swam on, his lithe, even strokes barely breaking the surface. Then, with deadly accuracy, single shots followed. One hit the boy's calf, another his hand. His body lurched, his good hand reaching out beyond him, as if grasping at the sea to save him. The sea, crimson with his blood, now began to engulf him. Those he had shared his painting plank with looked on in helpless pity and horror as, finally, a fusillade of gunfire shredded the boy's now-limp body, turning it into fish-bait.

After this incident, the relations between the crew and pirates became openly contemptuous and defiant. There were frequent scuffles and beatings, threats of death, withheld rations. If they were going to die anyway, why cooperate?

The pirate leader decided to make an example of one of them. At dusk, while the crew were eating rice and water, one of them was arbitrarily selected and dragged out in front of the rest. Two of the pirates, armed with *parangs* (long knives), set about hacking him to death. The blows were vicious and painful. Trying to fend them off, the victim fell to the ground as huge, bloody welts appeared over his body. He was not dispatched humanely, but left to die slowly and agonisingly from his wounds. This exhibition of public cruelty had the intended effect. Next day, cowed and humiliated, the crew went back to their work. The delusion of the remotest hope of being saved was marginally better than being summarily butchered.

Up on the bridge in the wheelhouse, the captain noticed that the barometer was dropping. Tuning into a weather station, he learned that stormy weather was forecast. In the South China Sea, this could mean anything from a sharp squall to a typhoon. It was imperative to get the job of painting the ship completed as quickly as possible. The pirates argued among themselves about the best way to cajole the crew into working faster. Their leader came up with a solution. Addressing the crew, he promised them that if they completed the task early (there was less than a day's work left) their lives would be spared, and they would be set adrift in lifeboats. None of the crew believed him, least of all the captain. Nonetheless, promise or not, they would certainly die if they didn't cooperate. As a last resort, the pirates could abort the hijacking, call their support ship and make their escape. Reluctantly the crew agreed.

As the swell rose, those on the hull planks found themselves dangerously swinging to and fro, and from side to side. It was enough to avoid being crushed against the hull, let alone paint it. Those on the bridge were having a similarly precarious time, sloshing on the paint as best they could as they swung pendulously above the deck. Paint cans were lost, some tumbling into the sea, others spilling on to the deck. Surely the pirates must have realised that, as soon as they entered whatever port they were bound for, the harbour authorities, noticing the haphazard and unprofessional paintwork, would be immediately suspicious. In the sinister world of sea piracy, however, it was more often the case that the port authorities, in one way or another, colluded in hijackings.

With much of the paintwork completed and the storm rising, the chief pirate decided that the ship was now sufficiently disguised. In the event, the storm was little more than a sharp squall of torrential rain, which came as a great relief to the crew who had spent the greater part of each day exposed to the sun and sweltering humidity. Typical of storms in this region, this one blew over just as quickly as it had come. Then, once more the sun emerged, and the heat and humidity spiralled.

The chief pirate ordered his men to round up the crew. Would the pirates now keep their promise and free the crew? When the captain insisted they did, he was marched off to his cabin and shot dead.

Meanwhile, the crew were ordered to collect furnace slag from the hold. Confused, and with growing apprehension, they obeyed. Finally deciding that enough slag had been collected, the pirates opened bottles of beer and started drinking, tormenting the crew about what they intended to do with the slag. When the pirates' chief appeared, they conferred briefly, then put down their beers and took up their guns. The crew, hearing the bolt actions of the rifles, instinctively huddled together as if to protect themselves. Lining themselves up in a firing squad, the pirates aimed their guns at the pitiful huddle of men. Short bursts of automatic fire followed. Some of the crew gasped as if winded, others cried out, a few, instantly killed, jerked back and lay still. The massacre was over in seconds. A few desultory shots followed as the wounded and moaning were dispatched. Fourteen of the original crew lay dead. The pirates were jubilant, one of them even taking photographs of his accomplices standing proudly over the strewn, disfigured and bloody corpses. That photograph was to prove a fateful error.

Afterwards, the pirates set about binding lumps of slag to the corpses before unceremoniously throwing them overboard. The bodies, they hoped, would sink without trace. The last evidence of the atrocity – the pools of blood on the deck – was washed away with a high-pressure hose.

What subsequently happened to the *Cheung Son* is uncertain. One thing is sure, however – it never arrived at Penang, its original destination. Most probably it returned to one of the many small ports on mainland China, where other hijacked ships had eventually been tracked down.

Ten days after the massacre of the crew, several of the corpses were caught in fishermen's nets, bloated and unrecognisable. The bullet holes and cuts testified to their brutal murder. However, it seems that no official investigation into their deaths was set up. Indeed, it's not even known whether the bodies were identified and returned to their families.

Awkward questions about the *Cheung Son*'s final destination remain. If the ship was sold, why didn't the port authorities (where it docked) become suspicious when the cargo was declared, as it surely must have been? The *Cheung Son's* unprofessional paintwork must also, as mentioned before, have aroused curiosity. And what about the ship's bona fide documents? Few, if any, of the original details, specifications and logs would have corresponded with the disguised identity of the pirated ship. In fact, everything pointed to an officially sanctioned hijacking.

Three other well-documented cases of piracy – the hijacking of the *Petro Ranger*, the *Anna Sierra* and the *Tenyu* (all cargo ships), all of which ended up in Chinese ports, renamed and re-registered – clearly implicated the Chinese in sponsored piracy. But the Chinese vehemently denied any involvement, blaming these acts of piracy on rogue elements in their military, or on criminals posing as Chinese Navy personnel.

Though China is a signatory to the Rome Convention of 1988 (specifically Article 10, which obliges all signatory countries to submit piracy cases for prosecution), until the arrest of the *Cheung Son* pirates, no pirates there had been brought to trial. Astonishingly, in the notorious case of the *Petro Ranger* (nicknamed the 'big heist'), hijacked on 19 April 1998 and carrying a $3 million (US) cargo of gas, oil and kerosene, the suspected twelve Indonesian pirates were released and repatriated. All requests to the Chinese government to act more thoroughly and decisively with piracy have either been ignored or shrugged off. In December 1999, the arrest of the *Cheung Son* pirates perhaps marked a change of attitude in the Chinese government.

The arrest came about when the photographs of the massacre taken by one of the pirates mysteriously came to light after ten of the gang were persuaded to give evidence against their accomplices. Was this simply a token gesture on the part of the Chinese towards the international maritime community? Whatever the reason, at Shanwei Intermediate People's Court, thirteen of the gang were sentenced to death, while the rest received commuted jail sentences and heavy fines.

A BBC TV crew filmed the thirteen condemned pirates as they were driven in a military truck to their execution. One was drunk and laughing boastfully. Was he Jia Hongwei, who had written a vividly graphic diary account of the massacre? If he showed no feelings of remorse on the day of his execution, his diary told a different story. Here is an excerpt, published in a Hong Kong newspaper:

> I will now walk down to hell for my sin. I hope I will be understood and beg the twenty-three dead men to forgive me. Even my soul feels the sin. I will accept all the punishment inflicted on me. I have the courage to face it . . . Through witnessing the deaths, I now realise the preciousness of life. But all is too late now.

Lashed to posts on desolate wasteground, Jia Hongwei, along with his twelve comrades, was shot dead.

Even if it were true that corrupt or rogue Chinese officials were involved in piracy (and that has never been proved), there had to be someone, a middleman or syndicate, organising the pirate gangs. To attack even a modest-sized vessel, especially one under way, takes considerable skill and know-how. Fast boats are required (in the case of the *Cheung Son* a Chinese Navy launch was used); weapons, and training in their use, have to be organised; a support (or 'mother' ship) has to be acquired, as well as a crew to man it. The logistics and planning needed for a hijacking are certainly beyond the means (and probably the imaginations) of most impoverished fishermen or farmers, or petty criminals and small-time rogues, who are frequently blamed for such attacks. There had to be a 'Mr Big', a mastermind.

– CHAPTER TWO –

I had arrived in Singapore to take up a job as a supervising script editor in the English drama department at Singapore's national television station (Television Corporation of Singapore) two days before Christmas 1998. John, a colleague and TV director there, had immediately befriended me. Perhaps feeling sorry for me (I had spent Christmas Day on my own, albeit happily sunbathing beside my apartment's swimming-pool with a large whisky and thinking of a bleak British winter), he decided, before the holiday was over and we returned to work, to take me on a sightseeing tour of Singapore.

It was a Sunday afternoon when John collected me outside my apartment block on Clemenceau Avenue. While I was waiting for him, I watched an old Indian chap jay-walking across the road (jay-walking is prohibited). As he wove his way among the traffic, he threw his cigarette into the road (littering the street is an offence). Finally reaching the other side, he spat out a wad of chewing gum into the gutter (gum is forbidden). In the space of a few metres, this man had contravened three of Singapore's plethora of rules and got off scot-free (Singapore is punningly known as 'fine' city). My earlier forebodings about living in this 'authoritarian' state all but disappeared. And, if John's car was anything to go by, Singapore had a sense of humour.

'Hop in, Bob,' John called as he threw open the passenger door of his Datsun Cherry, which looked as if it had just emerged from a blistering sandstorm with the odd rock thrown in. The interior was threadbare but serviceable. He pulled off from the kerb with barely a glance at the traffic. 'So what would you like to see?' John asked. I shrugged. 'I'm your guest. Show me what there is.'

We drove off on a coastline tour of Singapore, during which John filled me in on all the gossip of my prospective job. 'So-and-so's a wanker, but he's OK. She's a careerist bitch, but [wink, wink] loves the *ang moh* [a nickname for Westerners, especially the men]. Most of the writers, with a couple of exceptions, are crap. The technicians are great, but given half a chance they would skive off for an afternoon's fishing on a *kelang* . . .' And I had come halfway round the world to hear exactly the same gossip I'd heard in the British TV industry!

Driving towards the west coast highway, I suddenly caught sight of Singapore's massive entrepôt. I was astonished by the sheer size of it, so much so that I asked John to stop the car. Covering millions of acres, it offered anchorage to something in the region of three-quarters of the world's shipping. Apart from its size there was something almost magical about it, how its miles of latticework docks fingered their way into the glistening vastness of the South China Sea, studded with hundreds of miniature-size ships. I had seen docks in other parts of the world, and been impressed by them; but this one was not just impressive, it was a spectacle. And yet for some peculiar reason, it's not in the official guides to Singapore.

We passed through Little India, a densely built-up area of old shops, bars and restaurants, and alleyways, which over the next few months was to become a favourite haunt of mine. One of my weekly treats was to go shopping there for $5 (S) shirts, followed by a Tiger beer and curry. And I was never short of conversation. Indians must be among the most genial people in the world.

As we drove on through the skyscraper financial district, John glanced at me wonderingly. In typical clipped Singalese (in John's case, larded with Americanese – he had spent several years at an American university studying English) he asked me if I wanted a woman.

'I quite fancy a beer actually,' I said, wiping the sweat from my forehead. His Datsun Cherry had no air-conditioning. 'It's the humidity, Bob. You'll get use to it,' he said, sympathetically. Then, with a broad, lascivious smile he suggested we could have both – beer and women – in Geylang. 'Ever been to Geylang?' he asked. I hadn't. 'Then you've missed something,' he laughed.

Geylang is the heart of the sex industry in Singapore, where several streets are devoted to state-run brothels. There's nothing secretive or shady or unseemly about them – the brothels, clearly identified by their red numbers, are mostly new buildings and reminded me in an odd way of a bland suburban street in England. Outside each brothel was a miniature Buddhist temple complete with lit candles and bells. Before our excursion around them we went to a small restaurant for a drink and, in John's case, something to eat (I soon discovered that the Chinese, especially the women, like to eat every hour on the hour).

When the order came, John took up his bowl of noodles, held it to his mouth, and shovelled his food in with his chopsticks. He ate ravenously and in silence. I sipped my beer and gazed round at the thronging streets and bustling traffic. Singapore, it struck me, was one large marketplace that never closed. Its approach to commerce is an obsessively driven cultural habit.

When John finished, he wiped his mouth, pushed the bowl away and started talking immediately.

'You know what, Bob? You can get anything you want in Singapore. I mean *anything*.' He picked a tooth, then added: 'So long as you've got money.'

'Much the same as anywhere else in the world, I suppose.'

'Yes, lah, but it's all much cheaper here. Hi-tech stuff, electronic gear, branded clothes, even food. Much cheaper than in Britain, eh?'

'That's true,' I conceded.

'That's because we're the copy-watch society *par excellence*. You in the West invent the wheel, then we copy it and sell it back to you at half the price and,' he grinned, 'with a tyre on it!'

'So what d'you put this entrepreneurial talent down to?' I asked.

'Simple, lah. Money. It's the only God we worship here.'

I found this a strange remark coming from someone I knew to be a devout Christian, but John had already anticipated this.

'You're probably thinking that's a heretical thing to say coming from a Christian.'

'Well . . .' I began. He leant towards me earnestly. 'You see, Bob, our take on Christianity is a bit like the Catholics – you can sin yourself to fuck here but still get absolution. Our absolution is money. Like Iago, you know, in *Othello* . . . do you know it?' I nodded. 'Well, he's driven by what he wants – power. And, as you know, he goes to any lengths to get it. Ruthless? Unconscionable? Yes, but he's true to his nature, his instincts. He's no hypocrite. And who does he harm? Only those stupid enough to let themselves get screwed.'

'You've got a point, John. But doesn't Christianity preach brotherhood, compassion, generosity to others less fortunate than yourself?' I was trying to be a touch ironic.

'Yeah, but you can't give a starving man a loaf of bread if you haven't the means to bake it.' He thought for a moment. 'You have beggars in Britain, don't you?'

'Yes, we do,' I said.

'Well, we don't.'

On the whole, I came to like and respect John very much. He was in the vanguard of the new young generation of Singaporeans – confident, educated, worldly and unstintingly self-assured. His generation was putting new springs in the old board on which Lee Kuan Yew had launched his economic miracle back in the '60s. But I sensed in his arguments, as I think he did, a crude logic that needed some refining before he could sell his ideas to me . . . He had to put tyres on them.

The first brothel we went into, like all the rest, was cool, clean and pleasantly decorated. We sat down in the viewing room, with the girls behind a large glass screen. The manager apologised for the lack of girls. There were six. If we would like to come back later, he assured us, there would be many more girls to choose from. John was content and studied the girls as if he were about to make a selection on the horses. Rather than looking miserable and indifferent, as I'd expected, the girls waved and smiled at us. 'Take me, I'll give you a good time . . . I love you . . . You're very handsome . . .' I felt amused and rather flattered. The girls were all foreign nationals – Malay, Indonesian, Thai. They had been granted short work permits for the brothels. Most of the money they earned, I gathered from John, went back to their families.

'So which one do you want, lah?' John asked. I didn't want any of them. Still unaccustomed to the heat and humidity, I felt drained of energy and – if I'm honest – of sexual appetite. But to placate John I pointed at one of the girls.

John frowned incredulously. 'No, Bob. She's too skinny.' He pointed at another girl who could politely be called voluptuous. She was just fat. 'She's good, I promise you,' John insisted. But I declined.

After the fifth brothel, John got impatient with me. 'Look, lah. The next place has my regular girl and I'll have to go with her. Maybe you'll find a girl you like there.' As we entered, as if on cue, his 'regular' stood up and called to John. His eyes widened with delight. After he'd paid his money, they both dashed off together hand-in-hand. I sat down, but was soon subjected to a hail of abuse from the girls after they failed to elicit my attention. I couldn't understand what they were saying, but I guessed they were questioning my sexual orientation. I finally got up and went outside.

Across the street was a small Buddhist temple. The gates were open and an elderly woman was arranging flowers in highly decorative china vases. As I watched her, she looked up and smiled at me. I nodded hello, and she beckoned me in. I remarked how beautiful the flowers were. She explained that she was preparing them for a funeral. Would I like some tea and something to eat? (Did I look that drained and undernourished?) I accepted her offer of tea and sat with her while she finished her flower arranging.

In the months ahead, I came to have a great affection for the Buddhists, who customarily welcomed strangers with food and drink. My local Buddhist lodge off Clemenceau Avenue became another favourite haunt, especially on weekends around lunchtime.

John finally emerged and called to me. Saying goodbye to the old lady and thanking her for the tea, I joined John. He looked concerned, and as we walked off down the street he asked: 'Can you get AIDS from oral sex?'

'You were wearing a condom, weren't you?'

John shook his head. 'No.'

'Depends on whether she had bleeding gums,' I shrugged.

'Oh, fuck,' he muttered, and hurriedly excused himself, saying that he had to get home to his family.

'Thanks for a great day, John.'

'I'll give you a lift back to your apartment.'

'Forget it, I'll catch a bus.'

John nodded, but was obviously too distracted by what I'd said about him and the girl to insist on taking me back. So he left me there in Geylang – on one side of the road a brothel, on the other a Buddhist temple.

Most mornings before going to work on the number 50 bus, I bought a newspaper (there are two main papers in Singapore, *The Straits Times* and *The New Paper*) from a small Indian-owned kiosk across the road, then sat outside a corner curry house with a coffee. I always started off early, mainly to beat the humidity and heat, and was invariably joined by groups of migrant workers who were later picked up by trucks and taken off to the many building sites. The national bird of Singapore, so the joke went, is the crane.

On one of the Home News pages of *The Straits Times* was a full spread on sea piracy, describing yet another attack on a ship in the Strait of Malacca off the coast of Malaysia. The account of the attack was brief, but the article went on to describe the enormity of piracy in the area by exhaustively listing the number of ships attacked or hijacked over the last year. Astonishingly, it seemed that on average one or more a month was being attacked. The article called this an 'outrage' and claimed that piracy in the area had now reached plague proportions. It mentioned the murderous hijacking of the MV *Cheung Son* and said this tragedy marked a new turning-point in the ruthlessness and audacity of the pirates. It called for immediate action to be taken, accusing the maritime authorities and governments in the region of complacency.

I was fascinated by the article. All I knew of piracy, like most of us I suppose, was from childhood stories and Disney films of buccaneers and pirates like the infamous Blackbeard, Captain Hook and the sinister Long John Silver. They were equivalent heroes to the Billy the Kids and Wyatt Earps of the Wild West and provided hours of play for us as kids swinging from trees, with rubber daggers and patched eyes, onto unsuspecting girls. I remember my mother sending my brother and I to a fancy dress party at a neighbour's house dressed as pirates, with real axes from the woodshed. You can imagine the parents' consternation as two little boys walked in swinging these lethal weapons.

Piracy, I had read, ended with the Golden Age back in the sixteenth century. So who were these latter-day pirates, roaming and plundering the South China Sea with apparent impunity? And why had it got so out of control?

My local pub was the New Page, just round the corner from my apartment block. On a row of classical Chinese-style coffee houses, on which a conservation order had been placed, the New Page was a favourite watering-hole for journalists and writers. I spent many evenings in the pub with a jug of beer and a basket of monkey nuts ploughing through execrable scripts for the drama series I was working on. Its dark-stained teak furniture, bare floorboards and little natural light made it slightly gloomy, but it was a wonderfully cool place to escape the heat of the day. As I walked in, Sher Lin, who worked behind the bar, was placing an opened umbrella over the till. She did this when it threatened to rain. The roof leaked badly.

I sat on a bar stool, ordered a jug of beer and cracked open some nuts. Sher Lin was in her twenties, and like most Chinese girls of her age was exquisitely slim and petite, with a beautiful oval face that made her look almost doll-like. Her perfectly groomed jet-black hair shone in the light that cascaded down from the rooftop window. I put the newspaper I'd been reading that morning on the bar. When Sher Lin brought my beer, I asked her if she knew any of the paper's journalists, possibly the one who had written the piece on piracy. I showed it to her.

She looked at it and shook her head. 'No, sorry.' She poured me a glass of beer. 'Why not phone the paper and asked to speak to the journalist?'

It seemed the obvious thing to do, except in my experience contacting journalists about their stories was usually met with immediate caginess and suspicion, probably because they imagined I was another journalist trying to steal their story.

As I glanced at the paper again, the heavens opened. Sher Lin grabbed a sweeping brush, shrugged her shoulders and waited. The rain hit the glass roof with the impact of grapeshot, and down the shaft came streams of water bouncing off the umbrella and flooding the floor. She began sweeping the puddles towards a small drain-hole, her cheeks glistening with drops of water. After a few minutes the rain stopped, but in that time I reckoned several millimetres must have fallen.

'Why don't you get the roof mended?' I asked.

'Because the manager's never here when it rains. He doesn't believe the roof leaks. One day it will catch the electrics, then the New Page will be the *Last* Page.'

She went off to serve a couple of customers who had just come in and were shaking their umbrellas. Like most pubs in Singapore, the New Page was generally dead until around 9 p.m. By midnight until closing time, around 2 a.m., it was packed.

As I was about to go, Sher Lin returned and emptied the monkey nut shells I'd carefully placed in an ashtray on the floor. In a country that prided itself on cleanliness, I found this custom puzzling.

'I have a friend, Mary Lau. She works for a news agency. She might be able to help you. D' you want me to phone her?'

I was grateful.

She tapped in Mary's number on her mobile phone and waited. When Mary answered, they chatted away frenetically in Mandarin for a good five minutes. Finally, Sher Lin handed me her phone. 'She will speak to you.'

Taking her phone, I introduced myself and told Mary I was interested in researching a story about sea piracy in the area. Could she help with any information? She said she would look through the archives at work tomorrow and see what she could come up with. We agreed to meet at eight the next evening.

Thanking Sher Lin, I finished my beer and returned to my apartment, where I settled down with another batch of agonisingly awful scripts. We were due to start filming the first episode the next day. But it wasn't long before I was staring out of my apartment window, from where I could just glimpse the sea. Out there were the thousands of islands of the Indonesian archipelago, Sumatra and Borneo. It was an irresistible romance.

– CHAPTER THREE –

I arrived on time to meet Mary, but half an hour later, when she hadn't arrived, I became impatient. An hour later, I presumed she wasn't coming. This compounded the bad day I'd already had at work. In their wisdom, the casting department in English drama at TCS had, without my knowledge, cast a number of models (not actors) for the main parts. I'd protested when I'd seen the rehearsals, but was politely overruled when I was told that it was the corporation's policy in all drama to employ 'pretty' people. It was like asking the average man in the street (me, for instance) to give a rendition of equal virtuosity to Richard Burton's *Under Milk Wood*.

As I was leaving the pub, Mary walked past me. We both looked at each other with instant recognition.

'Are you Bob?'

'You must be Mary,' I said with a relieved smile.

Regrettably I'd forgotten Singapore's unofficial time-keeping convention – 'rubber' time. If you arrange a time to meet, expect your meeting to begin an hour later. Mary didn't apologise for being late, she just looked harassed and slightly intimidated by my abruptness with her.

I bought her a drink. Mary was in her mid-twenties, dressed in a light, casual, grey suit and carrying a stylish black briefcase. For all her suavity, there was a beguiling gaucheness about her, as if she'd much prefer to be wearing jeans and a T-shirt. Fumblingly, she opened her briefcase and took out a file.

'Here's the stuff I managed to find on piracy from our archives. I've also run off some articles on piracy for you from the net.'

When I saw the quantity of information she had brought me, I felt guilty. After all, she was doing me a favour, so I apologised for my earlier abruptness.

Gently reproaching me, 'You *ang mohs*, you're all the same. You can't stop being English wherever you are in the world,' she said.

Flicking through the information, I was impressed. But did she know any journalists who could possibly help give me a lead to find a pirate gang I could interview? She wasn't sure, but said she would ask around. Then her mood changed. 'These pirate gangs, they're very dangerous. You should be careful.' The impression I gave her, I think, smacked of foolhardiness.

I tentatively invited her out to dinner to thank her for her help, but she refused. 'I'm going to visit my boyfriend tonight.' I thought the word 'visit' a bit quaint. Then she added, 'He's in Changi prison.'

'Oh,' I said, not wishing to pry.

She continued: 'He was caught with a few grams of hash. He got a six-month correctional sentence.'

That struck me as rather harsh, but, as Mary said, he could have been caned as well. And for fifteen grams he would have received an automatic death sentence. I was tempted to condemn the Singapore government, but I knew anything I said would sound sanctimonious. I commiserated and left it at that. Mary collected her briefcase and stood up to go. I thanked her, shook her hand and kissed her on the cheek. She smarted at the kiss and pulled back. A gesture of gratitude had been mistaken as an act of intimacy – a cultural *faux pas* in Chinese Singapore.

Mary agreed to keep in touch and pass on any names of journalists who might be able to help me. As she left, I went back to the bar and ordered a whisky. It would be less lonely sitting in the pub reading the information Mary had given me than going back to my apartment.

I loved listening to the BBC World Service; in fact, most nights I'd fall asleep listening to it, then wake sporadically throughout the night to catch odd, esoteric pieces on subjects like arable farming in post-Balkan war Croatia, or the mathematical history of the square root of two. One morning, while treating myself to a fry-up, I heard a short feature by David Willis, the BBC's correspondent in South-east Asia (based in Singapore), on the crisis of piracy in the South China Sea. In his breathy, declamatory tone he presented a wonderful dramatic vignette which held me spellbound. It ended, as I remember, on a suitably ominous note, speculating on the radical measures that were necessary for authorities to take before piracy reached a point where the very economy of the maritime trade in this area was jeopardised.

I phoned the BBC office later that day to see if I could contact Willis, and perhaps arrange a meeting. But I was told he was recording a piece in Vietnam and wouldn't be back in Singapore until the end of the week. All the same, they took my name and phone number and said David would be in touch. He never rang . . .

I had arranged some leave and planned to spend a few days in Malacca, on the west coast of Malaysia. My reason for going there (apart from the area being highly recommended by my boss) was that during its colonial years it had been rife with piracy. It's situated on the Malacca Strait, still one of the most dangerous areas in the world for piracy.

As I checked my bag before leaving work for the bus station, John shuffled up in his inimitable, slouching way. His mode of dress was always meticulously down-market and passé. He wore open sandals, baggy trousers and an over-sized T-shirt. When I saw him, I did a double take. John had shaved off his hair and eyebrows, and didn't seem a bit self-conscious about his new look.

'Where are you off to? Had enough, have you?' he snorted. 'Not surprising. All you *ang mohs* soon get pissed off and leave.'

'I'm going to Malacca. Just for a few days.'

Ever annoyingly dismissive, John frowned. 'Why d'you want to go there? It's a shit-hole.'

I ignored him and carried on checking my bag. He stood there staring at me.

'So what's with the shaved look, John?' I asked.

He wiped a finger across one hairless eyebrow. 'D'you think I've gone a bit too far, Bob? It was meant to be an experiment in asceticism.'

'Oh, I see.' I didn't really want to pursue it. 'Well, I think your asceticism could run to some eyebrows without compromising the experiment.'

'Yeah, perhaps.' On that note, John shuffled off in his eccentric, apparitional way to haunt someone else.

I caught a taxi to the Lavender Street Bus Terminal, from where the Malacca–Singapore express left. The bus station was a frenzy of diesel fumes, dust and people. I had half an hour to wait before my bus left, so I bought a coffee from a kiosk at the station and sat down on my bag to watch the comings and goings. Many of the long-haul buses were full of migrant workers, either arriving or returning home. Those arriving, with only a few belongings wrapped in sheets or blankets or stuffed into cheap, threadbare cases, seemed either dazed and lost, or were arguing cantankerously with their companions. Those leaving, by contrast, seemed subdued, as if the prospect of returning home filled them with gloom. Other travellers were either going to visit relatives in Malaysia, or were Westerners backpacking around S.E. Asia. 'It was only when they were on the move that Americans could feel anchored in their memories,' wrote Norman Mailer. I don't know whether there were any Americans at the bus station that day, but all the travellers I saw there had the look of carrying a memory.

My bus left on time and headed north to Johor Bahru and the border crossing into Malaysia. Half an hour later we were crossing the causeway and entering Johor. It was a relief to get out of Singapore and see some decent squalor again. And Johor Bahru had plenty of it. Singapore's almost pathological obsession with public cleanliness, admirable though it is, makes the place look homogenised. Then again, I thought, after seeing a fat grey rat appear out of a broken drain right next to my feet as I sat at a coffee bar waiting for the bus to pass through Customs, perhaps I was being unfair to Singapore.

Once I was on the main east coast route, the countryside opened up. It wasn't just landscape, but a vast territory of unsleeping, lush, predatory vegetation. The gigantic density of it astonished me – the huge palm trees beside the road, and in the endless distance hills and mountains shimmering hazily in the heat of a vast tropical sky. As I stared out of the window at this spectacle, the man sitting next to me pointed at the telegraph wires beside the road. He chuckled, 'Look, monkey!' A monkey was sitting on a telegraph wire with one hand placed against its ear, looking as if it were actually making a phone call.

Somewhere around Batu Pahat the bus parked up for a tea-and-pee stop. Across the road from the restaurant was a family-run fruit and vegetable stall. I was invited to taste whatever I wanted and finally chose a prickly red fruit, rambutan, which, I was told, was very thirst-quenching. From behind the stall two children appeared, a girl and a boy, perhaps six or seven years of age. They were dressed in T-shirts and shorts, and they clamped their hands behind their backs and wiggled their shoulders as they stared at me. They were two of the most beautiful children I had ever seen. With their mother's permission I took their photographs, gave them some ringgits (which they fingered curiously) then went back to the bus.

As the bus entered Malacca City, a fury of dust blew up as the traffic increased in volume and density and the narrow streets slowed everything down. Either a laissez-faire system, or pure mayhem – either way, the traffic was, if nothing else, entertaining. But despite the chaos, there were no clenched fists to be seen or angry exchanges to be heard between the drivers, motorcyclists, cyclists, cart-pushers, rickshaw-riders (and one skate-boarder). Their systemless traffic 'system' was, believe it or not, based on politeness, patience and tolerance. It was an exhibition of national good temper.

I collected my bag and walked to the hotel I had booked. It was on the waterfront of the Malacca River, and I expected to spend the evening with a long drink overlooking a palm-festooned river and reading Conrad. I soon discovered that the room was poky with malfunctioning air-conditioning. As for the Malacca River, it was little short of a sewer. I went back to the bus station and explained my situation to a taxi driver there. Did he know of a decent, reasonably priced hotel nearby? He did, and the Hotel Puri, an old, renovated Peranakan manor house, turned out to be a real treat. The lobby was delightful, with a cool marble floor and beautiful old cane furniture. A stone bas-relief at the bottom of the stairs was home to a family of swallows.

My room had a desk and windows that opened onto a quiet courtyard with potted tropical plants. It was idyllic. I poured myself a large whisky and laid out on the desk all the files of information on piracy which Mary had given me.

Flipping through the International Maritime Bureau's 'Piracy and Armed Robbery against Ships' report (for the period of 1 January–30 September 1998) I came across a league table of worldwide regions beset by piracy. Top of the league was S.E. Asia, with Indonesia credited with around 250 actual and attempted hijackings since 1991. And these were only the reported attacks. As for the Malacca and Singapore Straits, the numbers were fewer but still alarming. Beside the files I spread out my World Continent, S.E. Asia map to study the geography of the coastline where, it appeared, most of the attacks occurred. I traced my finger down the Malacca Strait, where the official shipping lane ran, then into the Strait of Singapore (or Phillip Strait), an extraordinarily narrow channel between the Indonesian islands of Batam and Bintan, and Singapore itself. Millions of tons of shipping were literally being funnelled into a lane no more than a few miles wide, and the coastal geography conspired to make such a bounty an irresistible temptation.

In the same report there was a list of 'narrations' of actual attacks. In one month alone (April 1998), five ships were attacked by pirates in Indonesian waters – the *Swift Tiger*, the *Kwangtung*, the *Calatagan*, the *Calabria* and the *Virgin Pearl*. The attacks seemed to be indiscriminate in terms of what was stolen: valuable engine spares, rope, paint, a life raft, etc. However, there were several common logistical features of the attacks: apart from the pirates all wearing disguises and carrying weapons, the attacks were mounted on anchored ships from fast speedboats. Furthermore, there was certainly a difference between stealing a few cans of paint and stealing an entire ship. So were there two types of piracy operating – the hit-and-run pillagers, and the rigorously planned and organised attacks that normally resulted in a ship being 'phantomed,' like the *Cheung Son*? Whatever the case, the facts made it quite apparent that piracy was now endemic in the South China Sea.

Later that evening I went for a stroll, just to get a feel for the place. The very name of Malacca (or Melaka) resonates with piracy, as does its atmosphere. In fact, its history is one of a succession of 'piratical' colonial occupations, particularly Portuguese, Dutch and British. This accounts in large part for its whimsical hybrid architecture. The warren of streets down by the river was fascinating, and that's where I got truly lost. I finally emerged on a tree-lined boulevard and spotted a small Malay–Chinese restaurant.

I sat at a table and ordered a beer. The restaurant was part of one long room, the restaurant to the front, a shop in the middle, and at the back the family's living-room, where the children played and Grandpa sat twiddling a long single whisker on his chin (a good luck charm). The mother was cooking on a stove fuelled by a large gas cylinder. She was deftly peeling tiger prawns and hurling them into a sizzling wok. As she peeled and stirred she looked over at me and, smiling, indicated that I might like a dish. I wasn't hungry, but was interested to know what she was making. It was a prawn curry. She showed me the ingredients and how to prepare the dish. At the end of this impromptu cookery lesson, I thanked her and was about to return to my table when she suggested that I look around her shop (it was stacked with packets of spices, all home-made). Leaving her wok, she gave me a tour of the shop and I finally decided to buy some of her curry powder. Not content to let me sit down, she took me through to the living-room and introduced me to her family. Grandpa patted a chair next to his and invited me to sit down. The children found the hairs on my legs fascinating. Within minutes, their mother returned with a bowl of prawn curry and rice for me, also a beer. Speaking neither Mandarin nor Malay, nonetheless I gathered that I was now their guest. There was a Malay drama on the TV, and as soon as Grandpa was satisfied that I was happy, he returned to the programme. The children, I could see, were still intrigued by my bare legs and desperately wanted to touch the hairs. I leant down and, pinching a clutch, plucked them. Momentarily alarmed, they burst into fits of giggles.

I had arrived as a stranger and within an hour had become a guest of the family. During my stay in Malacca I ate there every night.

Down at the landing-stage where pleasure boats were tied up on the
Malacca River, I asked for the Captain. 'Captain George, I think his
name is . . . or something like that.' One of the hotel staff had given
me his name, and told me that he knew everything about piracy in the
region. Apparently he ran a pleasure boat on the river. The two men
at the ticket-office stared at me vacantly. Haplessly I repeated the
request, but only got a shrug and a nod in reply. I looked around the
landing-stage and noticed a sign for the departure times of the boats.
One had recently left and wasn't due to return for an hour. Perhaps
this was the Captain's boat. I decided to come back in an hour.

I walked downriver to where a group of barges, loaded with logs,
were tied up. On one of the barges, two men were brewing tea. They
eyed me suspiciously as I lingered there looking at the boats. Their
motorised barge was completely covered with a brittle excrescence of
rust. Further on were the docks, with a couple of cranes and
warehouses that looked dilapidated and abandoned. In a weed-strewn
corner of a broken concrete courtyard I discovered an old, rusted
anchor. On its shaft, still decipherable, was the manufacturer's name
and place – London. There was no visible date, but it looked as if it
had been there for centuries. Meanwhile birds flew silently among the
exposed raftered sheds, and the heat of the day dragged itself through
the place.

Back at the landing-stage I waited for the Captain's boat. I hoped
I'd got the right man. Still, the way the hotel manager had described
him (as 'funny'), I was sure he wouldn't be too hard to spot. Within a
couple of minutes, an old blue-and-white painted boat with a canvas
sunshade over the stern deck came into view. A short klaxon burst was
followed by an imperious announcement over a megaphone. 'Ladies
and gentlemen, I hope you very much have enjoyed this afternoon's
excursion up the Malacca River, one of the finest and most historical
in all the world. The Captain bids you farewell . . .' He then coughed,
cleared his throat and began to sing, 'We'll meet again . . .' As the boat
drew up alongside the stage, I could see the passengers suppressing
giggles and laughter. Who else could this be but the Captain?

I waited for the tourists to disembark, paid my fare and then
stepped gingerly onto the boat. The engine clunked idly and smoke

popped from the short funnel. The Captain, perhaps in his sixties, sat motionless in his cabin, hands on the wheel, a pipe sticking straight out of his mouth. He wore one of those white rope-and-anchor caps, the sort you find in seaside gift shops. His blue short-sleeved shirt was neatly pressed but faded. Pensive but concentrated, his expression reminded me of an old schoolmaster's. When the last passenger had taken his place, the Captain tapped his microphone, took the pipe from his mouth and introduced himself: 'This is your Captain speaking, who welcomes you all aboard. Good afternoon, ladies and gentlemen.' Upon which he gently revved the engine and signalled to the men on the landing-stage to cast off. 'You are about to embark, ladies and gentlemen, on one of the great river journeys of the world.' Then, with theatrical aplomb, 'The *magnificent* Malacca River . . .' The river was barely moving for pollution. It had an evil, sluggish, febrile look that reminded me of old engine oil edged with rind and boiling with mosquitoes. Several of the riverfront buildings (disused warehouses, I presumed) were inhabited. Lines of freshly washed clothes hung precariously over the river.

' . . . River of the great sultanates, of the Babas and the Nyonyas, of Portuguese and Dutch traders . . . and of the Great British Empire . . . Margaret Thatcher!' The passengers burst into stifled laughter at this, unsure whether to take the Captain seriously. 'The unrivalled Malacca River, the artery and life's blood of this grandiloquent city . . .' His floridly modulated voice, I reckoned, could hyperbolise the eviscerated gizzards of a chewed rat. Even the river seemed to wince at his paean to it. On the outskirts of the town, a small riverside *kampong* came into view. The houses were simple planked bungalows, each with neat picket-fenced gardens. Their pastel paintwork had bleached in the sun. Mothers and children sat on the porches surrounded by potted flowers, pet cats and dogs. 'A traditional Malay village,' piped up the Captain. 'Sweet Auburn! Loveliest village of the plain.' For once his ostentatious rhetoric had got it just about right.

Slowing down the engine, the Captain tapped the microphone, blew into it and announced: 'Tea time!' Upon which, he produced a small urn circa the 1950s. The china cups could be dated around the same period. We dutifully lined up to be served. The tea was made with sweet, concentrated Carnation milk. Seeing some of the passengers' lips pucker at the taste, I tipped mine discreetly over the side and was relieved that he didn't produce any cucumber sandwiches.

Since no one asked for another cup, the Captain – looking a little miffed – went back into his cabin and started to turn the boat around. We all leant back and silently took in the progressive squalor of the river as we returned. Scurrying along the mud-spattered stones on the waterside were the largest rats I'd ever seen in my life. I had initially mistaken them for beavers!

Back at the landing-stage, to show his appreciation of us, he burst into a less than virtuoso rendition of 'Ol' Man River'. Self-conscious applause followed as the passengers lined up to disembark. As the Captain lit his pipe and waited for his next passengers, I knocked at his cabin door. He opened it.

'Are you Captain George?'

He looked momentarily perplexed. 'Yes, I'm the Captain.'

I explained that I had been given his name as someone who knew about piracy, and that I was researching the subject for a book.

'Ah, piracy,' he exclaimed. 'Older than whoredom!'

I arranged to meet him later that afternoon after his last excursion. 'We will have tea together,' he smiled.

We met at a tea-room in the old quarter, just a few doors down from my hotel. The tea-room was a throw-back to the past, a hallowed museum-piece of colonial lifestyle. Spacious and quiet, it was palpably genteel with its snowy-white linen tablecloths and napkins, and fine cutlery. Overhead, antique fans whirred and clunked. Large porcelain figures stood on plinths in the corners – sultanates, pageboys, tigers. Shafts of mellow light turned the room sepia.

The Captain had served with the British Army as a batman during the Communist insurgence in the '50s. He had gone to Britain during a particularly harsh winter and returned almost immediately. After a series of local government jobs, he gave up work and bought his boat.

'I love the British,' the Captain said as he sipped his tea with his little finger extended. It was a sadly pathetic mannerism, one that would have been scoffed at in the Britain he so venerated. The

Captain asked for hot water for the teapot. As the obliging waiter went off to the kitchen, I reminded him of what we were here to discuss.

'Yes. Piracy.' He placed his hands together on the table and assumed a professorial earnestness. I felt a lecture coming on. 'If the Golden Age of Western piracy ended in the sixteenth century,' he declaimed, 'here in S.E. Asia, especially in China, piracy's most prosperous time was during the eighteenth and nineteenth centuries.' The waiter returned, placed the hot-water jug on the table, and smiled deferentially at the Captain.

'Is everything satisfactory?' the waiter asked. The Captain nodded brusquely, slightly annoyed by the interruption. The waiter hesitated and I caught his eye. He seemed impatient to ask me something. 'You are English?' I nodded and smiled. 'Where from?' I told him Manchester. '*Manchester United*!' he exclaimed exultantly, and threw his arms in the air.

Taking no notice of him, the Captain continued. 'The pirates formed a confederation to consolidate their power, organising themselves into combined fleets. At one point, they even took control of the opium trade by exacting protection money. The British tried to defeat them, but failed. Compromise was the only answer. The pirates were offered high-ranking positions in the Chinese Navy. But,' he added, 'that was not before their greatest military triumph . . .' Here he gathered his breath, and I could see he was imagining himself as one of the Kwangtung pirates. 'The invasion of the Pearl River.' I was putting all this down in my notebook, more out of politeness than interest. 'They were now, in a word, invincible. Do you know, they even negotiated with the Portuguese on ownership of territory they had captured?' I looked up from my writing.

'So they had become a significant political force?' I said.

'Yes, so much so that the authorities, under pressure from the British and Portuguese I dare say, had to offer them amnesty and reward. That happened in 1810, when around 10,000 pirates surrendered. From that date, effectively, piracy in the South China Sea came to an end.'

Appearing satisfied that he had given me a condensed but

authoritative account of piracy in the region, he poured us both more tea.

'But piracy still flourishes in the South China Sea,' I remarked, as the Captain dabbed his chin with a napkin. 'Thousands of tons of shipping and cargo go missing every year here. In fact, S.E. Asia has the worst record for piracy in the world. The Malacca Strait is a haunt for pirates.'

'Yes, but they are just petty criminals, banditti,' he said, quickly dismissing them. But did he know who they were, how they were organised? He shrugged his shoulders. 'I do not know.' He looked at his watch, and I could see he was keen to leave. As he stood up, he leant towards me. 'Be careful who you talk to; these men you are interested in are dangerous.' It was a warning I was to be given many times.

I thanked the Captain and shook his hand. 'My pleasure,' he smiled. Stiffening his back, he put his cap on and, waving behind himself to the waiter, left. This was the waiter's opportunity. He came over and excitedly reeled off all the names of the Manchester United team. Could I send him a shirt and Beckham's autograph? I was asked this so many times while in S.E. Asia that I eventually told everyone I lived in some unpronounceable, godforsaken village in Wales.

On my way back to the hotel, I stopped at one of the many antique shops in the area. Malacca is famous for its antiques, many of them coming from old shipwrecks. One that took my fancy was a clock shop. It was full of melodious chimes and tickings of every rhythm. The owner, a small, genial man, was immersed in a pile of clock parts. There were timepieces from every part of the world. One that particularly caught my eye had been made in Indonesia, a small mantelpiece clock with a delicately painted fishing scene on its face. 'You must have a great deal of patience,' I said to the owner, who was persevering with a couple of fine springs and wheels. 'I have plenty of time on my hands,' he grinned.

The Malacca Strait is around 500 miles long and is the main seaway connecting the Indian Ocean and the South China Sea. Varying in width from 11 to 200 miles, it's a treacherous passage. Shifting shoal banks and fierce currents, as well as the vicissitudes of the weather, have historically made this route a graveyard for ships (and, of course, a boon for Malacca's antiques trade). 'These conditions require the full attention of a vessel's crew, and the length of the transit is taxing and stressful. This is what makes it a prime feeding ground for attackers' (*Dockwalk.com 18/01/01*). In the year 2000, there were thirteen reported cases of attacks in the Strait. In every case (apart from those who were repelled) the pirates used high-speed boats, attacked the ship (usually at night) from the stern using grappling irons or ropes, and stole cash from the ships' safes and the crews' personal property. Significantly, however, none of these attacks was an attempted hijacking of the ship itself. These seemed largely to take place in Indonesian waters, where there was more suitable anchorage. It was an obvious difference between the two types of piracy – the small-time raiders (or banditti, as the Captain had called them), who seized their opportunities where they could, and the highly organised Mafia-style theft of ships and cargo.

This difference, it seemed to me, should surely have made it easier for the ship-owners and maritime authorities to decide on effective measures for dealing with piracy. But that seemed not to be the case, if the steadily increasing rise in both types of piracy was anything to go by. In recent times, the Malay Navy, after an embarrassing rash of attacks, began intensive patrols of the Malacca Strait shipping lane, after which piracy attacks significantly decreased. Yet for reasons of cost and manpower, these patrols had not been kept up. Consequently piracy had resumed at the same levels as before, with the ship-owners and maritime authorities now claiming that piracy had reached a crisis. If the countries affected (principally Malaysia and Indonesia, also Singapore) combined their efforts and resources with the assistance of the ship-owners and maritime agencies, and perhaps with international help, a highly effective anti-piracy unit could be established. Was there sheer complacency, or – as some had sinisterly suggested – collusion between the pirates and the authorities?

I decided to explore part of the Malacca Strait the following day. I needed to see it, and to come to some understanding, if only imaginatively, as to why piracy occurred there.

– CHAPTER FOUR –

A few doors down from the clock shop I'd visited the previous day was a bike hire shop. Most of the bikes could properly claim classic status. There wasn't a modern mountain bike amongst them. Despite that, at ten ringgits for a day's hire, they were a bargain. The one I chose looked as if it had been specially designed for those suffering from bad posture or low moral virtue. It was stiffly upright, and had to be pedalled (perhaps because of the buckled front wheel) with legs tight together. For the first few miles I rode it gingerly, half-expecting it to give up the ghost it was halfway to becoming.

In the event I needn't have worried too much about its age and condition. As I rode north out of the town along Jalan Tengkera, the busy coastal road that heads towards Port Dickson, just about everything else on the road that morning was an exhibit of equal decrepitude. I'd hit the morning rush hour, but in contrast to the manic driving we get in Britain at this time, everyone seemed extraordinarily good-tempered. Even a policeman waved to me. Eventually turning off the road towards the shoreline, I arrived at the outskirts of a modern housing estate, many of the houses as yet only half-built. Mostly breeze-block and concrete shells, they looked like an abandoned project. Even the road already in need of resurfacing. In a row of shops I came across (apparently part of an unfinished shopping centre), there was a small and largely empty restaurant. I stopped for breakfast.

A local fisherman was at the counter with a fresh catch of fish. He seemed to be haggling with the owner over the price and quantity. Finally agreeing, they shook hands and money was exchanged. With a half-pint glass of tea, the fisherman sat down at a table. His vest and shorts were stained with engine oil where he'd wiped his hands. His lean face, darker than the restaurant owner's, was leathery and weather-beaten. Lighting a cigarette, he gazed across the room with an abstracted, intent look – the result of staring at water for too long. Knowing the sea as intimately as he must have done, perhaps at night he took off with some fellow-fishermen in a skiff to attack a passing ship. Instead of nets, the boat would be laden with ropes, grappling irons, knives and masks. Manoeuvring at the stern of their victim, they would get in close enough to throw a rope or grappling iron, then shin up onto the deck and attack the crew. Believable? Yet this was the modus operandi described in so many articles I'd read on piracy.

Anyone who has seen a large cargo or container vessel at sea knows how high it can stand out of the water. It would take a Herculean effort to throw a rope onto its deck, let alone a heavy grappling iron. And under full steam, a ship can throw up a massive and turbulent wake, certainly enough either to overturn a small boat or at the very least to make it extremely uncomfortable for its crew. More convincing was that the pirates already had a contact onboard the ship, a crewman on their payroll. Not only would he help them to climb on board (perhaps by throwing a line down to them), he would be familiar with and knowledgeable about the ship – the number of crew, where the safe was located, where the crew's quarters were and, most important of all, how to make their attack a complete surprise before an SOS could be sent out, or some deterrent action taken.

Finishing his tea, and after a brief chat with the restaurant owner, the fisherman left. Climbing on his two-stroke Honda, on the back of which there was a large box with a couple of fishtails sticking out, he sped off. I thought of following him and finding out where he lived, and perhaps talking to him about what he might have heard, or even knew, about piracy in the Malacca Strait. My research methods have always been naïvely optimistic. In any case, my bike wasn't up to the chase.

I rode off in the direction of the sea along a cracked metalled road that finally became a dust track. Either side, the land seemed to be under reclamation. There were what looked like drainage ditches, but had latterly become useful refuse tips for abandoned car and bike parts, domestic rubbish, Coke cans and plastic water bottles. Here and there, brackish pools of stagnant water seethed with mosquitoes.

The dust track eventually led to a large *kampong*, one of the most delightful I'd seen so far. Its main thoroughfare was no more than a path along which kids raced their motorbikes with a kind of delinquent abandon. No one seemed to mind them. On the verandas of the stilted houses (traditionally the formal entertaining area), families sat passing the day chatting, playing, laughing. Washing hung on lines, and lean dogs scratched and sniffed themselves, while the thinnest cats I'd ever seen peered up expectantly outside the *dapur* (the cooking and eating area) at the rear of the houses. Compared to the soulless, concrete 'community' I'd just left, this place had life. Did these people aspire to doorbells, glass windows, locked doors, a garage? Did they just want to be left alone, however subsistent and frugal their living standards? Or was I, the *ang moh*, just being patronisingly sentimental?

At a small kiosk shop that had a few rickety old tables and chairs outside, I stopped for a drink. I supposed I wouldn't be able to buy a beer, but I was mistaken. Approaching me rather tentatively at first, but then recognising me as English, a young boy gleefully gestured with a mischievous smile that I'd like a beer. I nodded, upon which he disappeared round the back of his shop and just as quickly returned with a couple of cans of lager. Fresh out of an icebox, they were deliciously chilled. 'English?' he enquired. 'Yes,' I said, thirstily slugging back the beer. He grinned and mimed my drinking with comic exaggeration. Perhaps he was thinking, 'Ah, you English – all a bunch of lager louts! And so hilariously funny when you get drunk.' Then came the predictable football roll-call – this time not of players, but of English teams. After a tedious but impressive litany of names, he jubilantly exclaimed: 'Bradford City!'

The coastline was disappointing. I reached it along a muddy track that led through a scabrous mangrove swamp to a couple of dilapidated fishing huts, with several fishing skiffs moored alongside. The emerald-green sea I had expected was muddied and opaque with an oily sluggishness to it. There seemed to be no tide at all; instead the sea just leaked listlessly backwards and forwards on the beach. I was astonished at how large the Strait was. Somehow I had imagined it to be smaller, a sea-passage between the mainland and an archipelago of beautiful, wild islands. There was one island, about two or three miles out, but otherwise it was all flat, desolate sea. I could just identify a few ships on the horizon, glinting in the hot sun. Inside one of the fishing huts was an array of nets, rope, drums of dirty engine oil, a Primus stove on a table with tin mugs. The only window looked out towards the Strait. I inspected the skiffs that leant on their sides in the muddy sand. Their tilted engines were old and salt-scoured, much of the paintwork having peeled away. The boats themselves were about ten to fifteen feet long with a beam of about three feet, and were wooden. I couldn't believe they were suitable, unless in very skilled hands, for sailing far out at sea, let alone attacking a cargo ship.

Further up the coast was another fishing station with a couple of fishermen repairing a boat. The clunk of a blade against wood echoed across the bay. I picked up my bike and cycled towards them, the track now no more than a rutted footpath edged on both sides with high, dense grass. I had been warned about venomous snakes that lurked in this kind of undergrowth – the spitting cobra in particular – so I pedalled as fast as I could, hoping that the buckled wheel wouldn't seize. I had recently heard an alarming story about a family who, having gone on a picnic, were sitting under a tree when a large python appeared from its branches showing a very keen interest in the baby. The mother screamed and snatched the baby to safety while the father, brandishing a stick, beat the snake to death.

The fishermen looked up surprised as I arrived on my bike. Smiling, I waved to them. 'Hello.' They regarded me with suspicion, the one with the *parang* holding it tightly, while the other glanced nervously at his friend. The boat they were working on had various planks missing from its hull, to be replaced by the set of new ones they were crafting. Another boat, serviceable by the look of it, lay with its bows in the water. With a series of gestures I asked them if they could take me out to the island I had spotted earlier. I wanted the experience of riding in one of these boats out at sea, just to judge for myself their seaworthiness and whether they could actually be used for attacking a ship. The fisherman with the *parang* shook his head, and cast his arm in a shallow arc across the bay. Pointing out to the island, again he shook his head. 'No.' I understood what he was saying; the boat was only suitable for inshore fishing. My hunch was right. I took out a packet of Marlboro Lights and offered them a cigarette. Once lit-up, they seemed more relaxed with me, and in exchange for the packet of cigarettes they gave me a dried squid wrapped in an oily piece of sacking. I thanked them, pretending it would make a delicious meal. Squid, however prepared and cooked, has the consistency and tastelessness of soft rubber, and I immediately threw it away once I was out of their sight.

A short time later, the path I was on merged with a track that led through a glade of stunted palms down to a beach. I got off my bike and decided to walk. Out to sea, the Strait was as wide and featureless as before, but at least here the beach was sandy and the sea looked fresher. Along the beach mammoth lumps of timber lay in gnarled abstract forms, perched on by mewing gulls. Before long other less attractive things came into sight: large pieces of Styrofoam, frayed lengths of rope the width of my wrist, battered cans of soft drinks, plastic oil cans and the ubiquitous wads of tar. Much of this rubbish had come from the ships. It was a beachcomber's paradise and a conservationist's nightmare. Then I came across a few unwrapped packets of cigarettes of a generic brand. As I trudged on, more packets came into view, scattered over a wide area of the beach. There were cartons too, still in their wrappers. Altogether there must have been thousands of cigarettes. It must have been a smuggling operation that had gone wrong: either the ship had been intercepted by a passing Malaysian Navy customs boat, or the waterproof container in which the cigarettes had been sunk – and which was to be collected later – had broken from its mooring and split open.

There were ships on the horizon, perhaps five or more miles out, large cargo vessels heading south to where the Strait narrowed around the approach to Singapore and the South China Sea. These ships were the 'glittering conveyor belt of prizes' – a phrase used by a maritime investigator who had written an unusually controversial article on the reasons, as he saw it, for the high rate of piracy in this region. The essence of his argument was an economic one. Whereas the ships carried the rich consumables of the West, here on the land – along the coasts of Malaysia, Indonesia, Thailand and the Philippines – the people were poor. It was a universal equation: poverty results inevitably in crime; in this case, the Third World's envy of the industrialised nations' wealth and prosperity. Though crudely simplistic, his argument nonetheless had the merit of honesty. Effectively, he was saying: 'Flaunt your wealth in front of the poor by all means, but then don't complain if you become a victim of theft.' Good plain advice that no doubt would get wholehearted approval from the anti-capitalist movement, it was also clearly disingenuous. Who were these 'poor'? The fishermen, perhaps, whom I'd encountered earlier? The folk in the *kampong*? The kids I'd seen playing football on some rough ground outside Malacca? Were they so stricken with envy of the industrialised nations' affluence that they were all potential pirates? The only reason I could have imagined some of them becoming envious was if I'd been flaunting myself in a Man U. shirt. Their so-called 'poverty' was a relative measure of living standards, and who are we to so arrogantly suggest that the 'Third World' envies our standards of living? In any case, I wasn't at all convinced that piracy in the Malacca Strait was being carried out by rogue groups of amateurs – fishermen (or whoever) by day, pirates by night. The Strait was an awesome waterway, and if it demanded considerable seamanship from the crews of the vessels that sailed it, what would it be like for a gang of pirates in a small boat, however determined? These pirates, whoever they were, were well organised and professional.

I made my way slowly back along the beach, stopping now and again to pick up odd bits of half-buried flotsam, driftwood, pearl shells, rusted parts of ships. Over the palms that edged the beach large cumulus clouds stood hugely in the sky, turning pastel blue and crimson as late afternoon approached. The air and sea seemed as infinitely big as the sky, and the beach was my own. There is an irresistible romance about the tropics, a kind of natural lawlessness so suited to the imagination of piratical stories and swashbuckling adventures. In an abandoned, swaggering moment I dreamed of such adventures . . .

That evening, instead of going to 'Auntie's' restaurant, I went to a café in a back street near my hotel. It was quiet, very local, with the simplest food – and served the best black coffee that I'd ever tasted at five in the morning. I had some further reading to do, and it was the perfect place. Old men sat in corners sipping tea and talking, while others sat alone glumly smoking and thinking. The tables were Formica and the chairs plastic. On the wall hung faded and badly framed photographic prints of Malacca, film stars (Marilyn Monroe and James Dean) and portraits of (I assumed) the owner's family. Cigarette smoke and cooking smells filled the air. There was no air-conditioning, just the breeze and fumes from passing traffic. Throughout the evening, occasional deliveries of vegetables were made by harassed and tired farmers. They welcomed the opportunity for a break and joined friends for tea and gossip.

A particularly vicious act of piracy and one that convinced me that attacks were not being carried out by local people happened on 27 September 1998. A fisherman with his two children was fishing off Pulau Bohayan, Sabah, in East Malaysia. As the father was casting his net and his children were packing the caught fish into sacks, a fast launch approached them. The father was curious because he didn't recognise the boat, or the two men in it. As the launch came alongside, the fisherman drew in his net. One of the men in the launch demanded the fisherman's engine, but the fisherman refused. He grew angry and repeated his demand. Again the fisherman refused. The confrontation got nastier until, infuriated by the fisherman's continued refusal, one of the men drew an automatic rifle from the bottom of the launch and fired point-blank at the fisherman. He died instantly. His two children, fearing for their own lives, leapt into the sea and swam ashore. The pirates seized the engine, then attacked and robbed another group of fishermen in the area. The children raised the alarm in their village and soon a Malaysian Navy launch was on the scene. Spotting the pirates, the Navy gave chase but (as the report states), 'the pirates managed to escape into international waters and disappeared in a neighbouring country'.

The launch used by the pirates was obviously fast and seaworthy enough not only to outrun the Navy launch but also to take the chase far out to sea. Also, they knew where to take refuge undetected. And they had a high-powered, automatic gun. Such a launch and equipment were surely well out of the reach of ordinary local people. This was undoubtedly an organised gang. But what was truly puzzling was the Malaysian Navy's action – or inaction. Knowing as they must have done that the pirates were armed, they surely could have fired on them. Moreover, given that a clear act of piracy had taken place (not to say murder), the Navy had a legal right to pursue the pirates in international waters. Obviously reticent to do so in this case – for whatever reason – their option would have been to contact the Piracy Reporting Centre, or indeed alert the Thai Navy. Yet the pirates made an easy escape – too easy an escape, perhaps. Were suspicions of general collusion between the military and pirates justified? I was beginning to have my own suspicions . . .

Returning to my hotel, I was astonished to find that the street had been almost entirely sealed off with red and white tape. I immediately recognised the vans and trucks that lined it as film-crew vehicles. As soon as I lifted the tape, a young assistant director sprang to his feet and, waving his hand, brusquely told me there was no access. 'But that's my hotel over there,' I protested. Finally relenting, he let me through on the condition that I didn't hang around. 'Sean Connery's due on set any moment,' he said in a tone of camp reverence. 'The film's called *Entrapment*.' I wanted to say, 'I don't give a fuck. I came here to get away from the industry . . .', but instead I obliged him with a smile. I returned the bike to the shop and politely pointed out the buckled wheel. The owner shrugged indifferently as if to say, 'What d'you expect for ten ringgits – a limousine?' At which point, a limousine drove up and the legendary 007 stepped out.

Next morning, I checked out of the hotel and walked to the bus station down by the river. At the booking office I was told that the bus was going to be late; it had apparently had been involved in an accident. I heard later that a couple of male monkeys had got into a fight on the main road into Malacca and the bus had swerved to avoid them and hit a tree. So to kill time, I went and had coffee at a café on the square and decided to read up on the town from my *Periplus* Travel Map – one of the best maps I have ever bought. As well as being very clear, it has a superb résumé of the sights of Malacca, not just the usual tourist information, but anecdotal pieces like the mention of the cobbler Wah Aik (I'd visited his shop), who made exquisite replica miniature shoes for binding Chinese women's feet. He told me that the (barbaric) tradition was still practised in some parts of China today. Or the Chee Mansion (on the same street as my hotel), which boasted an eccentric mixture of Dutch, Portuguese, Chinese and English styles and was still inhabited by descendants of the Chinese merchant who had it built in 1919. I met one of the descendants. One place I regretted not having visited was the Proclamation of Independence Memorial, an onion-domed old drinking club where Somerset Maugham had been inspired to write *Footprints in the Jungle*.

By the time I'd read through the highlights of Malacca's history and drunk my coffee, the bus had turned up announcing its arrival with a series of fearsome blasts on its horn. The driver got out and inspected the front of his bus, then dusted it down where it had collected some stray palm leaves.

The return journey to Johor and Singapore was uneventful, apart from the startling scenery and the people along the way. Though, Malaysians might be thought of elsewhere as 'Third World' or 'developing', they seemed the happiest and most contented of people.

My reason for visiting Malaysia was principally to see the Strait of Malacca, one of the most pirate-haunted waterways in the world. I had gone there with the imaginative preconception that the coastline was infested with pirates, a hostile and dangerous place where snooping foreigners like myself went at their peril. And I had fully expected to stumble on a gang of pirates, masked and gun-toting men roaming the coastline on their junks looking out for an unsuspecting ship.

It was a preconception shared just as imaginatively by the world press. In some of the most respected British newspapers and journals, I had come across photographs of such men in taunting poses, like terrorists at a secret press conference. But those photographs were fakes, all popularising the myth of piracy in that old folksy romantic tradition of the outlaw, bandit and revolutionary. What effectively gave the lie to these photographs was the copy: nothing of it revealed anything truly significant about how the pirates operated, how they were organised or who their sponsors were. And you would have thought that with such graphic photographs, the copy would have been as revealing.

The pirates I was searching for would be as elusive as their myth would be tortuous to unravel.

– CHAPTER FIVE –

I arrived back in Singapore to a flurry of calls on my voice-mail, mostly from work, all anxiously querying something about one or another episode of the drama series. *Dreamers* was fast becoming an unmitigated disaster. The concept was interesting – it was the critical choices we all have to make in our lives, but the wrong one made usually had appalling consequences for the protagonist. And the decision to make the right or the wrong choice was aided by two earthling angels and a devil respectively. This fantasy element I found hard to swallow, but the Chinese (I was told) loved it. My real problem, however (after dealing with some astonishing shortcomings in the scripts), was with its artistic merit – or lack of it. The story element seemed of little interest to the programme makers, the realism of character even less. And performance was ignored. What solely preoccupied them, it seemed, was how technically accomplished and attractive the finished programme looked. In some scenes the camera whizzed about when it should have been static and focused on the character – but they all congratulated each other on the bravura 'choreography' of the camera work. I was also annoyed about the decision to use models from local agencies instead of properly trained actors.

John, sensing my frustration, sloped round to my office for a chat. 'You don't understand us, do you?' he said, with a slightly intimidating smugness.

'What don't I understand?' I asked.

'You've got a cultural problem with us.'

'What d'you mean?'

'We're obsessed with image here. Nobody gives a shit if the drama is lousy – it's the image that counts. Pretty faces, impressive pictures.'

John splayed his toes in his sandals and yawned.

'Go on,' I said. 'I still don't quite know what you're getting at.'

He looked at me uncomprehendingly. How could I be so stupid? 'It's about showing how successful we are.' He picked up one of the scripts of *Dreamers*. 'There's no difference between the devil and the angel in our society, because there's no bad conscience about being successful, however it's achieved.' Then, as a punch-line: '*Kiasu.*'

'What?'

'*Kiasu.* Loosely it means "grab" – aggressive acquisitiveness. If there's something "up for grabs" as you say, we grab it.'

I was growing impatient with him. 'John, you're being oblique. Get to the point.'

He raised his eyebrows – or what little of them had grown back since he'd shaved them off. 'If you really want to do a drama about us, then it should be about how we achieve success – about our ambitions.' He looked at me to see whether I was taking this in. 'Bob, here ambition and success involve no moral dilemmas for us. We don't get hung up about it. There's no tragedy or crisis or complication about it. Not like your British drama, where you all end up covered in blood or guilt. We just get a bigger car, live in a smarter place, start another business. Our lives are about *purchase.*'

I found John intriguing. He was one of the smartest, and one of the most aggravating, people I had ever met.

'Do you want to hear a real Singapore story, a story about us?'

I nodded. 'Yes.'

'There's this Chinese guy walking beside an HDB [Housing Development Board – high-rise apartments] when at his feet falls this suicide case. What does he do? Phone for a doctor? Call for help? See if he can assist the person in any way? No. He does none of these things. Instead he looks at his watch. He reckons it was about 10.34 a.m. when the body hit the pavement. As a group of people gather round, he asks them if they want to bet to the nearest minute on the death of the suicide. They all throw in their bets. And the upshot is, the family gets to grieve and our guy makes a lot of money . . . You see? We're just about opportunity, making every chance work for us. That's success.'

'That's pretty heartless, I'd say.'

'That's you not understanding us,' he replied chidingly, and shuffled off with a dismissive wave of his hand.

After that, I more or less abandoned the series. If I knew anything about English drama, then its values (moral and cultural) had no place here, it seemed. Yet what John had said to me was profoundly illuminating in another way.

One afternoon, at the wet market ('wet' because it literally is) in Chinatown, a stallholder went crazy. I saw him rushing towards me wielding a mallet, shouting in that piercing falsetto way only the Chinese, to my knowledge, can manage. Frozen with fear and guilt (what possible offence had I given him to merit such an attack?), I dropped my shopping bag of vegetables and watched in dismay as they rolled across the floor. Rather than make a run for it, for some perverse reason I knelt down to pick the vegetables up. As I did so, a large fish 'swam' past me in a lithe rolling motion, finally vanishing under an adjacent stall. Then I realised with heart-stopping relief that it wasn't me but the fish the stallholder was chasing. He tore past me, his eyes looking as if they were about to take leave of his head. Minutes later, his flailing arms seemed to be sinking in a tidal wave of creamy yellow and red apples. It was one of those bizarre incidents when your mind is shocked to its phantasmagoric roots. Eventually surfacing, he raised the writhing fish above his head in beaming triumph. There was tepid applause from the other stallholders. Returning to his stall, he hit the fish with several resounding blows until, deciding finally to behave itself, the fish expired. A stout Chinese lady, standing beside me and laden with bags full of bloody joints of meat, shook her head disapprovingly. It's not the Chinese way, I had heard, to make an exhibition of yourself in public.

After that incident, with rivulets of sweat leaking down my body, I sat at a food stall drinking a beer and watching the shoppers. They were inspecting the foodstuffs with an almost distrustful myopic scrutiny, turning and touching and holding everything, weighing it all with curious suspicion. The decision made, some form of haggling followed until, eventually, money was exchanged – or more like snatched. It was all very business-like, with no gossipy conversation or polite chatter.

Gazing around the market, a sign – rather oblique and hand-scrawled – caught my eye: 'Rare Species.' Intrigued, I wandered over to the stall. There were cages full of animals, large and small, which I'd never seen before. A man was in conversation with the stallholder, who appeared rather anxious and furtive. While talking, he pointed to a small cage on the floor, hidden away behind some boxes. It contained an iguana. The customer smiled delightedly when the reptile was taken from its cage and held up for his inspection. He turned to me.

'Very good for my wife's itchy skin,' he smiled.

'Eczema?' I asked.

'Yes, very itchy complaint. All up her arms.' He scratched himself to demonstrate the extent and irritation of his wife's problem.

The stallholder, nervously peering around, placed the iguana – now struggling fiercely – on his chopping-board and started hacking at it with such transfixing brutality that I couldn't keep my eyes off it. The poor beast's mouth opened wide as the blows rained down, doubtless in extreme agony. The customer smiled with barely contained satisfaction. He occasionally glanced at me as if to say, 'At last I'll get a decent night's sleep and my wife will be less irritable to live with.'

The butchering finally over, the pieces of iguana were hastily wrapped in a plastic bag, tied, and handed to the customer. A wad of dollars was exchanged and the business finalised. The iguana, I learnt later, was a protected species – so this transaction was in fact illegal. No wonder the stallholder looked uneasy while I was there.

Sickened by what I'd witnessed, I decided to leave the market and walk back to my apartment. On the way, two miles or so, I began to realise what had gone on there, forgetting the cruelty. What it had been was nothing more than a transaction (John's 'purchase' theory) whereby a customer had been satisfied and the stallholder paid. It was simple market economics where everything had a price and nothing was above monetary value. Everything in S.E. Asia, as I began to discover, was in one way or another just a commodity.

What John had so exasperatedly tried to explain to me had been amply illustrated in the market. If what I'd witnessed had taken place in a market in Britain, there would have been public outrage. In fact, the guy would very likely have been quietly dealt with by some Animal Liberation fanatic – and we would all have said good riddance. But here in S.E. Asia, by contrast, the *deal* was the only thing. Moral scruples didn't enter into it. If there was an unfortunate victim involved (like the iguana), then it was just tough luck. Business was business. And money is God. The more you had of the former, the closer you got to the latter. And piety and righteousness were index-linked. Such an ethic, fundamentally, could easily be applied, it seemed to me, to any form of business and commerce – including piracy.

I had read about ships being literally stolen to order, as I believe the MV *Cheung Son* had been (I discovered it was later sold to some businessmen for around $300,000 (US)). The fact that in the case of the *Cheung Son* a whole crew had been massacred was simply of no interest to those who had organised its theft. The ship was a commodity and someone had wanted it. The transaction agreed, the ship was stolen. Regarding it as a 'crime' was surely not how the thieves saw it. The ship was merely a means to an end – profit. Only if the deal had been reneged on, or if there had been some unsavoury double-dealing, would there perhaps have been accusations of criminality, or of being dishonourable, which amounted to the same thing, or worse. The deal transcended everything, and the money that accrued from it gave respectability. This seemed to me to be the culture in which piracy operated.

I didn't go back to my apartment, but decided instead to go to Mr Chum's hotel on Killiney Road. The Mitre Hotel was a glorious wreck of a place, endearingly seedy. Its sign was a piece of cardboard with its name scrawled on it, and its grounds were untended and overgrown. As a piece of real estate, it was worth millions of dollars to developers, but the hotel was apparently locked in some litigious family dispute, with Mr Chum stubbornly refusing to sell his share. So no renovations or improvements had ever been made to it, and architecturally it had remained the same since it had been built, well before the Second World War. Mr Chum still ran it as a hotel, and it had its regulars, mostly travelling contractors, technicians of one sort or another, and the odd broke deadbeat. Its best feature was its cavernous lobby and bar, furnished with threadbare chairs, battered tables and wobbly stools. There was no air-conditioning, only ceiling fans. As for the décor, it could best be described as atmospheric. The bright tropical light didn't reach the bar at the back of the lobby, which was shrouded in a gloomy, smoke-filled fug. If you stood at the entrance of the hotel's lobby, you could barely see to the bar.

Mr Chum had told me that during the war the hotel had been staff headquarters for the Japanese Army. Two officers were buried somewhere in the garden after being assassinated by the Singapore resistance. It always gave me an eerie chill when I walked up the hotel drive.

Mr Chum wasn't an hotelier by training, but a physicist. He had some long-standing and unresolved grievance against the Singapore judiciary, but I never found out quite what it was. Meanwhile, he lived in his own exile world in the company of drifters and drinkers. They liked and respected Mr Chum, as I did. He was a curious man, intensely taciturn but with an ironic sense of humour. And he dressed like his hotel – shabbily.

'Beer?' he asked, already opening a can. I sat on a stool with two men sitting opposite: Jan from Sweden (a cabling engineer), and George – originally from London – who ran a shipping line taking durian timber from Malaysia to Australia. (Incidentally, the durian fruit, much loved by the Chinese, smells like the contents of a baby's nappy.)

'No beer left,' Mr Chum told George and Jan, who had amassed between them the best part of a day's drinking. The bar was littered with empty cans.

George took out his wallet and gave Mr Chum a wad of notes. 'Here, go and get some more.' He looked across at me. 'What d'you prefer – lager or beer?' Remembering that we hadn't been introduced, he extended his hand. 'George.' I took his hand. 'Bob.' Jan, in turn, offered his hand. 'Whatever you're drinking,' I said.

'Lager, Mr Chum.' Mr Chum gathered up the money and disappeared, leaving the bar and till unattended. I felt embarrassed that I was the only one with a beer, so I offered to split the can with them. Jan waved his hand and George just smiled. 'Chum will be back soon.'

George was in his fifties, a heavy-set man who looked as if he had the strength of Samson. Jan, on the other hand, seemed rather effete with a wispy goat's beard and long, delicate hands. When Chum had gone, Jan told George that he was getting out of the hotel – he had drunk some tap water that he believed had made him violently sick the night before.

George shook his head in mock sympathy. 'Beer for breakfast, lunch and supper. You'll be pissed all day, but it's better than getting the running shits.' He emptied his packet of nuts and threw some to a mynah bird that was scavenging around for crumbs. Jan got up, feeling another bout coming on. 'Excuse me,' he said, holding his stomach. 'I think I'll go and lie down.'

George looked at me and shrugged. 'That guy's sick. He should go back to Sweden. It's not so much the water; it's the climate that's getting to him. Dehydration – you can see it in his face.' He cleared the beer cans away in front of him, emptied the drips from one onto the floor so he could use it as an ashtray, and lit a cigarette.

'D'you come here much?' he asked. 'I've not seen you here before.'

'Occasionally. What about yourself?'

'When I'm off the ships and the wife's doing her tai chi lessons. And you?' he enquired.

'I work at the TV station here – TCS.'

He smiled. 'Great people, the Singaporeans – but they can't make TV.'

Inclined as I was to agree with him, I was more interested in what he did.

'You're in shipping then?' I asked.

'Timber mainly . . . Durian. I ship it down from Malaysia to Australia.'

George and his wife had lived in Singapore for the best part of twenty years, running their shipping business from a small office in the Colonial District. He had originally come over here as a shipping agent, but then decided to invest all his savings in buying his own ship. He now had two, both running from Malaysia to Australia.

'I gather the South China Sea can be a pretty dangerous place,' I said.

George blew out a long stream of smoke then dropped the butt of his cigarette into the beer can.

'You can get some nasty squalls, but they tend to go as quickly as they blow up.'

'What about pirates? Aren't they a problem, too?'

He looked grimly ahead. 'They're worse.'

'Have you ever been attacked?' I asked.

'Harassed a couple of times and shot at. But so far I've been lucky.'

'What happened when you were shot at?' I asked, intrigued.

He tapped his cigarette thoughtfully. 'It was about 2 a.m. and we were fifty miles off the Malaysia coast. I was in my cabin asleep. The next moment, I woke to this ricocheting sound of metal on metal, and then I heard glass breaking somewhere in the ship. I thought some of the cabling had possibly snapped, but then I faintly heard the unmistakable rattle of automatic gunfire. Oh fuck! I thought, and grabbed some clothes and rushed up to the deck. It was mayhem. One of the deckhands had put a searchlight on the pirates, but then they'd shot it to bits. Fortunately, the young lad was unhurt. There were two boats, fast launches, at the stern, and I could just make out around seven to eight crew in each one. They seemed determined to get in as close as possible, presumably to fire grappling hooks.'

'Did you have any weapons on board?' I asked.

'No. We're not allowed to. Besides, I don't like carrying weapons, just in case one of the crew goes berserk. It has happened, you know.'

'So what happened next?'

'I told the crew to keep their heads down while I went to get some flares. I radioed up to the bridge to get the ship under full steam. We couldn't outrun them, but we could churn up enough water to make things difficult for them.'

George lit another cigarette and wiped his hand across a day's stubble of beard.

'Once I'd got the flares and the flare gun, I rushed back up on deck. The crew were still lying on the deck, and there were sporadic bursts of fire, and I was frightened that someone was going to catch a ricochet . . . Anyway, I loaded the first flare – a red phosphorus type – and fired it above their heads. The sky lit up and we could clearly see them, four in one boat, three in the other. They were dressed in camouflage gear, like paramilitaries. A weapon in each boat.'

Mr Chum returned with a couple of cases of lager, and put them on the bar.

'Your change,' he said to George who waved his hand at the money. Chum put it in his pocket and returned behind the bar. George opened a can and handed me one.

'Go on,' I said.

'I fired two more flares at the boats and they fired back at us. Have you ever been under fire yourself?'

I shook my head.

'I tell you, it's frightening . . . bloody frightening.' He took a long drink. 'And I'll tell you something else – they knew how to use those guns. They weren't amateurs. They were skilled seamen too.'

'But you managed to repel them?' I asked.

'Yes, eventually. I heard them shout at each other, and then they pulled away and sped off. After that we maintained a round-the-clock watch until we reached Australia.'

'Did you report the attack?'

'Not officially, no. What was the point? What could the maritime authorities do? We all know the risks we run out there with pirates. You've just got to be on your guard – which I wasn't until that attack. Now I'm very vigilant.'

Slumped in his armchair, Mr Chum began to doze, then snore faintly. George nodded at him and grinned.

'Look at Chum,' he said, taking another drink. 'If he had a care in the world, you wouldn't know it. Odd bloke.'

I told George about my interest in piracy and about my trip to Malacca.

'So who d'you think these pirates are? They're not local fishermen, I'm pretty sure of that.'

'Maybe some are . . . But the ones who attacked us that night, they were professionals.'

George opened another beer and handed one to me. It was four in the afternoon and a storm was building up. I could hear the wind gusting. Leaves started to blow into the lobby. Then it went still, and the mynah birds stopped singing. Lightning flickered around the walls, and a loud boom of thunder rolled overhead. Rain cracked on the tarmac outside, each drop the size of a puddle. Chum stirred in his chair.

'They're well-organised gangs,' George continued, 'and the reckoning is that they're part of the military – Malaysian, Indonesian, Philippine, even, some say, Singaporean. How else do you account for their skills and expertise, plus their equipment?'

'So you're saying these countries are colluding in, perhaps even sponsoring, piracy?' I suggested.

George glanced at me uneasily. Could he trust me not to repeat his allegations? But George had had too much to drink.

'There are too many rice bowls involved,' he said.

'Rice bowls?'

'Yes, and the governments don't want to break them.'

'Are you saying that the governments are directly or indirectly involved in actively sponsoring piracy?'

George became edgy again, uncertain whether to continue. 'Yes. Rogue elements of Navies, Coastguards, Customs . . . But look,' he insisted, 'that's only my opinion, and I'd be grateful if you'd keep this conversation to yourself. OK?'

George looked at his watch. 'About time I went. My wife will have finished her class.' He drank the remains of his beer, straightened his shirt and got up. He reached into his back pocket and took out his wallet. 'Here,' he said, handing me his business card. 'Keep in touch.' We shook hands and he left.

I had another beer before I left, and sat in an old armchair at the entrance to the lobby and watched the storm pass. The rain had stopped and rivers of water ran everywhere. Straight after a storm was the most comfortable time in the tropics. The air was fresher and the humidity less intense and debilitating. The mynah birds returned, as bold as ever, springing along the drive like po-going athletes, ready to feed on anything the rain had shaken from the trees. I could hear the cars swishing along Killeney Road and smell cooking in the air. Mr Chum was snoring more loudly now, so I tidied the bar and left some money tucked under a beer can.

Needing some more $5 'Banana Republic' shirts and something to eat, I caught a bus to Serangoon Road and Little India. On the way I took out George's business card from my pocket and placed it carefully in my wallet. Annoyingly, within a couple of days I had lost it. In any case, I doubted whether George would have spoken to me again about piracy – certainly not about who he thought was involved. Like any large business, piracy had its politics, and as yet I was only a novice. Besides, I couldn't afford to be indiscreet.

Serangoon Road blares with sound and colour: music, traffic horns, shopkeepers, curry, pornography, parrot-wielding fortune tellers and jasmine garlands. It's pure sensory indulgence, and in complete contrast to the rest of 'detollised' Singapore, or at least the areas where most tourists end up, Orchard Road and Boat Quay in particular. Like Mr Chum's hotel, Serangoon Road, the heart of little India, had a history and an easygoing scruffiness.

The shop where I bought my shirts was just off Serangoon. It was wall-to-ceiling shopping, with some clothes in cellophane wrappers or hanging from rails, but most dumped in piles on trestle tables and ranging in price from three to ten dollars. You just dug around until you came across a shirt you liked, giving it a cursory inspection before you bought it since the humidity tended to rot the cloth after a while. I bought a couple of white cotton 'Banana Republics' (in a diaphanous size 'large', which meant they dried quicker when you sweated).

The backstreets of Little India (alleyways really) fascinated me, especially those around the so-called seedy area off Desker Street. They had excellent coffee shops and restaurants where old men sat playing dominoes under umbrellas. There were tables set out with pornographic videos: 'English, French, German, American, Indian ...' the vendors would furtively tell you. Sex is sex, I thought, so what real difference does it make in what language it comes? And in dark open doorways sat sullen prostitutes watching TV and knitting.

'Hello, Bob, my married bachelor friend!' I was halfway through a delicious *roti pratha* (Indian pancakes with curry sauce) when 'Barry' turned up (I had mispronounced his Indian name as 'Barry' when we had first met, but he didn't seem to object). Barry was an Arthur Daley character, but with more wit about him. He liked to refer to himself as a 'businessman in luxury commodities: import & export'. I never discovered what those 'commodities' were that he dealt in, but Barry was always smartly dressed and encrusted with gold. Barry lamented the departure of the British in 1974, when, as he said, 'everything was cheap and life was good'. Of course, he hadn't done so badly since, as I often reminded him. He drove a Mercedes and wore handmade leather shoes.

Barry was exceptionally generous and always insisted on buying the beers, which he did with an ostentatious flourish of his well-endowed wallet. He sat down with me, ordered two Tiger beers and politely waited until I'd finished my meal. He was wearing a new Rolex watch, but it was a fake – I could hear it ticking. Barry's fraternal mission towards me was to fix me up with a woman – hence the term 'married bachelor'. I had told him of my family in Britain, but he insisted it wasn't natural for a man to live alone, as I did. I had to have a woman to 'look after me', and it perplexed him utterly when I told him that I could look after myself perfectly well. One afternoon, determined to fulfil his mission, he gave me a guided tour of a brothel in Little India. He recommended certain girls, others he grimaced at. Frustrated by my lack of interest, he eventually gave up. 'Ah, you Englishmen,' he sighed. 'I don't understand you. All you do is play with your balls!'

'So where have you been, Bob?' he asked as the beers arrived. 'I've not seen you round here for over two weeks.'

'Malacca,' I told him.

'Filming?'

'Researching sea piracy.'

He nodded thoughtfully. 'So why are you interested in piracy?'

'I think it's a good story,' I said as I poured my beer. 'Do you know that millions of tons of shipping and cargo are stolen each year around these parts? Let alone the number of lives lost in attacks. And in the West it's hardly discussed. We still think of pirates as kind of swashbuckling adventurers and freebooters.'

Barry smiled and relaxed his capacious belly.

'Piracy, smuggling . . . they are the old ways over here, the ancient trades.' He showed me his watch. 'See this?' he said.

I grinned. 'Yes, a Rolex. And if I'm not mistaken it's a fake.'

'It is. But it's a bloody good fake. And I only paid fifty bucks for it.'

I agreed with him that it was a bargain, and a good copy, although I found even the genuine Rolexes vulgar.

'I could take you round here now and show you more pirated stuff from the West than you could believe. Films, CDs, VCRs, electronic and hi-fi gear, brand-name clothes . . .'

'I was talking about sea piracy, Barry.'

'Stolen copyright, stolen ship – what's the difference?'

'Proportion, money . . . lives. That's the difference.'

'I would bet you that more money is lost through copyright and software piracy each year than because of sea piracy. As for lives lost, look around Singapore's construction sites and ask yourself how many migrant workers' lives are needlessly lost in industrial accidents?' He drained his glass and ordered two more beers. 'You know something, Bob, when you British were here, you were up to all sorts of rackets, probably piracy too! We don't hoodwink ourselves over here by calling things "administrative oversights" or "acceptable margins of loss" or whatever other euphemisms you used for keeping your hands clean. But scratch an Englishman and there's an Oriental underneath.'

'I understand what you're saying, but piracy – whatever form it takes – is still piracy. It's still a crime.'

'Ah, crime!' Barry rolled his tongue round his teeth and burped in polite mockery of my mention of the word. 'So why is it that most of S.E. Asia isn't facing some hugely crippling lawsuit from the West? I'll tell you why, and it's simple: we don't regard piracy as a crime. Our interpretation of "law" is very different morally from yours.'

It was the same sort of cultural argument I'd had with myself and, more confrontationally, with John. 'We're talking essentially about cultural differences, aren't we?'

Barry ordered more *roti pratha* and beer. Now he was in his stride. 'Yes, that's true, I suppose. But "culture" is such a baggy word – like a woman with a fine figure from the front, but a fat arse from behind.'

(Barry liked the English language. He said it was more expressively vulgar than his own.) 'Let's keep to the word law.'

I liked Barry's imperious way of arguing. He naturally took centre-stage, and became quite excitedly camp after a while. 'Let's do that,' I agreed as the food arrived.

'Our laws are designed not so much to prevent crime as to deter anti-social behaviour. Splitting hairs, perhaps, but there's a difference.' Barry lunged his fingers into the food and stuffed a whole *roti pratha* into his mouth without a drip of curry from his lips. 'If crime doesn't disrupt the social fabric of our society, or threaten it in any way – then it's acceptable. We tend to turn a blind eye, especially if it makes money. But anti-social behaviour is worse – it can lead to a breakdown in values and subvert society. And it doesn't make anyone rich.'

Barry leant back in his chair and began to pick his teeth. He was the sort of person who, once he had said what he had to say, looked around for something else to interest him.

'So what now, my married bachelor friend?'

Strolling back to my apartment, I reflected on what Barry had said. However much a crime in terms of *international* law (a fact Barry dismissed as a mere irrelevance: 'Who cares about laws made thousands of miles away?'), over here piracy was just another business, it seemed. And as long as it didn't exhibit or encourage any 'anti-social' characteristics, who was there to condemn it? Besides, it was a multi-million dollar business – and no one wanted to drop such a rich rice bowl. It was, like much else I'd experienced in S.E. Asia, part of a dual 'public–private' morality: what was unacceptable in public and so denied, in private was quietly acknowledged.

It was an ethical code of living that seemed to be at the very heart of Asian society, whatever the differences in religion, ethnicity or race might be. I'd seen it in other aspects of life in Singapore and elsewhere. Homosexuality, for instance, is illegal – yet there was a thriving community of gays, transvestites and transsexuals (some of whom were actually quite attractive!) in Geylang. Smoking hashish could land you in serious trouble, but it was relatively easy to obtain. Certain kinds of pornography were proscribed, but it was available nonetheless. And gum-chewing was forbidden, yet the young Singaporeans ate it almost openly.

The ubiquitous public signs that invariably began, 'It is an offence . . .' were effectively saying *Don't give offence*. They were not so much about law enforcement as reinforcing certain conventions of behaviour. As long as those 'conventions' were obeyed publicly, what you did privately behind closed doors was nobody's business. Or so it seemed. And as far as the difference went between civil and criminal law, there really didn't appear to be much of one. So was it the case then with piracy (any form of piracy, indeed) that, if it didn't offend the social mores of the society in which it occurred, it was generally overlooked?

I had to consider all this, because I felt I'd hit a crisis. If I didn't understand the culture in which piracy operated, then much that I said about it would be mere witness to the facts, or just silly supposition. I had come to a point where piracy itself really didn't interest me – as a maritime crime, that is. The facts and figures spoke for themselves. But as a phenomenon of this part of the world – as a way of life – it intrigued me.

– CHAPTER SIX –

I had not heard from Mary for several weeks. Then one day at work she phoned me. She apologised for not getting in touch after we had met in the pub that night, and explained that she had been away in Bejing doing some PR business for an IT company. She said she had an excellent contact for me – a local freelance crime reporter who had apparently covered stories of several recent hijackings. But when I asked her for his name and phone number, she suddenly became reticent. Perhaps, she suggested, it would be best if she gave him my phone number, then he could contact me if he wished. I asked her if there was a problem. 'There is no problem,' she said, 'but he must be careful . . .'

At the time, I didn't understand why Mary's friend had to be 'careful'. I had assured her that anything confidential he passed to me would remain so. She insisted that it wasn't so much a matter of trust as his 'circumstances'. I decided not to push her on the matter and waited for his call. But after a week I became impatient. I was about to phone Mary when a message was handed to me at the reception in my apartment block: 'Please contact me. Jasbir.' The number was his mobile phone.

I phoned him immediately but only got through to an answering service. I tried again later that day, but the same thing happened. I tried once more . . . 'I'm not available at the moment. Please leave a message and your number, and I'll ring you back.' It sounded like the voice of a person in a rush, with a slight tone of panic at its edge. And I thought it was curious that he didn't give his name. I had virtually given up on him when he rang me at my apartment.

'Mary said you wanted to talk to me about piracy.' There was something irascible about his voice that I found slightly intimidating at first, but as we talked his tone mellowed. I suggested that we meet for lunch, but he was adamant that if we met it should be somewhere relatively private.

'What about here at my apartment?'

'Maybe a hotel would be best,' he suggested.

We agreed to meet the next day at a hotel in the Financial District.

'How will I recognise you?' I asked.

'I'll find you.'

The conversation ended as abruptly as it had begun, and it unnerved me. I suspected that Jasbir wasn't his real name, and his reluctance to describe himself made me feel even more dubious about him. All the same, I was pleased that he had got in touch, and I had no reason to believe he wouldn't turn up the following day.

That night, rather than slog through another batch of execrable scripts, I decided to finish a piece I was writing for *The New Paper*, the tabloid sister paper of *The Straits Times*. It was for the ex-pat section and was about a group of Indian migrant workers I'd met at a coffee bar near Paya Lebar. They had invited me back to their 'home' for a curry one evening. Their 'home', it turned out, was a bleak room in an air-conditioning storage plant. Five of them lived there, sleeping rough on mattresses. One of them, who could speak a little English, told me that they had all come from villages in southern India after an 'agent' had extorted a large fee (around $S5,000) from their families to arrange visas and work permits for Singapore. Their wages in Singapore were derisory, and in order to send some money back home they had to live in this squalor. In fact, what they were being paid was a fraction of their initial outlay, so there was no realistic chance of reimbursing their families. They had been monumentally screwed.

I knew that I had to temper my outrage in order to get the piece published, so I wrote a bland, politically correct article about our convivial evening together, with a photograph of myself and one of the migrant workers with our arms round each other laughing. It's my one piece of journalism I'm least proud of, but I hoped the mention of their living conditions would needle a few consciences.

The next day I caught a bus to the Financial District and the hotel where I was due to meet Jasbir at midday. I got there half an hour early and had a beer and sat near a fan in the lobby to dry out. The humidity outside had saturated me. But here in the hotel, the coolness was like a balm, regulated to change the climate from equatorial to temperate. And the calming effects didn't stop there. The colour-coding of the furniture and the marble floor all helped to soothe and relax, as did the crisp unhurriedness of the staff. Even the pace of the lifts seemed languorous. If there is a human rhythm to technology, Singapore had just about got it right. It almost had a heartbeat. I often used to wonder how close the Singaporeans were in their technological expertise to curing all forms of human fallibility, from sweating armpits to mortality.

Minutes passed, and after an hour of waiting I was not so sure Jasbir was coming. But there was of course Singapore 'rubber time', so I held on, crunching my way through yet another bowl of peanuts and watching the endless flow of guests and staff, the check-ins and check-outs, the buzz of computer-issued bills, the hellos and goodbyes in a hundred languages. Then I noticed a large Sikh walk in and briefly gaze around. He must have been well over six feet tall, excluding his turban. His face raged with a large black beard and his stoutly built body looked quite definitely out of place next to the petite figures of Japanese and Chinese guests. He wore black jeans, sandals and a sloppy white shirt. Over his shoulder hung a perished leather case. There was no mistaking that this was Jasbir, and since I was the only *ang moh* in the lobby, there was no mistaking me either. Catching my eye, he made a beeline for me.

'Bob?'

I stood up to shake his hand, feeling dwarfed by his size.

'Jasbir.'

I offered to buy him a coffee. He glanced around nervously and suggested we went upstairs to the dining-room. It would be less crowded, he suggested, and quieter. I was intrigued by his sense of subterfuge.

Jasbir was right. The dining-room was empty.

'Two kopi-o,' I asked the waitress. 'Coffee all right for you, Jasbir?'

'Fine.' He was riffling through some documents in his bag, while keeping a watchful eye on the surroundings.

'Thanks for coming,' I said, hoping to relax him. 'How long have you known Mary?'

'Off and on for several years. We worked together on a couple of stories for a foreign news agency. She's a good journalist, but she got into trouble over an investigative piece we did . . . and decided to pack it in.'

The coffee came and I thought it an ideal opportunity to mention that Mary had told me Jasbir had to be 'careful'.

He shrugged. 'She's right. I do.'

'Any particular reason why?' I asked.

'I have excellent contacts in the police force, military intelligence, and the government. They give me good first-hand information on breaking stories – but there are others who don't like it.'

'Other journalists, you mean?'

'Yes . . . but also other people too.'

'Who?'

Jasbir became nervous again and looked furtively around the dining-room. 'The secret police, and others . . . Much of the time I'm being followed.'

'Secret police?!' I exclaimed, smiling with a look of incredulity that he obviously found irritating. 'If they are *secret*, how do you know they're following you?'

He grinned at my naïvety. 'When you're sitting in a restaurant or a pub, just look around for the dumbest one there. They're easy to spot.'

I wondered if this was just paranoia on his part, but he seemed genuinely serious about it. His nervousness became infectious and soon I was scanning the dining-room too.

'I gather from Mary that you've investigated a couple of piracy attacks.'

'Yes. Both ships I wrote about were hijacked in the Phillip Strait, somewhere between Bintan and Batam. You know the islands?'

I did. 'So what did you find out?'

'Both were phantomed and ended up eventually in a small port on mainland China. You know what I mean by phantomed?' he asked.

'Yes. They're ships that are re-registered and reflagged and then hired out fraudulently to shipping companies, whose cargoes are then invariably stolen.'

I felt Jasbir was testing my knowledge and interest in piracy to reassure himself that he wasn't wasting his time. Perhaps he also suspected my motives.

'How far did you get in your investigation?'

'I couldn't confirm it, but I'm positive both ships were hijacked by the same gang working from Batam. It's a syndicate – a Mafia organisation controlled from China or Hong Kong. Anyway, evidence of other things I came across proved more interesting.'

'Such as?'

Jasbir hesitated and once more glanced around the room. 'I'm not sure . . .'

'Not sure you should tell me?' I asked.

He sighed and looked hard at me.

'Jasbir, you can trust me.'

His size, like a natural defensive mechanism, began to relax.

'OK. It's only circumstantial evidence, but it's highly sensitive. You won't divulge it to anyone?'

I gave him my word.

'I'm convinced the Indonesian authorities and military are involved. And I'm damn sure the Singapore government is aware of it . . . in fact, it might even be involved indirectly too.'

'I've heard this before,' I said. 'But isn't it all largely rumour and hearsay?'

He knew that I was quizzing him for more than 'circumstantial' evidence, and he appeared suddenly humbled.

Finishing his coffee, he quietly cautioned me. 'Look, Bob, it's a very dangerous story. Let's just say I was warned off it when the questions I was asking got too sensitive for some people.'

'How were you "warned off"?'

'*Sufficiently.*'

This last remark was, I think, a veiled warning for me to stop my own investigation. But it had quite the opposite effect. Until I had met Jasbir, no one else seemed to have had quite the same serious attitude to piracy – even though his own investigation had been brought to an abrupt and inconclusive end. And, after all, as we both agreed, it was a good story.

'Do you have some contacts for me?' I asked.

He opened his bag and took out a scroll of papers. 'Some of these people you might find helpful. I've asterisked the names of those you can mention my name to. Most are in naval and military intelligence and Customs both here in Singapore and in Indonesia.' He passed them to me beneath the table and told me to put them away immediately. 'Whatever you do, please don't leave these names lying around. OK?'

Jasbir had other appointments, so we shook hands and I promised to keep in touch with him. As he left, he turned to me: 'Be careful,' he said.

I ordered more coffee and started to read the handwritten list of names. There were some high-ranking military people on it. Other names had 'spokesman' in brackets after them. And some were totally unpronounceable. Only two names were asterisked. I set about underlining and prioritising them, and ended up with ten names of people I thought most likely to give me the information I wanted. At last, it seemed, I had some definite leads, as well as people whom I felt sure could confirm, or otherwise scotch, the many rumours of who exactly was involved in piracy in the region.

Instead of using my apartment's phone (I had been told all phone calls were logged), I went down to a friend's office in an old tea-house in Tanjong Pagar, the media area of Singapore. Adam was setting up a small TV production business there and I worked for him on a casual basis, developing ideas and drinking with him a lot. I had suggested the piracy idea to him as a proposal for a possible series, and he was delighted for me to research it – for no money, of course. Charlotte, his assistant, was married to the 'egg man'. He delivered eggs in the district and was trying to teach me how to balance one egg on top of another. I never succeeded.

With the list in front of me, I started making the calls. An hour later, it was quite obvious that most of the telephone numbers were either defunct, or the person was no longer contactable for one reason or another. One person I did manage to contact – in Customs – became quite irate. He wanted to know how I had come to have his number. Since his name wasn't asterisked, I avoided mentioning Jasbir. He insisted I gave him my number, so I gave him a false one and put the receiver down. Livid with Jasbir, I called him, but he was unavailable. I left him a message.

Frustrated by the lack of results, I went for a beer at the curry house next door. I took the list with me, which was now heavily scored with crossings-out. I couldn't believe Jasbir had given me a duff list.

It was getting on towards five o'clock in the afternoon, and the bars opposite were beginning to fill up with the smart set from the Financial District and the various PR companies in the area. Most were Europeans and Americans and they loved the ex-pat lifestyle. They were a bearable lot, and preferred their own company. For many of them (though they never admitted it) Singapore was still a colony, ruled by their 'expertise'. They never expressed this openly, other than by a sort of brash confidence and a polite aloofness towards their Chinese counterparts. And their parochialism I found tiresome. If their conversations weren't about work and gossip, they were usually about their social diaries – parties, dinners, clubbing. They perfectly fulfilled the injunction, 'Here in Singapore, eat and enjoy yourself – but say nothing.'

I went back to the office and decided to phone a couple of numbers in Batam, a colonel in military intelligence and a Navy commander. The colonel's name was asterisked, but with a question-mark after it. I held out little hope. Finally getting the phone code right, I was put through to staff headquarters. The line was poor, and not speaking Indonesian naturally made things awkward. Nonetheless, I eventually got through to a 'colonel', though not by the name of the person on the list. He confirmed that he was in military intelligence. I told him that I was investigating sea piracy and wanted to know whether there were any pirate gangs operating on the island, as I'd heard.

'Yes,' he said.

I was astonished, as much by his answer as by the almost unsolicited way he had given it.

'How many gangs? One, two, three?'

'Three gangs,' he replied.

I pressed him for more information and asked him if he knew where these gangs operated on the island. But he became confused, and I could think of no simpler way to put the question. So I thanked him for his help. He grunted in a cordial way, and I put the phone down.

Charlotte had been listening to the conversation and she was not happy, especially when I told her I intended to leave for Batam as soon as possible.

'Bob, you are being very stupid. You are meddling in things that you do not know about and are dangerous.'

I shrugged and told her that this was the first real break I'd had and I wasn't prepared to waste it. She became angrier. 'The Chinese people are being victimised and killed there. Indonesia is a bad place.' I knew about the troubles in East Timor, but not about this. 'Yes,' Charlotte insisted, 'the Chinese are being driven out, their businesses destroyed, their houses attacked. We are like the Jews in Israel, surrounded by Muslim countries . . .' This outburst had little to do with me going to Indonesia, and I told her as much. She stared at me haughtily and told me I was a fool.

'I'm not Chinese, Charlotte. What's more, this is my job.'

I had a great affection for Charlotte, but after this incident our relationship deteriorated.

Before I left the office, Jasbir rang. He was very apologetic about the list of names, but when I told him of my coincidental success with the Indonesian colonel, he brightened and suggested we meet. 'Have you a map of Batam, Bob? I think I can show you where one of the gangs might be operating from.'

This time I persuaded Jasbir to meet me in a hawker centre near the office. Being very public places, they guaranteed anonymity. At least that's what I'd found; I'd spent many hours in them, reading or just idly thinking, and was never interrupted or disturbed by anyone. They were where you could see the richness of Singapore life, and especially how well ethnically and racially integrated the country was. And this wasn't down to government policy, but something much more mundane: the Singaporeans' obsession with food and cooking. In one alley of stalls alone, there was Indian, Chinese, Malay, Indonesian and Thai cuisine, and while there was fierce competition, there was never a hint of racial tension. Food enlisted a common appetite for social harmony. They worked together, matching each other's prices and quality of cooking, and all the stalls were generally uniform and the public seating shared. If there was ever an exemplary sociological paradigm of social integration, it was the Singapore hawker centre.

The unmistakable figure of Jasbir loomed above the mêlée of early-evening diners as he searched for me. His wild beard and turbaned head made him look very distinct, and it amused me to wonder how Jasbir, wherever he went, could possibly hope to be anonymous. His slightly furtive manner made him even more conspicuous.

'Excellent news,' he said, as his huge frame seemed to devour the stool at our table. 'How did you manage it?'

'I got through to someone in military intelligence and asked them. Simple as that.'

'Incredible.'

The only map I could find of Batam was in a traveller's guide, but Jasbir thought it adequate. Batam has four peninsulas or headlands on its northern side, the most westerly of which forms part of an archipelago of small islands. Jasbir studied it carefully and then pointed to the last of these headlands.

'*Kampong* Melayu is around here somewhere, and that's where it's rumoured piracy attacks have been launched from.'

The only roads to the north-east of the island, it appeared, headed towards a group of beach resorts.

'But there appears to be no road,' I said.

'There will be a track to it through the jungle. It's a very remote village, and one of the largest there.'

I wrote the name down and marked an arrow roughly at the point Jasbir denoted it on the map.

'Look at its location,' Jasbir continued. 'Strategically it's ideally placed for attacks on shipping. It's got excellent access to the Phillip and Malacca Straits, and I bet it will have deep water. And, as I said, it's very remote. In all that jungle and mangrove swamp you could conceal just about any amount of cargo. Even a ship.'

I was not entirely convinced by Jasbir's speculations that this village was involved in piracy. After all, his list of contacts had proved virtually useless, and he hadn't provided me with any substantial information on piracy or anything to support his suspicions about who was involved, despite his claims that he had investigated several hijackings. I liked Jasbir, but I was uneasy about his credibility as a journalist. I suggested that we both went to Batam, but Jasbir declined, saying that he was hoping to cover the troubles in East Timor. The last I heard of him, he was teaching in a secondary school in Singapore.

I went to a travel agency near Raffles Hotel and booked a 'long weekend' package in Batam.

'Are you going on holiday?' the booking agent asked. It struck me as a rather curious question.

'Yes. Why do you ask?'

'The Singapore Customs may be interested in your reason for going there.'

I wondered what she might have said if I'd told her I was going to Batam to investigate sea piracy!

'Just a short break,' I smiled. 'The longer you live in Singapore, the smaller it seems to get.'

She processed the details, handed them to me and wished me a pleasant holiday.

Since Raffles Hotel was only a block or two away, I thought I'd go and have a drink there. I remotely hoped to meet David Willis there, since I was told he was a habitué of the hotel, but I didn't see him. Until then I had avoided going to Raffles, despite its reputation for elegance and colonial nostalgia. If it had had any character once, now it was essentially a tourist trap, albeit a very profitable one. Some august writers had stayed there in the past – Conrad, Kipling, Somerset Maugham, Noel Coward and Gunter Grass – and I suppose it was for this reason that I was tempted to visit it. Under a sunshade in the garden is the place to have a drink – or beneath a frangipani tree, as Maugham had done while writing his quaint Asian tales. However, the story I liked best was about the hotel itself. Apocryphal or not, it was about the last tiger shot in Singapore – under a billiards table in the hotel.

Sitting in the garden, I wondered about what I was doing, about the whole piracy business. I reflected on Charlotte's warnings and her rebuke, and Jasbir's polite refusal to come with me to Batam. I thought of how others too had pointed out to me the dangers of what I was doing, and my rather heedless reactions. Danger, I've always thought, like the best and worst of all human passions, thrives on the extremes of a compulsive nature.

– CHAPTER SEVEN –

THE International Maritime Bureau (IMB) defines piracy as 'an act of boarding any vessel with the intent to commit theft or any other crime and with the intent and capability to use force in the furtherance of that act'. The definition is, it would seem, quite clear, and complies with international definitions. And coming from such respected organisation as the IMB, anti-piracy law should derive easily from that definition and be implemented effectively and successfully. But that apparently is not the case, and, as things stand, will never be the case.

Academics, marine lawyers, seafarers, ship-owners and agents, even governments, have argued for centuries – indeed as far back as the American Civil War – on a precise and universally acceptable definition of piracy. But the more they debate the matter, the further it appears to elude definition. And it's largely understandable, if an analogy is drawn, say, with the current controversy, post-September 11, over how to define 'terrorism'. Who, for instance, would accuse Greenpeace of piracy? Yet they were found guilty of piracy under international law by a Belgian court for engaging in anti-dumping protests at sea. There is even a complex sensitivity involved in the actual use of the word 'pirate'. As Samuel Pyeatt Menefee, a legal scholar on the subject, writes: 'The effects of decolonisation and the multiplication of non-Western legal viewpoints have resulted in attempts to recharacterise many activities historically designated as piracy, along with a general reluctance to apply what is viewed as a pejorative term to contemporary marine attacks.' As one example of this he mentions the campaign by Indonesian and Malaysian officials to characterise many local attacks as 'armed robberies' or 'robbery at sea'. Not as piracy. And this is hardly surprising since jurisdiction over piracy has largely become the responsibility of the individual coastal states it affects. The legal view across the high seas might be clear from the bridges of the ships academics and other boffins sail, but the waters through which they pass are deeply muddied.

Professor Menefee concludes his article with a convoluted but astonishing admission: 'In the light of far-reaching developments in the field of international law and foreign relations, the law of piracy is deemed to require a fundamental reconsideration and complete restatement, perhaps resulting in drastic changes by way of modification and expansion . . . It is recommended that the subject of piracy be entirely researched and the law bearing on it modified and restated in accordance with the needs of the times.'

Such is the confusion that the IMB, in particular, is made effectively impotent legislatively, only having any real impact in terms of reporting incidents of piracy, advising shipping companies on safety, and running seminars. One such seminar was held in Singapore while I was there, but unfortunately I missed it. Apparently it pointed out that criminals were profiting from the legal confusion that arises from acts of piracy and armed robbery, the latter having no clear legal definition whatsoever. Perhaps Menefee's recommendation for a comprehensive redefinition of piracy was long overdue . . .

I was reading this extract from Menefee's paper while waiting for the ferry to Sekupang, Batam, in the World Trade Centre. I wished Menefee had been with me, if only because some of the things he said tantalisingly touched on what I'd been thinking – apart from the cultural context which he, and others, had somehow extraordinarily overlooked. I wondered how Menefee and others like him would have responded to some of the arguments put to me about Asian attitudes to money, prosperity and wealth, and how they figured in their notion of 'crime'? How would they have responded to Barry's argument over his distinction between 'anti-social' crime, and crime that accrues individual wealth and respect, yet which does little or nothing to undermine or threaten social order and stability? How would they have reacted to John's 'purchase theory' and *kiasu*: the idea that the transaction (never mind the commodity) is one of the primary principle of market relations, and that to grab what you can is perforce socially acceptable? How would they have reconciled a devout Christian's attitude to money as God?

Of course, the argument must run that the worst acts of piracy, where people are injured and killed, cannot be considered as anything other than a crime, and that various notions of cultural relativism are no explanation. The wilful slaughter of the *Cheung Son* crew was by any standards a terrible crime. But in a pragmatic 'political' sense, what did those killings signify in terms of a threat to the countries off whose shores this incident occurred? In the event, only China it seems, since they were under considerable pressure to prosecute and punish the pirates in their custody (something they had been notably lax in doing before), and by virtue of that to show the international community that they were willing now to 'comply' with international maritime law (something they had shown little willingness to do before).

As I sat by the wharf waiting for the ferry to arrive, I thought about Menefee's lines: '. . . the law of piracy is deemed to require a fundamental reconsideration and complete restatement . . .' and realised that he was courageously ducking the argument by admitting that his scholarly investigation into piracy fell dismally short of providing any insights. Basically, he was saying with admirable honesty that he hadn't a clue.

My ferry arrived and departed on time. Such is the Singaporean way. It was clean, large and fast, with a pleasant sundeck over the main housing. Since we were to pass through the busy shipping lanes of the Phillip Strait I decided to take some photographs of the ships. We skirted Sentosa island, a playground for the 'beautiful young Singaporeans' and a booming tourist attraction (a theme park), and where (I was told) the British fatefully had their guns facing the wrong way when the Japanese invaded during the Second World War. It's still a source of considerable mirth among the older generation. The Brits, of course, have always denied it. Such is the British way.

We passed several small, uninhabited islands; but with the Singaporeans' commitment to various 'reclamation' schemes, I doubted if even the smallest of these islands would stay uninhabited for long. Pulau Ubin, on the east coast, and one of the last to remain as it originally was, with its delightful Malaysian *kampong*, was, I'd heard, designated for future 'development' – another tourist resort. Perhaps, before long, the inner coastline of Singapore will be desalinated and turned into a large swimming-pool.

Leaving the coastline of Sentosa, the ferry master revved the engines, and we began to speed out into the open sea. Already several ships at anchor were coming into view, but as we progressed a veritable armada could be seen, some in passage, others at anchor. They were of every type and size – tankers, cargo ships, freighters, containers – all with their different colours and flags, some gleamingly new, others just rusting hulks. I couldn't begin to guess at the tonnage of shipping out there, but it ran easily into the millions. Through this narrow Strait sailed more than half of the world's shipping. The density was alarming, and I wondered how they possibly avoided collision. Another thing struck me too – the majority of the ships were sitting targets for pirates. Most vulnerable, it seemed, were the heavily laden ships, low in the water and, if not at anchor, then slow-moving. At night, a well-equipped gang with a fast launch, could attack and board these ships with relative ease, almost unnoticed. And throughout the twenty-minute journey I never once saw a Navy or Customs boat. These ships were, it appeared, totally unprotected.

Soon Batam was on the horizon, with its myriad offshore islands and a long seam of coastline dense with vermilion jungle. I wondered if all these tiny islands, some no bigger than the circumference of a child's paddling pool, were counted among the 17,000 islands of the Indonesian archipelago. Somehow I doubted it. Mapping them would in itself be more than a lifetime's work. Besides, there was something magical and romantic about these small islands, sovereign in anonymity.

As the ferry manoeuvred in to dock, a large sign welcomed visitors to Batam. The port and customs house of Sekupang looked like a busy trading post, and starkly contrasted with Singapore's majestic World Trade Centre. All it consisted of was a large wooden office and a series of rickety timbered quays. Fishermen in skiffs were throwing out their arc-shaped nets close to the shore, while raggedy kids selling cigarettes, gum and trinkets waited eagerly on the main quay for the new arrivals. Even before landing I recognised something about Batam that I instantly liked. It was one of those instinctive responses we all have to a new place: either it throws us into horror, or else inspires a kind of whimsical good-humoured appreciation.

The arrangement through the travel agent was for me to meet a taxi driver who would be waiting at Sekupang to drive me to my hotel. The reception area in the customs house was chaotic, but controlled all the same with infinite patience by the various officials who were processing one tidal wave of people after another. My passport was stamped with perfunctory hastiness and a defeated smile. Among the crowds were young and old Singaporean guys over for a weekend of cheap sex, cheap booze and fun – they'd escaped for a brief time the watchful, paternalistic scrutiny of Lee Quan Yew, as well as Singapore's claustrophobia, and intended to find any form of baptismal ignition to set their minds – and loins – on fire. Then there were Indonesian girls off to Singapore to earn a quick buck illegally hosting in the clubs and karaoke bars around Orchard Road. There were businessmen looking hot, tired and bemused, peering round for someone holding a card with their name. A European couple dressed in catalogue safari gear were frantically fastening and double-fastening all their bags while being besieged by young boys competing to carry their luggage.

'Mr Bob!' A voice hailed me from across the concourse. I looked round to see a rather portly figure beaming at me. Assuming that he'd got the right person (he must have noted my surprise at a stranger knowing my name), he rushed up to me. 'Mr Bob, I am Yulius, your taxi driver.' We shook hands.

Yulius was in his early thirties, taller than the average Indonesian, and was wearing a loose tropical-coloured short-sleeved shirt and cotton trousers that concertinaed round his sandalled feet. He was ostentatiously polite, with an almost unctuous eagerness to please. He was immediately likeable, in a faintly suspect way.

'I will take your bag. My taxi is outside.' In this part of S.E. Asia, I'd heard it was very unwise to let anyone handle your luggage. You could become an unwitting drugs smuggler – and in Singapore that could cost you your life.

The taxi rank outside the customs hall looked like a rally of the oldest second-hand cars in the world. Most were Japanese models, whose guaranteed reputation for durability and reliability had long since expired. But their owners seemed proud of them, leaning on their bonnets, smoking and chatting to each other as if comparing valve capacities, torques and gear ratios. Meanwhile their engines ticked over, pumping out clouds of exhaust smoke that billowed into the humid and dusty air. Weaving amongst them, or haphazardly parked up, were the ubiquitous two-stroke bikes, with their owners – mainly young boys – keenly touting for business with the solicitous looks of male prostitutes.

Yulius's taxi was a Nissan people carrier, and stood out impressively against the others, if only for the fact that it had less dents and its paintwork was in reasonably good condition. As I was getting in, the European couple I had seen earlier were having trouble with their taxi. What had apparently happened was that as their taxi had driven off, its nearside passenger door had become unhinged and was perilously close to falling off. The woman bellowed at the driver to pull up; he did so, and on being made aware of the problem, nonchalantly stepped out, rehinged the door and with an obliging smile to his occupants drove off again.

Yulius was keen to discover why I was visiting Batam, but I was wary of telling him. All the same, I had to hire a taxi to get to *kampong* Melayu and I also needed an interpreter – and Yulius's English was good. As we pulled out onto the main road heading towards Nagoya, Yulius drove along the dusty hard shoulder until he decided to join the traffic, more on a whim than a calculated decision.

'Do you know *kampong* Melayu?' I asked Yulius.

'You want to go there?'

'Yes.'

'I take you there. One hundred dollars.'

'Fifty.'

'OK, Mr Bob.'

That sorted, Yulius relaxed. But I didn't. His driving was almost pathologically erratic. His foot plunged down on the accelerator with the same enthusiasm as he talked. The road was a carnival of traffic – buses, lorries, motorbikes, cars, cyclists – and no one had priority. It was the same experience I'd had in Malaysia, except this time I wasn't sure if there were any rules, codified or otherwise. The traffic just seemed to swerve with idle abandon, always at the last moment and with no acknowledgements or courtesies. Space and motion were all that counted. It was like dodgems during an earthquake.

On one side of the road was thick jungle, with large palm trees and dense undergrowth. I had always imagined jungle to have that uniform olive colour, but beneath the canopy it had a brown, desiccated, lifeless appearance. On the other side, there was no jungle at all, just vast swathes of empty landscape, deeply scarred by an earth-moving plant, the result of some large building development that had either been suspended or abandoned. It was an arid, dun-coloured wasteland, marred by deep cuts of russet soil.

Nowhere else in the world had I seen the two-stroke bike used so inventively as here. On one bike I saw a family of four, one child sitting on his father's lap as he drove and a baby wedged between the father and mother, who was riding pillion. On the rear luggage rack was a large bamboo cage full of scrawny chickens. They waved to us as Yulius, now impatient, overtook them on the inside.

Yulius seemed intent on impressing me with his driving skills, and on one occasion decided to overtake a slow queue of traffic. Without looking in his rearview mirror he pulled out, rolled his backside further into the seat, and accelerated. A few hundred metres ahead a large water-carrying wagon approached. We were, it seemed, on a collision course, and as I turned my head away and closed my eyes, Yulius swerved onto the opposite hard shoulder, scattering some very surprised motorcyclists. Once more back in the correct lane, Yulius shrugged and sighed, and I invoked God with a string of beseeching expletives.

'Batam is fun island, Mr Bob. What fun do you like? Batam has every type of fun.'

It might be fun, I thought, to stay alive. 'Whatever fun's on offer, I suppose,' I replied. 'What fun do you suggest?'

'We have fine restaurants, the best KTV bars, disco and music, many water-sports, and golf. Batam is for tourists, and we cater for every taste,' he beamed proudly. 'Nice women too!'

As we approached Nagoya, Yulius pointed towards a small jungle-clad hill. 'That is Smiling Hill.' (I think that was what he called it.) 'Every Saturday night many Batam people go there to make love.'

'Why there?' I asked.

'It's a tradition – a place of love-making.' He looked at it with amorous reflection. 'All through the week the people here work very hard. But on Saturday night, many couples go there, all naked, and make love.'

I pictured in my mind an erotic nudist colony where naked buttocks and flailing arms and legs rose in a cacophony of orgiastic groans.

'You mean, they do it in public?'

'Yes, Mr Bob. But there are cabins there for those who have the money.'

Sex in the open air may be pleasurable, but I balked at the idea of sharing my buttocks (and other tender parts) with swarms of mosquitoes, let alone making a public exhibition of myself.

'Many Japanese women come to Batam for the men,' Yulius smiled salaciously.

I have always been amused by the fact that when sex is raised in a conversation, it generally follows the logic of a non-sequitur.

'Oh, why is that?'

'Us Indonesian men,' he winked, 'are *very* proud!'

I assumed that word had the same connotation here as in the West.

Entering the town, we joined a wide boulevard, with shops, restaurants, hotels and cafés on both sides. The few trees stood pathetically along the pavements, besieged by dust and suffocated by traffic fumes. As before, the traffic was dense and chaotic. Most of the buildings were concrete, and nearly every one – to a greater or lesser degree – seemed fissured and pockmarked. In places it looked like the aftermath of some sort of civil disorder or skirmish by rival gangsters.

Yulius explained. 'The concrete,' he said, throwing up his hands. 'It is no good.'

What I'd seen so far of Batam suggested that there were few, if any, building regulations here. If that were the case, the concrete would be the first material to be 'corrupted'.

'A very bad mix of concrete,' Yulius elaborated. 'When it dries, it's . . . fucked.'

Stopping at some traffic lights, a young boy ran into the road, knocked at my window and fixed me with the familiar solicitous smile, edged with desperation. He was a newspaper vendor, selling one of the two national newspapers, the *Sijori Pos*. Yulius brusquely waved him away before I had time to buy a copy. As soon as he disappeared, another took his place, this time selling cigarette lighters and trinkets. Neither could have been more than eight or nine years old. I was later told that these street kids were organised in gangs, and spent most of their time preying on tourists. The café and restaurant owners in particular despised them.

My hotel, with a drive that set it back off the main road, was an imposing modern Dutch-style building with a grand entrance decked with plants and flowers. I arranged with Yulius to meet me there at ten o'clock the following morning. He gave me his card and we shook hands after I'd given him $S20 as a deposit for the trip the next day. He assured me that he would be on time. Then he drove off into a maelstrom of traffic and fumes.

Decorated in subdued colours, the hotel was rather gloomy, but the staff in their chic red uniforms gave it a brisk, efficient atmosphere. I checked in and was taken to my room via the stairs since the lift was out of order. The room was luxurious, if sunless, and overlooked a building site. After a quick inspection, I poured myself a large whisky and turned on the TV. Flipping through the channels I came across the film *The Fugitive*, starring Harrison Ford. He was about to make a death-defying leap down what looked like a precipitous waterfall. The picture, however, was of such poor quality and the transmission so jerky and spasmodic that it was plainly a pirated copy. The film had just gone on general release in Singapore. Interested to find out what else my hotel had to offer, I glanced through the tourist brochure I had been given on arriving. Written both in Chinese and English, it had all the usual anodyne stuff about what attractions there were on Batam. 'Water-sports fans would enjoy the water scooter, water skiing, wind surfing, sailing, speed boats and para *failing*!' The hotel itself offered 'exquisite local and international cuisine', as well other as excellent services, etc. '*She* is always ready to receive you warmly.' An unusual use of the feminine pronoun, I thought.

There was a light knock at my door. It was one of the staff, a sturdy-looking woman in her thirties. She wanted to know if I was happy with my room. I told her I was, but she insisted on coming in to check everything. I mentioned the building site and asked her what time they started work. She shrugged and smiled. She didn't know. After cursorily looking round, she mentioned that the hotel had a massage service which I might like to take advantage of. I politely declined her offer, but she persisted.

'Very nice massage.' Her eyes glinted suggestively.

'No thanks,' I replied, and walked to the door to show her out.

Glancing coyly at my crotch she made a masturbatory action with her hand. 'Very relaxing massage,' she hummed seductively.

Her hands, large and calloused, looked as if they had been ringing the necks of chickens all day, and I winced at the idea of my penis being engaged in a similar activity. Impatiently I shook my head and she finally left.

Yulius had given me a better map of Batam than the one I had in my tourist brochure. It showed all the main islands to the south of the Strait – Batam itself, Bulan island to the west, with its myriad of smaller islands, Bintan (the largest island) to the east, and the archipelago of smaller islands, Rempang and Galang, to the south of Batam. They effectively formed the adjoining corridor between the Malacca Strait and the South China Sea, and given their remoteness, it was little wonder crews of ships passing through these waters felt nervous and exposed. This extract from a captain's log testifies to that unease:

> Position north-east of Batam Island. Local time: 02.50. I have ordered a night watch, each watch compromising four crew to change every three hours. The searchlights are to be fully operational and manned throughout the hours of darkness.

Each watch is under strict orders to inform me of any suspicious vessels in the area. In the event of a hostile approach, the ship will maintain its course . . .

The steely doggedness of that final sentence might well have been uttered by a ship's captain in the sixteenth century. Except in those days the ships were at least armed, and if attacked by pirates could put up a fight. Searchlights and such defences as barbed wire and other anti-handling devices on today's ships are no match for rocket-launched grappling hooks, *parangs* and AK47s. It stood to reason that any ship passing through this region of the South China Sea should be armed. But here there is a mixture of reluctance and uncertainty: reluctance because weapons on a ship could be used by a disgruntled crew, and uncertainty because an armed ship might only provoke pirates to use larger and more sophisticated weapons. Less controversial anti-piracy equipment is available to ship-owners, but for some reason – perhaps cost – they're not inclined to use it.

I decided to get something to eat and went down to the restaurant. It was empty and had that 'hotel restaurant' atmosphere of piped music and pot plants and eager waiters in the wings who hassle you with fawning politeness. I dashed their hopes of being their first customer and decided to go and find a food court. Outside the hotel, lined up along the pavement, young taxi motorcyclists hailed me for business. Taxi drivers roared up and tooted their horns to get my attention. Had I been in London or Manchester, I would have been impatiently straining an arm now to stop a cab. I told one of the motorcyclists that I wanted a food court. He smiled and nodded and patted the pillion seat. I hopped on, assuming he knew where I wanted to go. With a swift manoeuvre we were out in the thronging traffic, my driver nipping in and out of the cars and lorries with such expertise that I had no time to be frightened. This was literally seat-of-the-pants travelling, and with the breeze billowing out my shirt and whipping back my hair it was exhilarating – the best air-conditioning service I'd had all day.

Some two miles or so outside the town centre, my driver suddenly made a sharp right turn, and perilously crossing the path of two lanes of traffic drew up outside a large, floodlit food court. I paid him and assumed he would get on his way. But he insisted on waiting for me. I tried to tell him that I would be some time, but he wouldn't go.

The food court was much like the ones in Malaysia and Singapore, with stalls of sizzling food and public seating, and each stallholder anxious to get your custom. At each stall I lingered at I was offered small helpings, appetisers that came almost to a full meal. The attraction of the food court was that the meals were cheap and well cooked. Eating here, you stood less chance of waking the next morning with a gut like a fiery cauldron. In the end I chose a plate of Indonesian satay and a beer. Sitting at a table, drinking and waiting for the meal to arrive three young prostitutes appeared, grinning lasciviously through heavily rouged lips. Their hair was garishly styled and heavily lacquered. I glanced at my taxi driver who was watching me attentively. He smiled and cheekily patted his pillion seat and pointed at the girls. It seemed they all wanted a ride of one kind or another.

The meal would have been excellent had it not been for the wheedling propositioning of the girls and my taxi driver's insistent gestures that he could accommodate the five of us comfortably. Western travellers, especially lone men, were harassed constantly for sex here, and I could sympathise with the way some women feel about the persistent attention of drunk men. It was a similar and intimidating experience. There was something in the region of 2,000 prostitutes in Batam, and while I could understand their plight in terms of little or no other work, their aggressive solicitousness more often than not made me lose my temper. However many erogenous zones there are on a man's body, his wallet is the only one they want to stimulate.

Rather than going straight back to the hotel, I walked the last half mile through the backstreets. The lack of street lighting and the broken pavements made walking a dangerous business. And the litter and open sewers gave the streets an intoxicatingly putrid smell. I sat in a small café under a tarpaulin and had a beer and watched the street scene. Everyone was involved in some kind of business – cooks, waiters, shop owners, taxi drivers, prostitutes, shoe-shine kids, hawkers and pick-pockets. It seems a peculiar Anglo-Saxon habit (perhaps just an English one) to sit alone and quietly contemplate things. At the other tables, plenty of energetic conversation was going on, things were being discussed, serious debates were in progress, deals were being hammered out, there was laughter and taunting. If Batam could harness and convert this energy to electricity, I thought, its street-lighting problems would be solved instantly. Looking around at how rundown and shabby it all was, it seemed to me that the whole infrastructure of the island was either on the point of collapse, or had collapsed; yet the life of the place had an irresistible vivacity. Batam was self-regulating chaos.

Back at the hotel, I took the lift (now repaired) to my room. As I stepped in, the masseur lady got in too. I fumbled for the floor button and pressed the wrong one.

'You are on the fourth floor,' she grinned, with vampiric predatoriness.

'Thanks,' I said, smelling her heavily scented body.

'You would like a massage now?'

'Maybe another time,' I told her as the door opened.

The corridor of my floor was dimly lit, and I half-expected to hear her voice behind me as I unlocked my door: *You would like a massage, a very nice massage?* It resonated in my mind like the opening line of a David Cronenberg horror movie.

Once safely inside my room, I turned on the TV and caught the last few scenes of *The Fugitive* – the ones that were discernible at least. As the credits rolled, the music skewered into a weird discordance, then the screen went blank. Obviously someone from the hotel had trekked over to Singapore for the matinee showing of the film, recorded it on a cheap VHS video camera, and caught the last ferry back. I wondered what the bosses of the studio that made the film would have had to say about this blatant act of piracy. I could imagine them raging at the reception desk of the hotel, and the staff looking confused and bewildered, and the masseur lady eventually calming things down by offering them *a very nice massage*!

Next morning I went out early to buy a newspaper and have a coffee.

Batam, like most Asian countries, never sleeps. Even at 5.30 a.m. everything seemed on the move. Cafés were being hosed down and brushed, deliveries were being made, tired and unshaven taxi drivers lingered on the street corners, the traffic was gridlocked, young newspaper vendors were standing on the road verges and islands, and stray dogs and cats dozed or scratched as the sun got up. I decided to buy a copy of the *Sijori Pos* (there is no English paper in Batam), not for the news (I couldn't read it anyway) but for the photographs. Handing the vendor a small denomination note, he frowned at it and dug his hand in his threadbare pockets for change. The huge quantity of notes I received back starkly demonstrated how totally out of control Indonesia's economy was: its inflation rate must have been in three figures.

Just off the main boulevard was a small coffee stall with some labourers having a quick snack before going off to work. A couple of rickety chairs and tables stood on rough ground. The coffee was black and thick as molasses, but excellent. Disappointingly, the newspaper was thick with text, and the few photographs it contained were, I supposed, of local dignitaries and politicians. Half an hour before Yulius was due to arrive, I returned to the hotel to collect and load my camera and gather up a few pens and a notepad. Surprisingly, Yulius turned up on time looking flushed and slightly agitated. He explained that he had had a last-minute booking to collect some tourists from Sekupang.

'Maybe we stop for coffee, Mr Bob?' he suggested.

I agreed, and we set off, with Yulius driving in his customary, oblivious way, weaving frantically among the traffic.

'How long will it take us to get to *kampong* Melayu?' I asked.

Yulius had an unnerving habit of looking at you while he talked, instead of watching the road.

'Maybe an hour, Mr Bob.'

We drove out of the town, and the same scarred and arid landscape began to appear again. Scattered among the plains of excavated land were the shells of concrete buildings laced with rusting wire cable. More abandoned projects, I assumed. Batam's ambition to become a thriving tourist centre seemed either doomed or misguided. If they couldn't get the mix of concrete correct, what hope was there?

'What is at *kampong* Melayu that you want to see, Mr Bob? It is just a fishing village. Nothing more.'

Though reticent earlier about telling him, I now had to come clean. 'I'm told that a gang of pirates operates from the village.'

'Pirates!' Yulius looked alarmed.

'I have it on good authority that there are three gangs operating on Batam, one of which may be at the village.'

Yulius regarded me earnestly, and slowed down. 'Mr Bob, these men . . . they are dangerous, very dangerous.'

'I only want to ask questions, not make accusations.'

To Yulius, however, that distinction was academic. He insisted that I be very careful and, rather than ask questions, merely look around the village.

I ignored him. 'I need you to interpret, Yulius.'

After much persuasion, he reluctantly agreed, but he was plainly anxious about the trip.

'Let's stop for breakfast soon.' The mention of food quickly improved his frame of mind, and spotting a restaurant Yulius pulled up.

The restaurant was plainly furnished, cheap and appeared to do little trade. It was part of a new development, a complex of shops that looked similarly down-at-heel. A couple of old Datsuns sat baking outside in the heat offering a little shade to some scrawny chickens which, I guessed, would soon be served up as a meal, their sinewy meat disguised in a rich, curry sauce. The restaurant owner, dressed in T-shirt and shorts, sauntered over to us, his misshapen and calloused feet slapping along the floor in an old pair of worn-out sandals. Yulius ordered coffee and a selection of pastries. Noticing how flyblown the food counter was, I told Yulius that I was more than happy with just coffee.

'So what is your interest in pirates, Mr Bob?' Yulius asked as the restaurant owner shuffled off.

'I think it's a good story.' It was the standard cliché answer, but I couldn't think of a better or more honest one. At other times when I had been asked this question, my attempts to explain my interest usually ended in a kind of embarrassing reductiveness, as if the more I talked about it, the less interesting the story seemed to be.

When the food came I paid for it, and Yulius tucked in with an appetite. For a moment I felt slightly guilty about involving him, as if I had deceived him into coming with me, which effectively I had. Yulius lived on the island, and if there were to be any dangerous repercussions from my investigation I knew I would be responsible for any harm that came to him.

'Are you married?' I asked.

'Yes,' he said, wiping his mouth. 'I have two small children, a girl and a boy. And you?'

'Yes. I have two girls.'

'Does your family know what you are doing?'

'You mean the piracy? No,' I said.

'Why have you not told them?' he enquired.

'I'm not sure they would be interested.'

'And what if anything should happen to you?' He looked at me in a rather accusing way, as if I was being extremely irresponsible.

'I don't know . . .' I replied.

A hawker, who had been hovering around us for a few minutes and trying to catch my attention, joined us. When I looked at him, he quickly sat down beside me and opened a small leather suitcase. It was full of trinkets, watches, rings, bracelets and other garish artefacts, mostly famous brand copies. He was the stereotypical, comic hawker, so beloved in colonial English literature: diminutive, wheedling, and inexhaustibly sycophantic. His sales pitch was delivered with such sly self-effacement it was difficult not to feel sorry for him.

'You like a watch? Sekonda, very good. You like a ring? Best gold . . . nine carat. You like a lighter? Electric . . . very expensive, but cheap to you . . .'

Yulius advised me to ignore him; then he would go.

But the hawker's pièce de resistance had yet to come – a tiger's penis.

He could see that I was intrigued, and to indicate its aphrodisiac powers, he made a circle of his index finger and thumb and placed his other index finger through it.

'Good for fucky-fucky!'

The 'tiger's penis' was caramel-coloured, about six inches long and pointed. I inspected it closely, felt it and handed it back.

'You buy this in Singapore and it will cost many thousand dollars. But I only ask you for fifty dollars.'

'It's plastic,' I replied.

The hawker was momentarily outraged and glared at me, but thought better of accusing me of insolence when Yulius interrupted and told him to leave. With a deferential, simpering smile, he packed up his wares and left.

There are only four petrol stations on Batam and I glanced at Yulius's fuel gauge to see that he had enough petrol. If where we were going was very remote, I didn't want to end up walking for miles in the scorching heat for fuel.

'Every day I fill up,' Yulius smiled reassuringly. 'And there are the unofficial petrol stations . . .'

The road had now become more of a trail, its surface a composite of compacted dirt and old tarmac. Some heavy commercial lorries passed us and when their nearside wheels caught the edge of the road huge dust storms exploded, blotting everything out for a few moments. Motorcyclists miraculously emerged from these storms with their eyes closed and heads down. It reminded me of those classic scenes in the film *Grapes of Wrath* when the convoy of battered trucks and cars hit the road and a wake of dust blew up behind them sealing them off from their past lives forever.

'This is where we go to the *kampong*.' Yulius indicated a rugged dirt track and turned sharply on to it. Kids on bicycles shuddered to a halt as Yulius breezed past them, banging on his horn and waving. More shells of houses stood in rubble-strewn wasteland, other abandoned projects. Impoverished cabins, with washed clothes hanging from lines, and families sitting on the porches with mangy dogs and cats, stood half-concealed by jungle.

'One day maybe Batam will be a rich country,' Yulius smiled with sad optimism. 'But until then we must work hard and always smile.'

It was another way of saying that Batam had to look on the bright side of things, and it was this happy resilience – however deluded perhaps – that kept its population going. But it was apparent to me that if there was money in the island's economy, it certainly wasn't ending up in the right places.

'Maybe you need a more democratic system of government.' I avoided using the word 'corruption', an allegation constantly levelled against the ruling élites in Indonesia.

Yulius smiled. 'This is Indonesia, Mr Bob. And Batam is just one small island.'

'What do you mean?'

'Indonesia is a big country, but it is all islands, many thousands. We are Batam people, but we are not our *own* country.'

The desire for self-determination (which Yulius I think was alluding to) was a sentiment I'd heard uttered elsewhere – in terms of Indonesia becoming a loose federation, that is. But the interests of the numerous rival parties came first – to rule rather than to represent. And if that coincided with some form of democracy, all well and good. Here it patently did not, if the disparities in the island's economy were anything to go by. Batam seemed to exist on a cheap deal made elsewhere. But I appreciated Yulius's stoic optimism.

The jungle became denser as we drove on, and the track bumpier. The harsh sunlight was now reduced to flickerings and shadows in the thickening enclosure of vegetation. I wound down my window and caught the tangy, arresting smell of the jungle, a mixture of humidified mould and fleshy greenness; the smell of fertility, almost sensual. In the Malaysian jungle, or here in Indonesia, it made me wonder why the biblical story of Eden had as its mythical setting usually a very pastoral 'English' landscape, instead of the writhing, almost celebratory sexual ambience of the jungle.

The track made its way along the edge of a mangrove swamp, and in a clearing I saw two wooden fishing skiffs moored up. Opposite, and set back from the track, was a small stilted house, and a fisherman repairing a boat. His little daughter, in a gaily coloured frock and bare feet, played nearby.

'Pull up, Yulius. I'd like to speak to him.'

Yulius parked the van, and as we walked up the path to the house the girl ran to her father and grasped his leg. Yulius greeted the fisherman in Indonesian. He was holding a long, sharp knife (a *parang*) with which he was carving strips of wood to repair the damaged sections of his boat. We shook hands and his daughter tucked herself around the back of her father's leg, and stared at us with entrancing hazel eyes.

I asked Yulius to ask him if he knew of any pirate activity in these parts. After a brief conversation, Yulius turned to me.

'He's not heard of anything. He says that his boats are only for in-shore fishing, and he would never take them out to sea.'

He pointed down the track. 'At the next village,' he told Yulius, 'they have a big ship and fast boats. The water is deep there and they go far out to sea. I think maybe you should talk to them.'

'That will be *kampong* Melayu,' Yulius said.

After thanking the fisherman, we got back in the van and drove off.

A short while later I noticed a deep, single rut in the track imprinted with tyre markings. As we approached the village, a group of young boys on motorcycles came tearing up the track in our direction. Some had their feet on the saddles, their knees tucked under their chins. Others rode side-saddle, their wrists twitching on the accelerator grips to maximise the bikes' traction. It was quite apparent that they were expert riders, and as we were painfully bumping along, I rather envied them.

The village was a traditional *kampong*, with stilted 'houses' (more like huts) built along the bay and linked by a series of plank walkways. The houses, all made of wood, were extremely modest – basically just one large room with an open matt door at one end and a similar opening at the other. There was a kiosk shop and a small restaurant (a hut with a few chairs and tables), and lying about, all the usual paraphernalia of village life: abandoned kids' toys, clothes-lines, domestic wares, a couple of old rusting trucks, and litter. At the end of the stilted landing-stage a large ship was docked, and beside it sat fishermen mending nets and listening to music on a portable radio. It all looked very idyllic. The song, Yulius told me, was a lament to dead fishermen.

While Yulius talked to a friend who owned a house just outside the village, I sat at the restaurant with some of the village boys. I bought them Cokes while I had a beer (Muslim countries are often more hospitable regarding alcohol than some English pubs). We communicated in gestures of mutual misunderstanding, me trying to explain who I was, them mimicking me and laughing in return. While they played with my camera, giggling and snapping each other, I glanced round the village and saw how strategically perfectly located it was to run pirate operations from. Set in a remote bay and surrounded by mangrove swamps and jungle, it had deep water and direct access into the main shipping lanes. And, as the fisherman we'd earlier met had said, it had a large ship. Obviously the ship was used for fishing, but equally it could have been used as a pirate 'mother' ship from which to launch attacks.

Yulius had arranged for me to speak to the headman of the village. He lived in a small house on the edge of the bay by the landing-stage. Unlike the other villagers' houses, his was glazed, air-conditioned and wallpapered, and was – by the standards of the others – quite sumptuously furnished. I offered to buy him a drink at the restaurant, but he refused. Throughout our discussion he sat steadfastly in the doorway of his house. Perhaps in his mid-forties, his face was hard and inexpressive, and he held me with an unflinching gaze, his eyes dark and deeply set, and a mouth that barely moved. His countenance gave the impression of a highly ruthless character.

He wanted to know what my interest was in coming to the village, and I told him through Yulius that I was investigating sea piracy in the area. He glanced at two men who sat impassively beside him. The mention of piracy clearly made him agitated, and his eyes narrowed and became furtive. Did he know anything?

'I do not know,' he said, glaring at me.

'I've been told that there are three gangs of pirates operating from Batam, and one of the gangs is in this area.'

His face stiffened. 'I have not heard of any pirates in this area.'

I pointed at the ship. 'Is that a fishing boat?'

'Yes.'

'Where do you fish with it?'

He pointed in the general direction of the Phillip Strait, then waved his arm as if to indicate everywhere. 'We fish.'

'Has your ship been used for any other purposes?' I saw no reason not to push him for information.

THE AUTHOR ON THE ISLAND OF BATAM, INDONESIA

JOE

ON A PANCUNG — THE PIRATES' FAVOURITE CRAFT

THE PHILLIP STRAIT

BELAKANG PADANG ISLAND WITH A VIEW OF THE PHILLIP STRAIT AND SINGAPORE IN
THE DISTANCE

BELAKANG PADANG VILLAGE. ONCE (AND PERHAPS STILL?)
A HAVEN OF PIRATES

LEFT: GOMAN AND DAUGHTER, BELAKANG PADANG. A REPRESENTATIVE OF PIRATES?

BELOW: 'ENI' CAFÉ, BELAKANG PADANG.

MR WONG (RIGHT) WITH HIS LAWYER, MR DAHLAN. BATAM PRISON

ONE OF WONG'S GANG IN BATAM PRISON

JOE HOLDING A PARANG

THE AUTHOR WITH NAVY INTELLIGENCE, BINTAN ISLAND

PANCUNG

'We are just fishermen.'

'So you know nothing of piracy in this area?'

'Nothing.'

I asked if I could take some photographs of him and the village. He shook his head angrily. 'No photographs!'

Yulius discreetly gestured to me that we should stop asking questions now. I thanked the headman and offered to shake hands, but he declined. It was apparent that he wanted us to leave the village.

I walked back with Yulius into the village. A group of children sat contentedly playing in the dirt, drawing pictures with their fingers. An old man lounged in a chair on the porch of a house, his wizened face smiling thoughtfully out to sea. At a safe distance from the headman, I turned to Yulius.

'What do you think?'

'I think he knows much more than he's telling.'

'You reckon he's involved in some way in piracy, don't you?'

Yulius's usual jolly expression had now become grim, almost frightened. 'I think we should leave now, Mr Bob.'

I told Yulius that I wanted to look round for a while; I too had my suspicions, and was sure that the headman's nervousness was because something was going on or was about to happen that he didn't wish us to see. Yulius decided to wait for me in the van.

I walked along the maze of connecting walkways among the houses, peering into them and waving at the occupants. The houses reminded me of a beach hut I'd rented on the island of Sibu off the south-west coast of Malaysia. They were very rudimentary, with just one room, no furniture, and mats on the floor. They smelled of confined living, and had no visible sanitation, water supply or electricity. In one hut three generations of one family were living – the grandfather, son, his wife and their two children. Yet they seemed remarkably content, without the domestic frictions and resentments you would normally expect. Rather than breeding contempt, this closeness seemed to have the opposite effect: it encouraged tolerance, consideration, sharing. It was a way of life easy to idealise, but they, of course, had no choice in the matter.

As I looked out towards the sea, through the palm-fringed window of one of the houses I'd been invited into, suddenly piracy was the last thing on my mind. The fishermen were still singing to the music as they mended their nets, and the sea breeze had a tropical coolness that made me instinctively push my head forwards into it and briefly close my eyes. There are moments of personal epiphany we relish, such as that moment, feeling the simplicity of things, the sea breeze on my face, the singing, and the smell of how these people lived. It was like reaching a blissful distance after a very short step. If it hadn't been for a distracting incident, I could have remained in that reverie all afternoon.

I heard several outboard engines being started up in the direction of the ship, and saw blue exhaust smoke sweep out from behind its starboard side. Then three skiffs appeared, all laden with boxes. With their engines ticking over, they made a slow arc across the bay, and then headed in towards the village. The skiffs were all driven by women and, as they approached, one of them waved towards the shore. Suddenly I spotted, concealed in a mangrove swamp a hundred metres or so outside the village, three Indonesian Navy launches, their crews, all in uniform, idly sitting about, smoking and talking. One of the crew waved back to the woman. I hurried to the end of the walkway to get a better view. The contents of the skiffs were quite visible from where I stood – cardboard boxes clearly marked Sony and Panasonic. There were four or five boxes in each boat. As they landed, other women came out to meet them. I watched them unload the cargo, each woman taking one box, placing it carefully on her head then walking towards what I had presumed was a boat shed. Moments later they returned to collect more boxes. It was obvious to me that what was occurring was a smuggling operation, and right under the noses of the Indonesian Navy. They could clearly see what was going on, but they appeared not in the slightest bit interested. Someone else was interested though, and not so much in what was happening, but in me: the headman. Catching his malevolent glare, I quickly moved away, pretending that I had seen nothing. I hurriedly tried to take some photographs before the last box was unloaded, but in my excitement I managed to jam the film.

Yulius was waiting for me in the van. Climbing in I asked him if he had seen what had been going on. He nodded grimly.

'I think we had better go, Mr Bob. It is not wise to stay here any longer.' He started the engine and thrust it into gear.

'Wait a moment, Yulius,' I said impatiently. 'I need to change the film in my camera. I need photographs.'

Yulius shook his head and drove off. 'The headman said no photographs.'

I suggested to Yulius, who was clearly frightened, that he drop me off outside the village and I would walk back alone. But he refused and drove on. Some way out of the village, Yulius slowed down and relaxed.

'The Indonesian Navy were there. Did you see them?' I said.

'Yes.'

'And that was obviously a smuggling operation, yet they weren't interested.'

'I told you, Mr Bob. That headman knew more than he was prepared to tell us.'

Arriving back at the hotel, I paid Yulius and suggested dinner later. He agreed. In the meantime he had several taxi runs to make, and we arranged to meet at eight o'clock. As Yulius drove off, I wondered whether he himself knew more than he was prepared to tell me.

In the hotel lobby, a basketball team from Australia had recently arrived. Most of the players were well over six feet tall and dwarfed the hotel staff, who were frenziedly trolleying in their kits-bags and gear. For the masseur lady, who was excitedly moving among them, her Valhalla had come. Her hands, I guessed, would be literally full tonight. I bought a beer and sat down on one of the large, dark leather sofas under a tall plant to write up some notes. But my notebook and pen had been so contaminated by sweat that the pages were stuck together and my pen had leaked. As for my camera, its lens was completely fogged by moisture. Even if I had managed to make it work at the *kampong*, it was unlikely I would have got any decent shots.

Were the Indonesian Navy involved in piracy, I wondered. They were, as far as I could see, complicit (if only by virtue of turning a blind eye) in the smuggling that had obviously been going on in the *kampong* that afternoon. In any case, why were they there? There was nothing to suggest anything remotely like a naval base in or near the village. If they were on some kind of exercise, they looked surprisingly relaxed. Perhaps they were making a routine visit to the *kampong* – but then why choose a muddy mangrove swamp to land your boat when there was dry and ample mooring at the village? I was sure that Yulius could have confirmed my suspicions, but his reluctance spoke for itself. He was frightened.

Not liking the solitude of hotel rooms, I went out to a local market to browse around. I wanted some clean shirts, and the Indonesian men wore some pretty fancy ones, highly patterned and brightly decorative. The market was very much an impromptu affair, with stalls made of anything from bits of rug or carpet to old collapsible tables. I expected to see someone's granny with a price tag round her neck. It was the same eclectic mix of goods I'd seen in Kuala Lumpur and in the thieves' market in Singapore. The vendors sat by their stalls on rickety chairs or sat on the ground with a makeshift tarpaulin over their heads to protect them from the sun. I eventually came across a shirt stall, and the vendor (a delightful old man in his sixties) insisted I try on every shirt that attracted me. He was a superb salesman, and ten minutes and the same number of dollars later I'd gone native with half a dozen shirts. I would liked to have thought of them as metropolitan chic, but they could not have been worn anywhere else than in Indonesia. They were de rigueur tropical.

I was in the bar when Yulius arrived at the hotel. He was late and seemed agitated and was effusively apologetic. He excused himself with some vague and garbled reasons related to his work. Nevertheless, he'd managed to get home and changed, and looked just this side of dapper – a bright, flowery shirt and dark trousers.

'Do you know of any good restaurants? You choose where we go,' I said.

'I will take you to a restaurant where they serve excellent Indonesian food. Have you tried our food?'

'Apart from your satay, no.'

As we left the hotel, Yulius casually remarked that at the restaurant there would be some people who wanted to speak with me.

'Who? What about?' I asked.

'I do not know, Mr Bob,' he shrugged in an exaggerated way. 'Maybe something to do with your interest in piracy.'

'Who are they?'

'I do not know who they are.'

'You must do,' I said.

Yulius didn't want to be questioned; he climbed in his van and, with a concentrated expression that told me not to quiz him further, he drove off. 'The food will be very good, Mr Bob. It is one of the best restaurants in Batam.'

But I could see that Yulius was quietly anxious, almost as if he had been ordered by someone to take me to the restaurant. I sat still, wondering what was going on. I had faith that Yulius would not let anything happen to me – but then I had just met him, and only the Customs knew I was officially in Batam. Neither of us spoke as Yulius turned from one street into another, each street dimly lit only by shops and restaurants. We were driving into the backstreets, where everything seemed to deteriorate into grubbiness and destitution.

'Are we nearly there?' I asked Yulius.

'Yes, Mr Bob. The next street.'

As we drove into the street, there was one building lit more brightly than the others. It was two storeys, and the light emanating from the windows, though subdued, seemed to be coming from table lamps. There was no name above the restaurant's door. Parked outside it were fairly new cars, and a number of taxis were arriving and departing. It struck me as very odd that this was, according to Yulius, one of the best local restaurants; the area could hardly be called prosperous. And apart from a few straggling groups of people, there was next to no one on the street. Litter rolled along the edges of broken gutters, and the telephone and electric cable lines that crisscrossed above sagged heavily. It was disconcertingly eerie, and I was tempted to suggest to Yulius that we went elsewhere.

Despite my reservations, I followed him into the restaurant. It was surprisingly quite pleasantly furnished, almost sumptuously so compared with some of the places I'd visited. The tables had clean linen cloths, each with a small lamp and polished cutlery. Though open-plan and unimaginatively designed, it had a nice intimate atmosphere, with couples and groups at corner tables, their faces warmly lit by the ochre lights. While Yulius went to talk to the owner, I glanced around the restaurant to see who it might be who wanted to meet me. But there was no one in particular who caught my attention, or even glanced in my direction. Yulius finally joined me and suggested a table upstairs. I mentioned that there were empty tables where we were, but he insisted that it was more pleasant and comfortable upstairs. Except for being totally empty, it was no different. Yulius ushered me to a table at the far end of the dining-room and handed me a menu.

'Do you want me to translate the dishes?'

I glanced at the menu. It was all written in Indonesian.

With some difficulty, Yulius explained each dish, and suggested what I should order. (In Indonesia, you order as many dishes as you like, but you only pay for the ones you eat.) I deferred to Yulius's suggestions – a selection of fish, pork and chicken with rice and vegetables.

'What about yourself?' I asked.

Yulius nervously explained that he would join me later; in the meantime, perhaps I would like a beer while he put my order in. Puzzled, I agreed and Yulius walked off. After he had gone I moved to a seat where I could see the whole restaurant.

A little while later, a young waitress arrived with my beer. She lingered, smiling coyly and wriggling her hands by her side. She was waiting for a tip. I gave her a couple of notes, which she looked at disappointedly. I gave her more and she left, beaming. I sipped my beer and waited patiently for Yulius to return. I was now convinced that he was up to something, but whatever it was he seemed under some duress. I was about to leave when my food arrived on a large tray carried by the same waitress. She placed one small dish after another on the table, each one looking much like the other and covered in a thick curry sauce. By the time the final dish had been placed on the table, my appetite had all but gone. I gingerly picked at a couple of dishes, almost expecting them to jerk alive. They had been reheated and I was glad that I had packed medicine for upset stomachs. I was going to need it.

In a state of excitement, Yulius finally appeared.

'You are enjoying the food, Mr Bob?'

I pulled out the chair beside me and asked him to sit down.

'What's going on, Yulius?' I asked. 'I thought we were meant to be having dinner together. Where have you been?'

Yulius glanced down the restaurant then, in a confidential tone, told me that he had been speaking to the men who wanted to meet me. They were downstairs and as soon as I had finished my dinner I was invited to join them. Abruptly I explained to Yulius that I'd be finished in ten minutes. He nodded and went off to order me another beer. When the beer came, I tipped the girl, paid my bill for the dinner and angrily marched off down the stairs. This silly game of subterfuge had now gone beyond a joke, and I was in no mood for it. Before I had reached the last step, Yulius appeared from behind the bar.

'You have finished, Mr Bob?'

I showed him the bill. 'Forty dollars for what I've eaten is excessive.' I handed him the bill and his face fell. 'What's more, unless these guys I'm meant to meet are here I'm going.'

'I will write you out another bill. This one I think is wrong.'

It was obvious that Yulius, with the owner of the restaurant, was out to fleece me.

'Now I will take you to meet the men.'

They were sitting in a dimly lit alcove that I had overlooked when we arrived. Both were Indonesian, and in their late thirties or early forties. Smartly dressed, both wore crisply ironed white short-sleeved shirts and dark, well-pressed trousers. Their manicured hands were adorned with jewellery – heavy gold rings, wrist chains and chunky watches. One had a thin, well-trimmed moustache. Both were smoking American brand cigarettes and both had mobile phones and black briefcases.

The one with the moustache got up and offered his hand as Yulius introduced me.

'Bob? Yes?' We shook hands. 'Would you like to join us for coffee? Here, please, take a seat.' With an elegant sweep of his hand he pointed at the chair on the opposite side of the table.

I sat next to the other man who cursorily greeted me. Neither offered their names.

The one with the moustache told Yulius to fetch me a coffee. Yulius's expression was exaggeratedly deferential, yet barely concealed his fear. Whoever these men were, Yulius was eager to please them. With a smile of suave politeness, I was offered a cigarette. Both were well educated, especially the one with the moustache, whose English was almost pedantically impeccable. He pronounced every word as if he were giving an elocution lesson. The other one, more taciturn, had a sort of gruff, smouldering voice, and tonally ended every sentence as if it were a question. He chain-smoked and extinguished each cigarette in the growing mound in the ashtray with a heavy, thoughtful sigh.

'So how do you like Indonesian food, Bob?'

'Unforgettable.'

He laughed, understanding that I hadn't enjoyed my dinner. Yulius brought my coffee, and, with a self-conscious grin, departed.

'May I ask who you are?' I thought it about time they told me.

'We are just businessmen, Bob. And you, I believe, are a journalist?'

'Amongst other things, yes.'

The other man watched me with lugubrious eyes, as if he were listening out of obligation to his colleague. His heavily set face gave a solid bearing to his mouth that almost fixed it into a scowl.

'You want to speak to me. Is that the case?' I asked.

'We are always interested to speak to people who visit Batam, especially English people.' He paused, and in a slightly self-deprecating voice, asked: 'How do you like my English?'

'Very good,' I told him. 'Where did you learn to speak such good English?'

'I learnt it well at school. Also my friend here.'

This blond and strained convivial chatter was beginning to bore me, but, like them, I intended to remain politely enigmatic. Then the man beside me asked if I was enjoying my visit to Batam and if I was on holiday.

'Yes. Just a short break from Singapore; I'm leaving tomorrow.' I felt they were now getting to the point.

'Batam is a very beautiful place, don't you think?'

'I haven't seen enough of it to judge. But I'm sure you are right.'

'As a journalist, do you intend to write anything about Batam?' the man beside me asked.

'You mean as a holiday destination?'

He smiled and lit another cigarette. 'Yes . . . And maybe about other things?'

I declined to answer him and sipped my coffee. I could almost have anticipated what he was about to say.

'What is your interest in sea piracy, Bob?' the mustachioed one asked, without a hint of inquisitive irony.

'I think it's a good story.' I saw no point in asking them how they knew I was investigating piracy on the island. Yulius had, of course, told them.

'And how is your story going?' He asked me in a way a tutor might ask his student about the progress of his thesis.

'Why are you interested?'

Both men glanced at each other, their expressions briefly changing into a kind of mean candour.

'You should understand that it is very dangerous for you.'

'So what do you two know about piracy?' I asked.

They chuckled cagily, caught out momentarily by my forthrightness. An embarrassed silence followed. One fidgeted with his phone, while the other fingered the sugar bowl. In a low monotone, the one with the moustache repeated himself. 'It is very dangerous for you.'

'I'll bear your advice in mind.'

'That's good.'

They were men whose small-talk had consequences, and whose politeness hinted a threat.

Deciding it was time to go, they collected their briefcases and left money on the table for the coffee. Either I was a lost cause and they had failed to convince me, or I had understood their 'warning' and would leave the island and forget the story. It was one of those ambiguous partings where the significance of what should have been said was left, like the coffee cups, for someone else to clear up. I never saw them again.

As soon as they had gone, Yulius came up to me. 'Was your discussion interesting, Mr Bob?'

'Who were they, Yulius?'

Yulius shuffled his hands together and looked uncomfortable. 'I don't know.'

'They said they were businessmen. So why are they interested in what I'm doing? Unless of course their businesses involve piracy?'

I could see that Yulius was not prepared to divulge anything about these men. Either he had been threatened, or else he was simply trying to placate them. I suspected the former, and therefore I was not going to get anything out of him. I suggested he take me back to my hotel. He looked at me with visible relief.

'You look tired, Mr Bob,' he said. 'I think I should take you back.'

Our return journey was in silence. I leant against the window and watched the streets passing like a series of fading lights and transient shadows. I hoped that Yulius might finally tell me who those men were, but each time I glanced at him, his expression was resolute. I was convinced that they were either pirates or military intelligence. Perhaps even both! The secretive, Byzantine world of organised crime (if that is what I had now stumbled into) seemed like a Restoration play, so many guises and disguises, so much shifting of scenery and voices whispering off stage. And Batam offered the perfect backdrop, with its poorly lit streets, its volatile temperament and its crumbling economy.

At the hotel, I asked Yulius in for a drink. But the bar was crowded with the basketball team, so we decided to find a coffee shop. Yulius was my only contact in Batam and I couldn't afford to lose him. The coffee shop we stopped at was delightful, if rather scruffy. The lights flickered temperamentally and gusts of wind blew litter in. A storm was on its way. Yulius seemed more relaxed now and suggested I might like to go to a KTV bar after our coffee. He, however, had to get home.

'If you're free tomorrow, Yulius, I'd like to tour along the north coast of the island before I catch the ferry back to Singapore.'

'I may be very busy, Mr Bob.'

'But if you're not, would you take me?'

He handed me his business card and suggested I phone him in the morning. It was his taxi business number. I suspected, though, that he wouldn't be free to take me, even if I offered him more money. I avoided broaching what had happened earlier, and we talked about his work and family, Batam's politics and its future, and Yulius's ambitions. I began to like Yulius and to respect him. He was as cunning and duplicitous as the next, but that was the way everybody seemed here. But I knew he loved Batam, its history and culture, and it was deeply saddening that Yulius's life, like so many of the people here, was destined simply to scratch a living, to make meagre ends meet, and to be obligingly humble.

As the storm blew up, Yulius thanked me for the coffee and left. I decided to stay on and thought I'd go to a bar later. The storm was ferocious, but no one in the café paid it much attention. Fissures of lightning spread like an electrified root system across the sky, spurts of long tendrilous jagged fingers, and then the thunder that sounded like the harsh crashing of metal on rock. The rain swept everything into near invisibility. When the lights failed in the café, I left and inched my way along the street, ducking the rain by sheltering in doorways and under tarpaulins. Ahead of me I saw a small neon light that flashed KTV bar and decided to go in. The doorway had a string of small coloured lights surrounding it, and I could hear loud Western music playing. It was hot and sticky inside and packed with people. The bar was doing a brisk trade with mainly Japanese and Chinese men jostling to be served. And everywhere there were young women provocatively dressed in tight short skirts and revealing tops. These girls weren't like the street girls; they were much more sophisticated and predatory. I finally managed to buy a beer (at an outrageous price), found a table and sat down to watch this flesh festival. There was a continuous up-and-down flow of men and girls on a steep, dark and cramped stairway that presumably led to the rooms where they had sex. For KTV in S.E. Asia, read brothel.

One of the girls had already spotted me and came over to my table. In the gloominess of the place, she appeared at first quite attractive – slim, petite and wearing a dark-blue silk dress. She was Indonesian, with tantalising hazel eyes. But as the dim yellow light from the table lamp caught her face, she seemed to metamorphose. Her naked shoulders, like her legs, were oily, and her features lacked the freshness of her age. Her face was bunched and fleshy, with wet garishly painted lips that were almost molten. Her lacquered hair shone and glittered. She appeared almost ghoulish.

'Are you looking for a woman?' she asked in a quasi-American accent.

'No, just having a beer.'

'Would you like me to bring some girls over?'

Her face was curiously engaging, and I found myself staring at her.

'If you would like me, buy me a drink, and then we'll go for a fuck. Eighty dollars.'

'I'll let you know,' I said dismissively.

She got up and left and went to join a group of girls who had corralled a bunch of Japanese men at the end of the bar. I'd heard that Indonesian girls favoured Japanese men for sex. Another girl soon joined me, but I initially mistook her for a customer. She was blonde and European and was wearing a kaftan-style dress. She glanced coyly at me and smiled.

'Hi,' she said and extended her hand. 'My name's Judy . . . and I hate it!' she laughed.

I shook her hand, amused by her introduction.

'Where are you from?' I asked.

'Originally Australia.'

'Originally?'

'Yes,' she shrugged and pursed her lips in a slightly sad way.

'Where do you live now?'

'Here in Batam.'

'So what are you doing in this place?'

She hesitated and looked embarrassed. 'I work here.'

I bought her a drink and she told me she had left Australia a year ago to travel with her boyfriend. Her father had abused her and her mother had left home. Her boyfriend was taking a gap year before going to university and had persuaded her to go with him. Within two months of arriving in Indonesia her boyfriend was dead, the result of a diving accident. Rather than return to Australia, Judy had decided to stay.

'I managed to get odd jobs in the hotels. Bintan was the last island I worked on. I tried to get work in Singapore, but they're stricter than here about work permits. But the money in the hotels was lousy, so I decided to do what the other girls did . . .' She smiled with a beguiling girlishness. 'Provide an extra service for the men.'

For a moment, feeling rather prudish on her behalf, I was tempted to admonish her for working in this bar as a prostitute, but it was none of my business and anyway I was pleased to have her company.

'So how did you end up here?' I asked.

'I came here to try and get into Singapore, but as I said I didn't have a work permit so I found work in one of the hotels. Then I met some girls who worked in this bar and they introduced me to the owner. It was a bit scary at first, but I started making more money than I'd ever had before.'

I was curious. 'How much do you earn?'

'Depends,' she said, straightening her blouse. 'We charge clients around eighty dollars, but it can be negotiable if the punters are down. Then of course we have to pay rent for the rooms, but I can still make several hundred bucks a week, a lot more than most people earn in Batam.'

'Do you think you'll go back to Australia one day?'

She sighed heavily and smiled. 'Perhaps. When I've made enough money. Maybe I'll go back to college, or try and start some sort of business . . . I don't know.'

Judy was the typical runaway. I'd met them in Singapore and Malaysia. Europeans, Australians, Americans, all seeking a hide-out in S.E. Asia, a refuge from some hideously embarrassing situation at home about which they never wanted to talk. Like Judy, they tended to be loners, and appeared to be just about coping with the ghosts of their pasts. They worked hard and lived alone, and when things became too familiar in their lives again, too close to who they really were, they got frightened and disappeared. No forwarding address, no letters of resignation, no hastily written messages of explanation. They just disappeared.

'So what brings you to Batam?' Judy asked.

I wondered whether to lie, and just tell her that I was over here on a short break from Singapore. But she had been honest with me, and since she wasn't Indonesian I felt less circumspect.

'I'm investigating sea piracy.'

'Wow! You mean people who steal ships and that?' she said with astonishment.

'Yes, that's about it,' I smiled.

'Wow!' Her eyes widened with fascination and intrigue. 'Have you met any pirates then?'

I told her about the smuggling operation I'd witnessed at *kampong* Melayu and the two men I'd met in the restaurant earlier, who I believed were involved in some way in piracy. I avoided boring her with the facts and statistics of piracy, and told her various stories I'd read about hijacked ships and the Mafia-style organisations I thought were behind piracy. She seemed enthralled, and I suspected her imagination already had her embarking on a new life as a sort of pirate's moll – another escape, another adventure into an illusory exile.

She looked thoughtful. 'You know, I'm sure I've heard of a girl working in one of the clubs here who was the girlfriend of someone who was rumoured to be a pirate. Some Chinese guy who owned a ship that he kept anchored off Batam.' She paused and placed a finger on her lips. 'But I can't remember which club it was, nor her name.' She wracked her memory, but then shook her head. 'All I know is that she lived with him for a while in one of the hotels here, but then he used to just disappear for weeks on business, and when he returned he spent a lot of money on her. Then one day he disappeared altogether.'

'Well,' I said, 'if you do happen to remember her, perhaps you could let me know. I'd certainly like to talk to her.'

I gave her my address in Singapore and asked for hers. She evasively declined, but said that she would ask the other girls if they knew where this girl was. She promised to contact me if she had any information. I offered to buy her another drink, and told her how much I appreciated her company. Her demeanour suddenly changed, and she gazed vacantly around the club.

'Thanks,' she said. 'But I'd better get back to work.' She touched my shoulder and looked at me with almost comical amorousness. 'Unless you . . .'

'Nice of you to offer, but I'm going in a minute. Besides,' I added, 'I haven't got eighty bucks.'

We shook hands and I watched her move off into the smoky mêlée of the club, her kaftan dress and her blonde hair suddenly dissolving in the vaporous gloom of the place. I hoped she would contact me, but like everything in Batam, nothing could be depended upon.

Walking back to my hotel, a thought suddenly struck me. I was sure that the two men I had met in the restaurant must have found out where I was staying, and if they were who I suspected them to be, there was every chance that they might have acquired my key and searched my room. In a panic I quickly itemised in my mind everything that was there, but couldn't think of anything remotely compromising or too valuable – apart from my passport. All the same, I felt I had to get back quickly and check my room.

When I got to the hotel, the only thing I noticed was that my room had been tidied and the bed made. I opened the desk drawer where I kept my passport, ferry ticket and notebook. They were all there, and the only things that had been moved were the room's furnishings – the TV's remote control, a glass, some travel brochures and a telephone directory. I poured a large whisky and lay on the bed, feeling exhausted by the day's events as well as by an almost indulgent sense of paranoia. I had persuaded myself that I had nothing to fear from what I was doing, no matter what I had been told or however much I had been advised to be careful. For a while I listened to the workmen outside (working in the cool of the evening under arc lights) hammering away and chattering, slow meticulous work that seemed to be making little or no progress, just enough to keep the boss happy. I turned on the TV and another pirated film came on, this time with such a poor soundtrack it was virtually inaudible. I tried to find the BBC World Service on my radio, but every station seemed to crackle with static or morse. I had with me some fictional stories of modern-day piracy, written by an American author, but only published on the Internet. I had leafed through them already, but had not found them especially interesting. Without anything else to do, I decided to look at them again.

All the stories (including some that just seemed episodic narratives, and others that ended with illustrative fictionalised interviews) were titled only with the year in which they were set, the first in 1998, the last in 2009. The first story was about a family of Indonesian pirates – improbably named Juan, Uncle Jeff, Gry and Toeday. Humble fishermen, they and their village (and in fact the whole island) were beset by that age-old Malthusian problem of overpopulation and not enough work in the towns to go around. So to make ends meet, they decided to attack and rob a passing yacht. The hijacking, however, was foiled by some of the crew, and a fierce gun battle broke out. Our poor and humble heroes are soon brandishing, with considerable expertise, 9mm pistols and machine-guns, and speaking like B-movie gangsters. The story ends with an inevitable blood bath, and our heroes finally setting the yacht adrift and making off with their ill-gotten loot. A daft story, but it cheered me up.

Another story, much more convincing, had a Chinese Navy frigate intercepting a cargo ship. There was a rancorous exchange between the two captains before a warning volley from the frigate was shot across the bow of the cargo ship. Once on board, the frigate's captain ordered a search of the ship for contraband. A small amount of marijuana was found, also some pornography. Since the ship was in Chinese waters, the Chinese captain felt it was within his authority to detain it. A scuffle followed and the captain was shot dead. The discovery of the drugs and pornography was – so the author seemed to imply – pretext enough to officially pirate the ship and then sell off the cargo once in port. Perhaps these were the same military the Chinese authorities branded as 'rogues' when the International Maritime Bureau got uppity about the Chinese sponsoring piracy. From what I'd heard about the Chinese Navy, this story was perhaps not too far from the truth in the way a ship was deceived into being hijacked.

Though badly written, it struck me as being closer than the other stories to the truth of the 'culture' of piracy in S.E. Asia: an exiled, homeless and desperate people turning to crime, and a ready market for their hauls in a country on the verge of becoming a commercial world player, a country where organised crime was 'legitimised' – so long as it earned money and didn't transgress any cultural rules. Whether controversially China was in fact 'sponsoring' piracy – and as I've said before, there is no hard evidence to support this accusation – pan-Asian economics, with all their stark national contrasts in terms of wealth and prosperity, and the First World competing to penetrate these markets, it would seem inevitable that China, now recognised as the leading power in this sphere, might be tempted to take advantage of these commercial opportunities, legitimate or not. After all, it's an economic truth, applicable to the West as well, that where there's wealth, crime prospers. Russia is an obvious example. Every country has its equivalent rice-bowl theory.

Next day, I tried to phone Yulius, but was told that he wasn't in the office. Impatiently I rang several more times, but each time I was told that Yulius was 'out'. I pondered hiring a motorbike taxi to take me along the north coast, but I needed an interpreter as well. After last night's events, I suppose I wasn't unduly surprised that he was avoiding me. Before going out, I rang Yulius's office once more and told the girl to leave a message for him to get in touch with me at the hotel. In any case, he was due to take me to the ferry at Sekupan for the early afternoon sailing back to Singapore.

I went for a coffee, but was anxious to see more of the island. I hired a motorbike taxi and went off to Waterfront City located on the broad bay of Teluk Senimba. It was a gruelling but thrilling ride, the storm the night before having strewn dangerous mud slicks across the roads. They would dry by midday and be turned into blinding dust. My taxi driver would occasionally turn his head round and beam at me, probably checking that I was still with him. Oily smoke billowed out between my legs, and the vibration of the engine, along with the shot suspension, set every nerve in my backside ringing. I couldn't imagine how old the bike was, but it felt as if it had covered many more miles than it had been designed for.

I had expected Waterfront City to be a thriving resort where, as my brochure declared, 'The Fun Never Ends'. Apart from a few tourists and locals, it was empty. It was obviously a new development, and had almost succeeded in reaching completion, except for tell-tale signs like roads that went nowhere, expanses of wasteland and only one pleasure cruiser in the unfinished harbour. It seemed the fun had in fact never begun. Perhaps I had come in the wrong season, but the place had an atmosphere of dying expectancy. The promise of hordes of tourists, like other promises in Batam, was resoundingly hollow. I walked up to the only hotel I could see to get a beer and wash the road out of my throat. The hotel was modern, functional, open-plan and entirely featureless. Its marble lobby was expansive and cool, with two departing tourists at the desk. A bored girl, primly dressed in her hotel uniform, approached me and asked me where my luggage was. I disappointed her by saying that I had only dropped in for a drink. She politely directed me to the bar. Pleasantly furnished, the bar had a good view of the sea, but was completely empty. The sea breeze rustled the potted palms, exaggerating the silence of the room. A waiter appeared and poured me a beer, silently. I took a chair by a window with a view of the bay; beyond was a broad glistening sea dotted with small deserted islands. There wasn't a swimmer or water skier in sight. This was quite the most peaceful resort I had ever visited.

'Is the cruiser for hire?' I asked the waiter, who had brought me another beer. A cruise along the north coast for a couple of hours was what I had in mind.

'There must be six or more people before the boat will go out,' he told me regretfully.

I had only seen two people up till now, and they were leaving. At that rate I was sure I was definitely out of luck. Finishing my beer I walked down to the landing-stage to see if there was perhaps something else I could hire – or purloin for an hour or two. The cruiser looked as if it hadn't been out to sea for days; its hull was grimed and scaled, and its deck was in need of a good scrub. Sitting on top of the cabin, I pondered what to do. There was no other boat in the harbour, not even a dinghy. Then I heard in the distance the unmistakable sound of a high-powered outboard engine and a skiff came into view, entering the bay from the north-east. It was moving fast, perhaps at twenty knots. As it approached the landing-stage, the Indonesian boy steering it suddenly throttled it back and I saw the wake wave plunge forward under its hull and bounce the boat uncomfortably.

In the front of the boat sat a man, and I could just make out that he was Japanese. As they drew alongside the cruiser I offered to take their line. The Japanese man, in his early forties and slightly built, smiled thankfully and cast the line to me. The boy was swarthy, with a dour, suspicious look about him, but he handled the boat beautifully. I tied the boat, with the boy watching me intently to see that I'd got the right knot. The Japanese man got out and told the boy to wait for him, and then introduced himself.

'I'm Michael,' he said. He had an immediately likeable manner, genial and warm. He asked me whether I was waiting to go to his island, which appeared to have no name, and pre-empted my answer by apologising for the poor ferry service, assuring me that it would improve.

'No,' I smiled. 'I was just passing a bit of time.'

Michael told me that he had some beer and groceries to collect from the hotel, and suggested we meet for a drink at one of the small bars along the road into Waterfront City. He pointed to one, a hut with a corrugated roof, and we agreed to meet in quarter of an hour.

The bar was dusty and flyblown, but it had more character than the hotel bar. The owner, an indefatigable old man dressed in filthy vest and shorts, was throwing diced fish into a wok while chastising his children and giving his wife an equally severe earbashing. She was pleased to see me, if only to get out of range of the domestic strife for a moment or two. I was about to sit down when she abruptly took my arm and guided me to another table, shaking her head exasperatedly at the one I was about to choose, and explaining that her good-for-nothing oaf of a husband couldn't be bothered to mend it. I ordered two beers. Thinking she now had an ally in me, she harangued her husband violently as she took two bottles from the freezer. Meanwhile, their two children gazed vacantly heavenward, as if this was a daily occurrence and to be endured quietly.

I was relieved when Michael finally joined me.

'So what are you doing on Batam?' he asked with an enthusiastic, genuine interest.

'Looking into a story about piracy.'

Michael nodded his head slowly. 'Very interesting. You probably know that it's big business in this part of the world?' he said in an almost confidential tone.

'I'm beginning to discover that.'

He drank his beer and looked thoughtfully out to sea. 'Have you managed to find any pirates to speak to?'

I took it as a rather ingenuous remark and wryly laughed. 'You can't exactly find them in a telephone directory!'

'No, of course not,' he smiled. 'I only ask because I have heard that on an island near my own – Sendora I think it's called – there are some men who were sent to prison for piracy.'

I immediately became interested. 'Are you sure about this?'

'Some locals I employed to help me build the chalets on my island were talking about them one day, and I heard them mention Sendora.'

I had no reason to disbelieve Michael, and was astonished at the sheer coincidence of our meeting; also at the information he gave me, however uncertain he was of its reliability.

'How far is Sendora from here?' I asked, already considering going there.

'Oh, about half an hour, perhaps more; I'm not sure how to get there myself, but the boy could take you.'

I looked at my watch – it was midday. My ferry was due to leave at four that afternoon and I still had to get back into town. A trip to Sendora wasn't really feasible, not if I wanted to do some interviews. Michael also thought I might be pushing it a little, and suggested that I came back at the earliest opportunity. He gave me his card, and I told him I would be back the following weekend.

Michael was a civil engineer, and he and his wife had worked and lived in Tokyo before uprooting to Indonesia. They had earned a lot of money and had a typical, affluent middle-class life. Michael adored snorkelling and water-sports, but because of the pressures of his work he rarely got time to indulge his hobby. His wife dreamt of a tropical island paradise, and frequently indulged this dream (as we all do) while staring out of her office window. When they managed to take a holiday, they returned to the same seaside resort on Batam, where for a brief couple of weeks a year they indulged in paradise and snorkelling. When they heard that they could buy one of the numerous deserted islands off the coast they packed in their jobs, cashed in their investments and, one day, arrived by skiff on their very own tropical island and started to build a resort – dedicated to water-sports and tranquillity. Not long after I visited Michael's island, it all went tragically wrong.

Back in town, there was a message waiting for me at my hotel. Yulius was sorry that he couldn't make the arrangement, but would collect and take me to Sekupan. After taking a shower, I packed my bags, paid my bill and waited in the lobby for Yulius to arrive. The Australian basketball team was also checking out, with the masseur lady supervising their luggage, her hands no doubt emboldened to the task by all the money and flesh that had been pressed into them. I caught a brief wistful look from her, as if a few furtive moments of ecstasy behind a potted palm or in the laundry-room was not out of the question.

Flustered and apologetic, Yulius greeted me with a torrent of excuses as to why he couldn't meet me earlier. I told him not to worry and that I'd spent the morning at Waterfront City. Did he know of an island called Sendora? He thought for a moment then shook his head.

'I've not heard of it, Mr Bob. Why do you ask?'

'I met someone at Waterfront City who told me that he thought some pirates who had spent some time in prison lived there,' I said.

Yulius shook his head again, his expression suggesting that he would rather not discuss piracy any more – certainly not in a public place like the hotel lobby. We left the hotel and headed out of town to Sekupan and the ferry.

Yulius employed his habitual driving skills on the way, cutting up other drivers and overtaking on the hard shoulder of the opposite lane. At one point I was offered a dead chicken from a motorcyclist who gamely grabbed hold of the van's door and dangled the scrawny beast at my window. 'Delicious chicken. Want to buy it?' The chicken's neck was a good few inches longer than it had been that morning, and Yulius's manoeuvre to get rid of him almost had the same effect on the rider. In the mirror I watched him career off the side of the road, still holding the dead chicken aloft.

We reached Sekupan in good time, and instead of rushing back to town Yulius decided to wait with me. I thought it an ideal time to square things between us, since I was sure I would need Yulius again. In any case, I liked him.

'I'm thinking of coming back to Batam next week. Will you collect me?'

'Sure, Mr Bob. You just ring me.'

'And if you hear of anything . . .' I cut myself short, realising Yulius's sensitivity about my research and how frightened he was about getting too involved.

With a kind of earnest sympathy, he turned to me. 'Mr Bob, it is too dangerous. I have a wife and family. You must understand.' His doleful, regretful eyes penetrated me.

'I'm sorry, Yulius.'

I grabbed my bag and shook his hand. 'I might just buy some duty-free before I get on the boat.' I opened the van's door.

Yulius placed his hand on my arm. 'You understand, Mr Bob, yes?'

'Of course I do.'

'But if I hear of anything,' he said. 'I will be in touch.' It was an appeasing gesture.

I shook his hand again and thanked him.

The ferry was full of returning day-trippers, travellers, businessmen and male Chinese sex-addicts. It pulled out of Sekupan amongst fishing skiffs and other ferries and passed a large, white, luxurious cruise ship that had just put into port. Within minutes we were out at sea and I went up to the top deck with my duty-free litre bottle of Scotch. Remnants of ash-coloured storm clouds were folded into the horizon, as if they were being posted away over the edge of the world. Whether it was an illusion, or the fact that we were practically on the equator, the curve of the earth seemed nearer and more visible here, as if this part of the world was smaller, or had somehow contracted. Or perhaps it had something to do with the vastness of the tropical sky, which seemed to magnify and diminish distances simultaneously, especially when huge mountainous anvil-shaped clouds gathered. They gave the tropics an almost vertiginous landscape among so much flatness of land and sea.

Ray, a telecommunications specialist from Singapore, joined me. He had been advising a company in Batam on how to update their internal communications systems. I found a couple of plastic cups and some ice and we sat in the hot sunshine drinking whisky. He said he was glad of the drink, after the confusion of Batam. Employed by a large international Sino-American corporation that was trying to make inroads into Indonesia, Ray had the onerous job of getting contracts. Exhausted and harassed by his week on Batam, he said he was glad to be going back to 'civilisation' – meaning Singapore.

'Don't get me wrong,' he said, rattling the ice around the cup, 'I think the Indonesians are great people, but they're hamstrung by so much corruption. Every deal comes with someone's own personal agenda, usually involving money.'

'Can't that be said of much of S.E. Asia? Even Singapore?' I suggested.

'Yes, but the Singaporeans love their technology, and they understand it too. They're innovative, and that always helps to wrap up a deal fast and efficiently. But the Indonesians . . .' He drank deeply, 'Jesus Christ!'

Ray was a sort of technopolitan whose supreme mission was to 'wire up' the whole world, to make the concept of the 'global village' a reality. I had met many people like him in Singapore – rootless, stateless people, 'technomads'. From the age of conception they had roamed the world, growing up there, educated here, and had an office in every quarter of the globe. Home, family and identity for them was the corporation. They lived for their work, and their leisure time was devoted to maintaining the corporation's image in the host country. In solitary, reflective moments when something almost human touched them, their mobile phones would ring.

As we arrived back in Singapore, Ray looked noticeably relieved. The monolithic skyscrapers and glittering hi-tech energy of the place was Ray's vision for the world. When the ferry docked, Ray got off a little unsteadily, and thanked me for the whisky. Insisting on repaying my hospitality, he invited me to join him at some exclusive country club where he was a member. I thanked him, but had no intention of taking up the invitation. For me, coming back to Singapore after Indonesia was like returning from a pleasant camping trip in the outback, and I found the prospect of the view from my eighth-floor apartment of a panoramic geometry of orderly and efficient living suddenly depressing. My story was now in Indonesia, not in Singapore.

– CHAPTER EIGHT –

THERE was a small parcel waiting for me when I got back to my apartment. It had been sent from home. I opened it and found a cassette. The label was marked 'BBC – Piracy story'. I dumped my clothes in the washing machine, poured myself a whisky and put the tape on.

'Reported cases of piracy on the high seas have reached record levels this year,' the piece began, 'and Captain Newton is one of the statistics . . .'

Newton, the captain of a P&O cruiser, was attacked in 1992. He was on a voyage from Singapore to New Zealand. Twelve hours from Singapore, off the coast of Bintan (an Indonesian island just west of Batam), his ship was boarded by nine pirates using grappling hooks. 'They came up to my cabin, accosted me and robbed me of all the money in the safe . . . $20,000 and my personal valuables.' Instead of tying and gagging him while they made their escape, they took Newton down to the stern quarter of the ship. 'I was rather expecting they were going to throw me overboard into the shark-infested waters,' he said. 'Obviously they didn't,' remarked the presenter. She continued: 'It sounds like they were a highly trained gang.' Newton agreed. 'They were extremely highly trained and professional and I'm absolutely convinced they were rogue military elements who were operating outside their remit.'

The presenter then introduced a spokesman from the International Maritime Bureau. What was his explanation for the rise in piracy in S.E. Asia? 'Mainly because of the growing problems in Indonesia with respect to law and order,' he replied, 'low-level criminals are finding it more attractive and less risky to attack vessels . . . than to attack premises ashore. And it is for this reason that we are calling on the governments in that area to take firm action against the pirates,' he stated. 'The attacks may take place aboard vessels, but they have to come ashore. Intelligence-led law enforcement exercises should catch these pirates, and we need the will of the governments to put them on trial . . .' It was a perfect piece of platitudinous PR.

The feature went on to discuss 'low-level' acts of piracy, like the attack on Newton's ship, and the 'high-level' stealing of entire ships and their cargoes by organised gangs. Regarding the latter, the IMB spokesman was adamant that the governments of the countries (Indonesia and Malaysia especially) off whose shores piracy attacks mainly occurred should commit more resources to guarding and policing their waters, and generally take a more serious attitude to the capture and prosecution of pirates.

But it was clear from what Newton had to say that he suspected the military of those countries to be directly involved in piracy, and was implicitly scathing of the IMB spokesman's unwillingness to address his suspicion (curiously, the presenter failed to spot this). 'Talking about increasing naval patrols,' Newton said, 'in Indonesian waters and elsewhere in S.E. Asia, they're the patrols by day and pirates by night.' I was expecting this controversial allegation to be put to the IMB spokesman, as it should have been, but the item came to an end, and the presenter went on to talk about belly-dancing . . .

Was the Navy unit I'd spotted in *kampong* Melayu during the smuggling operation one of those 'rogue elements' that Newton had mentioned? If so, how in all practicality could they be so? And was the phrase 'rogue element' just a diplomatic way of explicitly accusing the Indonesian authorities – like the Chinese – of directly sponsoring piracy? The unit I'd seen, whether they were on patrol or on exercise, must have been under the orders of some command structure and thus were obliged, at the very least, to report regularly their position, whereabouts and activities. They must have had a brief. Moreover, if they were a 'rogue element' their uniforms, hardware, boats and fuel had to be provided by someone, and presumably with the consent, tacit or otherwise, of the military. (Quartermasters' stores are not military surplus shops.) If, as Newton had suggested, these 'elements' were 'acting outside their remit' by committing pirate attacks at night, even on a 'low-level' scale, where and to whom was the stolen money and valuables going? The unit at *kampong* Melayu was a wretched bunch, and one haul – such as the attack on Newton's ship – could have set them up nicely in a country where $(US)20,000 goes a long, long way. The hijacking of an entire ship and cargo would have been the equivalent of a large lottery win. If 'rogue' meant freebooting, then such units as the one I had seen were obviously acting under the auspices of the military authorities themselves.

I listened to the tape several more times, and started writing down some of the phrases used by the presenter and contributors, phrases like 'law and order', 'low-level criminals', 'intelligence-led law enforcement', 'the will of governments', 'responsibility of the shipping organisations', 'acting outside their remit', 'highly professional' and so on. The context was also significant – a small feature on a BBC magazine programme broadcast from London. The terminology was characteristically and referentially Western, articulated with a kind of smugness that befitted BBC editorial policy and made the contributors seem authoritative and sincere. I wondered what the result might have been if this feature had been made on location in *kampong* Melayu as an open-forum discussion with the villagers, the headman and the Navy unit as invited contributors?

From an Eastern point of view, such terminology – not to put too fine a point on it – is alien. Even the word 'pirate' would leave them puzzled. What's more, I couldn't imagine even trying to explain to the ordinary Indonesian that piracy was a crime, let alone attempting to convince them that it needed the commitment and will of its government to eradicate it. Yulius had called pirates 'dangerous men', but I had never heard him once refer to them as *criminals*. And to explain the distinction between 'low-' and 'high'-level piracy would be like trying to persuade a prostitute that she was 'acting outside her remit' by having sex. As for the slogan 'law and order,' as resonantly high-minded as it might sound in the hallowed chambers of the British parliament, in Indonesia it meant little more than the police switching armbands of loyalty depending on which party election rally they were attending. Piracy in Indonesia is a crime of convenience – convenient to all who benefit from it, and only a crime if it's embarrassing for the government. The 'grey' market – which is the only true market in S.E. Asia – is just a shade greyer in Indonesia.

I had dinner with Adam that night and told him about my experiences in Batam and how I intended to put a proposal together on piracy for the Discovery Channel, which had an office in Singapore. He was excited, but he himself had little news to tell me about the various projects he was working on, one of which was a cookery programme starring a local Chinese actor. This went nowhere finally, like all the other projects he invested so much hope in. Adam had come to Singapore to train TV cameramen, but had lost his 'eye'. He was in his fifties and had hit a crisis of professional confidence. He enjoyed the ex-pat life, but in the end fell victim to all its delusions, the cardinal one being that he thought Singapore needed him more than he needed Singapore.

I worked on the proposal for the rest of the week, sometimes in Adam's tea-house office in Tanjong Pagar, at other times in my apartment. I had broken it down into three parts, the first dealing generally with the history of piracy in the South China Sea; the second on the myths and legends; the third part on modern-day piracy. It was written in caption style, with bullet points, teasing headings, and evocative anecdotes and quotes. Proud of the finished piece (though it bore no resemblance to the experiences I'd had in Malaysia and Indonesia), I delivered it to the Discovery Channel office, a few streets away from Tanjong Pagar. There was never a response, not even a letter acknowledging its receipt. Back in Britain two years later, unemployed and sitting in a pub one lunchtime, the Discovery Channel was on the TV, and I watched with astonishment a programme entitled *Piracy in the South China Sea*. What a coincidence!

My contract with the Television Corporation was due to end, and apart from tidying up a few affairs and paying an extortionate bill for 'damage' to my apartment, I was free to return to Indonesia. Adam suggested that I worked for his company full time, initially on a nominal salary of $5,000(S) a month. Accommodation in Singapore is generally expensive, but otherwise everything else, especially food, is very affordable. So I agreed. Besides, I had no work to return to in Britain. In the end, however, apart from occasional handouts, I was never paid a cent. Adam's loyalties were ambiguous, and his business sense was negligible.

Towards the end of the week, I phoned Yulius and gave him the arrival time of my ferry at Sekupan. He was happy to hear from me and told me that he had some interesting news. He wouldn't go into detail, but the excitement in his voice suggested it might be significant. I searched for Michael's card also to let him know I was coming, but found I had lost it. Just about everyone in Singapore I had met, in Malaysia and Indonesia too, had given me a card, and I had either discarded them, or put them safely somewhere and later forgotten where they were. But I was sure I could find Michael's island. A Japanese man with a passion for snorkelling in Batam shouldn't be too hard to find, I reckoned.

Arriving too early for the ferry, I decided to get something to eat at a large hawker centre that overlooked the terminal. It had just gone four o'clock and the place was crowded, mainly with Chinese. Their reputation for hard work is surely surpassed by their fierce appetite, since seldom is a restaurant ever empty, day or night, in Singapore. Besides money, eating is the nearest thing to an official religion here. Once, at a coffee shop in Tanjong Pagar, I had seen a Chinese man asleep at a table with a half-eaten bowl of noodles in front of him and chopsticks still in his hand. It was 5 a.m., and I supposed he'd been there all night. I ordered fish-head soup with noodles, an inexpensive and filling meal, though the bits of boiled fish (eyes included) floating around in it can be a bit disconcerting. And it's a torment to eat, even with a spoon. In the end you have to resort to eating as the locals do – picking it up with your fingers, stuffing it into your mouth, chewing the edible bits, and indecorously disposing of the rest in a pile on the table. Opposite me sat an old man who had cleanly picked every morsel of flesh off the fish bone. The skeleton lay complete on the table, head to tail. For all their copious eating, I rarely saw food left on plates or in bowls. I doubted whether it was because the Chinese were always ravenously hungry; it had something to do with the national psyche. Tidiness was certainly a part of it, but also a type of utilitarianism, especially among the older generation, who frowned on any form of wastage. The direct beneficiaries of this philosophy were not the young Singaporeans, who were flagrantly consumer-oriented; they were, in a comic way, the mynah birds who anxiously hopped about from table to floor, like alarmed curates, squawking their mantra: *Waste not, want not.*

At Customs, a young, surly officer scrutinised my passport and wanted to know my reason for returning yet again to Indonesia. He flicked the page of my last stamped entry back and forwards.

'I like the place,' I said.

He thrust my passport back to me, and with a sharp nod of his head let me through. I was sympathetic to Singapore's tight immigration rules, but I rather resented the officious, even rude way, some of the Customs people dealt with travellers. Besides, I wasn't a Singapore citizen.

I was glad to be back on the ferry and out at sea again. For all its air-conditioned modernity, the humid claustrophobia of Singapore was stifling. It was, as I liked to think, an 'in-law' state, with a comfortable Britishness about it, but not in the family's direct bloodline. Out at sea and looking back at its impressive skyline, you would imagine it was the gateway to a huge continent. But you can leave it at breakfast and be in Johor Bahru for morning coffee. Or, as I was doing, be in Indonesia in twenty minutes.

Like the last time, I sat on the upper deck watching vast fleets of shipping passing through the Strait. There were ships from just about every part of the world, and it made this slim stretch of water feel very cosmopolitan. It was an ancient sea route, but with a New World appeal to it. In fact, in economic terms, the New World began here and expanded throughout the South China Sea to the whole of Asia and a potential prosperity to dwarf the West. I fancifully imagined, at some future point, the pirates in this region becoming unofficial maritime toll-keepers, levying a 'tax' on the increasing shipping in this Strait, and becoming rich potentates to rival their piratical ancestors.

At Sekupan, Yulius was nowhere to be seen. As usual the Customs hall was in a state of complete chaos, with the officers in their shabby uniforms stamping passports as if they were bouncers inking the hands of arriving revellers at a nightclub. As for security, it appeared not to exist. The security officers I did see were lounging at their desks smoking and talking, and waving people through with a listless flick of the wrist. Outside the hall, the same wrecks of taxis were there, and the motorbike boys hailing everyone. Indonesia was full of fumes, dust and squalor – and one of the wackiest and most invigorating places I had ever travelled to in the world. Within an hour or so of switching off the air-conditioning in my apartment block in Singapore, with its own private luxury swimming-pool, I was once again in the outback, in a frontier land of hustlers, pimps, prostitutes, peddlers, sleazy plutocrats, and some of the kindest people I had ever met.

You could muse on life in Indonesia for a lifetime and get nowhere nearer to defining it than baffled amusement.

'Mr Bob,' a voice came out of the cacophony of traffic and horn-blowing. Yulius strolled up to me.

'Sorry I am late. The traffic!' He threw up his hands. 'So many madmen on the road.' It was like a compulsive thief being indignant about a rash of burglaries.

I put my bag into the back of Yulius's van and climbed in.

'What's the news you have for me?'

Yulius rifled in his glove compartment and pulled out a cutting from the *Sijori Pos*. 'Pirates, Mr Bob.' He handed it to me with a sort of uncertain glee.

It was a lengthy feature on the front page with a black-and-white photograph of a cargo ship. Underneath it the caption read: 'Uncovered – a syndicate of pirates.' I tried to make sense of the opening paragraph, but it was written in Indonesian. I suggested to Yulius that we stopped for a coffee and he could translate it for me.

At a small roadside restaurant that looked as if it had been industrially scarified, Yulius pondered the article, his translating skill evidently being tested to the full. 'It is about a pirate boss, Mr Wong. But that is not his real name. It is Chew Chiang Kiat, I think. The ship in the picture is the pirates' headquarters. They have been arrested by the Indonesian Navy . . .' He stumbled into incoherence and began shaking his head. 'I cannot make sense of the rest, Mr Bob.' He put the newspaper down. 'Sorry.'

'Does it say where the pirates are in prison?' I asked.

Yulius scanned the article again and shook his head. 'I think Wong and his gang are in prison in Jakarta.'

That was depressing news. Even if I managed to get to Jakarta it was unlikely I'd get permission to interview Wong. Yet why it never occurred to me to go straight to the *Sijori Pos* office and find out more about the case, I will never know.

I found a cheap hotel on the outskirts of the town. Its air-conditioning was not working and the room was unbearably hot. The floor was linoleum-tiled and the bed was solid. All the same, it was clean and serviceable. I asked Yulius if he would take me to Waterfront City the next day, but he claimed he was too busy. I sensed that he simply did not want to associate himself too closely with me now, especially since the events of my previous visit.

That evening I went out to try and find the bar where I had met Judy. Perhaps she had managed to find the girl who had lived with the pirate. But after two hours of fruitless searching, I gave up. Every KTV place I went into cost me a fortune, and being continually harassed and propositioned for sex was aggravating. Eventually I found a quiet restaurant and had some satay, rice and a beer, and looked at the article Yulius had given me. There were names of ships I recognised as ones that had been pirated, notably the MV *Atlanta* and the MV *Petro Ranger*. Both had been phantomed, the latter being a highly controversial case.

The *Petro Ranger*'s cargo of kerosene and gas oil was worth millions of dollars. It had sailed from Singapore on 16 April 1998 and was due to dock at Ho Chi Min City (Saigon) in Vietnam two days later. It never arrived. The concerned owner informed the IMB in Kuala Lumpur and a warning was broadcast immediately via Inmarsat C-EGC 2 safetyNET to all vessels in the region. A special alert was also transmitted to selected ports and maritime authorities. On 1 May, the IMB investigators tracked the vessel to Haiku, a port in China. It had previously been sailed to Hainan Island, off China, where its cargo had been unloaded. The Chinese had detained the ship with its crew, as well as the twelve pirates – all Indonesians. The reason for detaining the ship, so the Chinese authorities alleged, was because they thought it was involved in smuggling. The ship's name had been changed to *Wilby* and it was flying the Honduras flag. Astonishingly, instead of the twelve pirates being prosecuted, they were repatriated to Indonesia. Was this Wong and his gang?

I flung open the window of my stiflingly hot bedroom, but this only invited in a squadron of insects and mosquitoes that sizzled around the room patiently waiting for me to fall asleep, whereupon they would feast on me. Another feast was in progress in the room next to mine – a sex orgy. I could distinctly make out the voices of three men, Dutch I think, and the same number of girls. There was a great deal of laughter and squealing and the clinking of bottles and glasses. This was followed by a series of grunts and heavy breathing and the rhythm of a mattress. It went on at intervals throughout the night, and sleep was impossible. By dawn my bedroom wall was a massacre of insects and next door was a haven of peace and sexual gratification. Scratching fiercely, I paid my bill and left.

I was relieved to get on a motorbike taxi and head off to Waterfront City. The cool air from the ride and the fear of ending up under a lorry made me forget completely the awful night in the hotel. Reaching the sea was an unrivalled delight. At the hotel, I asked the receptionist about boats to the islands, and told her about Michael. She called the manager. A lithe and sprightly young man, with a reassuring smile, came to the desk.

'Can I help you?' he asked.

I explained my problem, and though he had not heard of Michael he suggested I wait at the harbour for a fishing skiff.

'They come in all the time and they will know your friend.'

Remembering the night I'd had in the hotel in town, and to show my appreciation for his help, I booked in that night. Since the hotel looked empty, I reckoned that whichever room I had, neither orgies nor mosquitoes would bother me.

Confident that a boat would eventually turn up, I lay on the upper deck of the cruiser, which had gained a few more crustaceans and grime since I'd last been there, and dozed off. Before too long, I was woken by the shrill sound of an outboard motor and looked up to see a fishing skiff skimming into the harbour. As the boat docked, I couldn't believe my luck – it was the same boy who had brought Michael to Waterfront City the week before.

'Michael? His island. I want to go there,' I told the boy, but he just shrugged a scowl at me.

Ludicrously I mimed snorkelling and swimming and then pulled my eyes up at the sides and said 'Japanese'. At first the boy gazed at me with spellbound incredulity, and I watched him mimic me as he put his fingers tentatively at the sides of his eyes. Then he nodded and pointed out to sea.

'Island?'

I smiled and nodded in the direction he was pointing. 'Yes.'

He signalled to me to wait by his boat while he went off to do some errands. I couldn't have put an exact age to him. He was small and slight, but had a ragged toughness about him and a defiant, scowling expression that made him look older than I had imagined him to be. His sinewy, tawny-coloured skin was dry and salt-scoured. He reminded me of the fishermen in *kampong* Melayu, with those same intense but glazed eyes, ever alert and watchful, and impenetrably wistful.

Beneath his boat a shoal of silvery fingerlings darted amongst the dazzle and flicker of the waves, their swift spontaneous movements all at once appearing in a flash then vanishing, to reappear again metres away. They had that same mesmeric evanescence of the tropics – airy and insubstantial, yet with an absorbing, timeless presence.

When the boy returned an hour later, he was carrying several boxes of soft, iced drinks. I offered to help him load them, but he shook his head and held them more tightly. Perhaps he thought I intended to steal them. Nimbly stacking the boxes, he turned to me and pointed at the prow of the boat. Stepping in, I thought how remarkably balanced and sturdy the boat was, and while it might not fair well out at sea, around the islands and inshore waters, it was the ideal craft. With a quick jerk of the starter rope, the engine burst into life, and a gossamer pool of oil spread round the boat. As we roared off I wondered if the boy really understood where I wanted to go, or whether I was off on some expedition on which, like those little fish, I would vanish and end up somewhere completely unknown, my last address being some scabrous little hotel in downtown Batam.

My uncertainty became more pronounced as a whole vista of small islands opened up around us. All I could be sure about was that the boy obviously knew where he was going. On our way we pulled in at a floating fuel station, a kind of raft with large drums of fuel on it. Manning it was a sinister character who looked as if he'd spent most of his life marooned on this raft, and grown liverish with the stench of the oily air. I paid for the fuel and we set off again, going deeper into the solitude of the sea. It was like entering an infinite pantheon of water and sky, with small islands and coral reefs breaking the surface like castaway bits of land. The sea seemed to gather vastness. It was like passing beneath successive bridges, each one taller and more expansive than the last one, and each revealing a more immense view. After half an hour or so, the boy looked round at me and pointed towards an island. It looked much like all the other islands until, approaching it, I noticed a small wooden landing-stage and a promontory of stilted huts sinking away into the sea. There appeared to be a castellated bamboo wall, and a palm-covered hut, and miscellaneous pieces of Chinese Buddhist architecture, notably a confection of miniature pagodas. It was oddly surreal, and I never expected to encounter such a place in the South China Sea.

As the boat drew in I saw Michael watching from the palm-covered hut, which was in fact a bar. Recognising me, he walked down to the landing-stage and waved. I apologised for arriving without phoning him first, but explained I'd lost his card. He was pleased to see me and offered me a beer.

'What a weird place,' I said.

Michael laughed and told me that he'd built his resort in such an eclectic style because of the smallness of the island (I walked around it in less than a minute). 'The old Buddhist architecture gives a wonderful illusion of grandeur and space – partly perhaps because of its ornateness. That's the illusion I needed to create here.'

He gave me a 'guided' tour of the island and showed me the chalets he'd built for guests. As an engineer he certainly knew how to exploit the smallest space, but privacy was clearly out of the question. All the same, there was no chance of ever getting lost on his island, and stumbling back to your chalet after a lengthy session at the bar wouldn't pose much of a problem. Michael enthusiastically subscribed to the fashionable 'philosophy' of feng shui, though I could see nothing random, divine or otherwise, about his resort – apart from the island itself, perhaps. The idea of living on the island for good, as Michael and his wife intended, made me feel almost claustrophobically uncomfortable. I'd find the monotony of my own company unbearable, even broken by visitors. Michael had bought thousands of dollars worth of sophisticated diving equipment, and he reckoned within two or three years he would recoup his money. Three months later, however, his island was ransacked by a local Indonesian gang and Michael himself was beaten up.

I mentioned to him about going to Sendora, and Michael went off to arrange for me to be taken there by the young boy, who was patiently waiting in his boat. Before departing, I thanked Michael and promised to stay in touch. But like so many of the fleeting acquaintances I had made out there, I never saw him again.

Whether I was to meet pirates or not, it was an illuminating experience to be sailing in this remote part of the Phillip Strait. Though it was relatively narrow, there was no map that I knew of that included all the islands we had passed, nor gave any real impression of the nature of this coastal region. I could only imagine that much of this area was totally uncharted, and that the only people who could navigate through it successfully were the fishermen and islanders. It was an ideal area for smuggling and piracy. And I suspect any Navy unit on patrol in this area would approach their task with some trepidation. By now, even I was beginning to feel uneasy at the prospect of going ever deeper into this mysterious and dangerous part of the world. I knew that if the boat was holed by a concealed reef of coral or overturned in a freak storm, there would be little or no chance of surviving. Apart from the wilderness of the place, there were also vicious currents and not a few sharks for the hapless sailor who fell overboard to contend with. For the first time in several months of being in S.E. Asia, I quietly began to yearn for home.

Sendora eventually came into view, and looked larger than I had expected. Thick, deep-green jungle fringed its rocky shoreline of coves and inlets, and a bald-headed eagle flew loftily above a ridge of palm trees. The sea began to get rougher as we approached the shoreline, and as we rounded a craggy headland I could just make out the beginnings of a village huddled away under a slurry of dark jungle. The young boy turned to me and abruptly signalled the village with his hand. I noticed a deep scar on the back of his leg that looked like a knife slash. I wasn't surprised. That smouldering, surly aggressiveness was bound to have made him enemies. I gave him $20(S) and he responded with a grudging smile.

At the wooden jetty where the boy pulled in, some children were fishing with lines, ecstatically teasing each other as they pulled up small silvery wriggling fish. It reminded me momentarily of crab fishing in Cornwall. I saw one girl slap a boy on the head, which he took with a cheerful laugh. There were fishermen lugubriously emptying their nets of fish into buckets, and women dreamily lingering around the doors of their houses or leaning out of windows. The pace of life here was accurate to the slowest notion of time. But then why should it be any faster when the climate never changed, and there was plenty of wood to build or repair a house or a boat, and enough fish in the sea, and one pair of shorts sufficed all year round? The young boy got out of the boat, tied it and disappeared.

Wandering along the jetty in my white shorts and shirt, wearing sunglasses, with my old Nikon swinging round my neck and a pen and scraps of paper in my back pocket, I was stared at with a mixture of puzzled amusement and silent curiosity. Kneeling on their haunches, the children kept firmly still as I passed them, as if the shadow of some elderly, disciplinarian spirit had fallen on them. They whispered and pointed behind me after I had gone. At the end of the jetty there was a bar with a few chairs and tables and a palm-leaf thatched hut serving sweet tea, cold drinks and sweets. I bought a Coke and sat at a table, thinking it would be best if I let the entire village observe me at first, then let them approach me once I'd reassured them I didn't bite. A few minutes later a group of men joined me at the restaurant, after – presumably – having first asked the young boy who had brought me what my business was here. They skulked around me at first, waving and smiling and looking at my camera. Disarmingly, I invited them to join me with a flourish of eccentric English bonhomie. I pulled a buffoonish face and laughed. It was like buying a round of drinks in a rough London pub and pretending to be affably drunk just to ensure that you left in one piece. When I took out my wallet and ordered drinks for them, their timidity turned to gloating avarice. While I got their drinks, they wasted a whole roll of film playfully snapping each other with the lens cap on.

Since I had no interpreter, I took the scraps of paper and pen from my back pocket and, with their attention, drew something resembling a ship. They must have been thinking, 'First he buys us drinks, then we fuck up his camera, now he wants a ship!' I pointed out to sea, then at the drawing – 'Ship!' One tentatively muttered ship, and I rapturously nodded and patted his shoulder. A few more curious onlookers arrived. Then, even less skilfully, I drew a small boat (or *pancung*), following the lines of a skiff and placed several men in it wearing masks and holding guns. It was so detailed as to be unintelligible. They looked at each other, and from what they were saying it sounded as if they were trying to figure out who the men were in the boat. They all shook their heads and looked disappointedly at me, as if no more pats and no more drinks would come. I had an idea and, pointing at the men in the boat, drew one on a larger scale, this time donning a mask (with slit eyeholes) and holding the emblem of universal modern weaponry – the AK47 (with an exaggeratedly curved magazine). 'Pirate!' I exclaimed. More consultative muttering followed. Again they shook their heads. It was time to play charades.

Getting up from the table I pointed at the picture of the ship. 'Ship!' they all yelled. I smiled. Then I pointed at the pirate drawing and pretended to don a mask, load my gun, sit in the boat (my chair) and, acting the part of helmsman, made a whining noise like an outboard engine. They all looked rapt, as if they were at the cinema watching the first part of the plot unfold. Hoping they hadn't forgotten what part I was playing, I then pointed at the ship and made as if to climb on board it. They must have thought I'd changed into a monkey, since one of them let out a shrill monkey-scream and drooped his arms in prehensile fashion. The others laughed, but were fixated on the next part of the plot and turned back to me in expectation of the following scene. Once on board the imaginary ship, I pointed the gun at the crew and menacingly demanded money from them. And that was about as far as I could go . . . or almost. Finally I placed myself in jail, sullenly holding the bars of my cell.

'Pirate,' I said and, exhausted, sat down.

They had all gone silent, and I noticed that two of them looked curiously guilty. I was convinced they knew what I was trying to explain. Then a young boy pointed sheepishly at one of the men and nodded. The man responded nervously, as if he had been pointed out in an identity parade. He glared at the young boy, then glanced at me. I showed him the picture of the ship and the masked man with the gun.

'You?'

He nodded slowly. I drew a prison cell with bars. Again he nodded, as did his friend sitting beside him.

Painstakingly I managed to piece together their story. They and five others had attacked a ship and stolen money and valuables. But subsequently there had been some sort of double-cross. Their 'boss' had become angry, possibly accusing them of concealing some of the haul for themselves, and had threatened to kill them. But they swore they had taken nothing for themselves, and that the 'boss' had everything. Disbelieving them, but unwilling to kill them, instead he informed the police and they were arrested. Apparently, the police had offered them a deal for their release – some amount of money. But they had no money, so the court sealed their fate. They each received two or three years in prison.

They were just a couple of wretched, impoverished fishermen – not 'professional' pirates. I suspected that they had just been used as part of a network to spy on the position of ships, as well as for their knowledge of the coastline. Undoubtedly they could handle a boat, and if they had taken part in the attack, unless I was mistaken they had only crewed the boat, not actually boarded the ship. So who was this 'boss'? Was he on the island?

'Boss?' I asked them in Indonesian. They shrugged and pointed beyond the island. It was clear enough to me – he wasn't here on the island.

'China?' I asked.

'China,' one nodded. 'Singapura.'

I understood. They were saying the boss was a Chinese Singaporean. I wanted to find out his name, but the convoluted way in which I tried to ask them just created confusion.

At the back of the small crowd that had gathered around me, I saw a man who had an instantly dislikeable face. He was staring at me in a very unsettling way. I bought some more drinks for my companions, and as I did so he wandered up to me and, with a sharp gesticulating finger, told me to leave. He was the headman. I ignored him and returned to the table with the drinks. He persisted, and the crowd gradually dispersed, believing perhaps that there might be trouble. Like the headman at *kampong* Melayu, his appearance and clothes suggested that he was comparatively well off, and that his income didn't derive solely from the village and fishing. Perhaps the young boy who had brought me here had told him that Michael had mentioned pirates on the island. All the same, I realised that it would very unwise to antagonise him further. You could dispose of a body out here, I thought, with very little trouble.

I asked the young boy to take me back to Waterfront City, though I had a faint premonition of ending up somewhere completely different. As we sailed back, I concentrated on identifying some of the various features that had caught my eye on the way here so as to reassure myself that we were going in the right direction. Few of us have a charmed life, but I've always thought that if my end came unnaturally it would happen in a moment of humorous self-irony. If it happened here, I consoled myself, it would at least add a romantic touch. Tragedy and death, in those Conrad novels set in the tropics, had always seemed to me more majestically pithy than those set in cold, grim *fin-de-siècle* London. So I lay back in the boat and relaxed, and watched the boy steering the boat, and the beautiful flight of a bald-headed eagle that effortlessly glided above on the thermals. If it had not been for the roar of the outboard engine, I could effortlessly have dreamed myself into the elemental tranquillity of the place.

Turning a headland, Waterfront City came into view. It seemed that, after all, this prying Englishman was not to be jettisoned into a watery grave. But I was certain that my presence on Batam and what I was investigating must surely have come to the attention of the authorities, and my growing belief that they were either involved in piracy or had turned a blind but interested eye to it made me feel more sensitive and vulnerable. If piracy formed a significant part of the grey economy here, and on its sister island Bintan, too (though some would say that because of the endemic corruption in Indonesia that it's *all* black), my persistent digging around would, I assumed, have consequences for me.

As I expected, the hotel was wonderfully quiet. I had specifically asked for a room overlooking the sea, and was offered a choice of five. The one I finally settled on had a panoramic view of the bay. Pulling a chair up to the window, I watched the evening draw in with its characteristic blue-mauve and vermilion light, and a breathless air that seemed languorous after the day's heat. The night happened suddenly (there is no dusk to speak of in the tropics), and the sky filled with stars. The sea became eerie with patches of opalescent light distilled from bright constellations of stars, and where it met the land, almost tidelessly, it was black. I thought about the day's events, and how the sea here wasn't just a geographical feature – it was these people's home and livelihood. For thousands of years, perhaps, the inhabitants of these remote islands had worked and harvested the sea – trading and fishing, being born by it, growing up with it, and dying in it. Nor was the sea here just a country's territorial water (Indonesia's); it was a way of life, with all the attendant myths, customs and traditions. Why should these people care about articles of international maritime law, even if they knew about them? And were they ever consulted about the various shipping lanes designated by officials and bureaucrats sometimes thousands of miles away? Were they compensated for the pollution caused by all the shipping that passed their islands? It's estimated that piracy in S.E. Asian waters costs the shipping insurance industry $100 million each year. But if a fraction of this were paid as a kind of 'toll' (at the narrow Phillip Strait) it would, I imagine, be a very effective way of discouraging attacks on ships, or at the very least help towards paying for better policing of the most dangerous areas. This might sound like 'buying protection' but it would be better understood in Indonesia than a bunch of obfuscating laws. However, the hijacking of whole ships was, I realised, in quite a different league, and the article Yulius had given me from the *Sijori Pos* on the mysterious 'Mr Wong' and his gang of pirates was the lead I needed to undercover it.

– CHAPTER NINE –

BROKE, I returned to the UK and spent the next several months scrounging around for work in London and Manchester. I wanted desperately to return to Indonesia and Batam to follow up the story, but I had to raise the funds and at the same time placate my family. Nothing is less easy in this country than wanting to be off on some adventure in a remote corner of the world. There is always someone who thinks you're either crazy or irresponsible, or both. I had begun to find England peevish, smug and dismissive. And I wanted to get away from a bad-tempered British winter.

I sent the *Sijori Pos* article to the Indonesian Embassy in London with a covering letter requesting a translation. A few weeks later I received a pleasant reply with a full translation of the piece:

UNCOVERED, A SYNDICATE OF TANKER PIRATES.
Their boss is a Singaporean, and the receiver/buyer of the stolen goods is in China.
Tanjungpinag, Sijori.

GUSKAMLA ARMABAR (a command of joint operations) has succeeded in arresting a significant pirate of international calibre in Batam waters, Indonesia. Chew Cheng Kiat, alias Mr Wong (age 56) and a citizen of Singapore, is suspected to be the brain (the head) to operate piracy of tankers in the international navigation lanes around Malacca Strait and Singapore and has been captured through a thorough and well-organised intelligence operation.

'If we have to wait, it is almost impossible to catch such a world-class pirate red-handed, as their system of operation is very clever. Therefore, only through several methods of intelligence operations have we at last apprehended their head of piracy,' said the Commandant of the GUSKAMLA, Commander Sumardi, answering questions for the *Sijori Pos* yesterday.

According to Sumardi, the MV *Pulau Mas* (*Golden Island*) and some of her crew were successfully arrested on 20 November 1998 while they were on board the ship in the Nongsa Batam waters. The ship had also been used for their headquarters while operating piracy around this navigation lane.

The MV *Pulau Mas* is a 399-ton ship. On board the ship, the GUSKAMLA ARMABAR have succeeded in uncovering evidence, among which were 15 units of handcuffs, 14 units of masks (balaclavas), 3 units of bayonets, one unit of Immigration stamp of Sekupang Batam, one unit of date stamp, 8 units of printing (sablon) of the ship's name, 12 boxes of paint of different colours, and one unit of speed boat with an engine capacity of 200 HP.

According to Sumardi, and based on the information he has received, during the period of November 1996 and 1998, 21 piracy attacks occurred in this area Out of that number Mr Wong's gang have admitted that they plundered the following ships – the *Atlanta*, *Petro Ranger*, the *Suci*, *Pendopo* and the *Plaju*. The *Atlanta* had been phantomed and its name changed to *Am Way*. With its new documents it had then been taken directly to China.

Why was the ship taken to China? According to Sumardi, it is suspected that Mr Wong's boss is in China. 'That seems to be the case since this international navigation lane is their operating area, and it is from here that they take their loot to China where the ships and their cargoes are sold,' he said.

Judging from their modus operandi, Sumardi suspects that Mr Wong is only one of a group from the network of world piracy. 'If their Big Boss is in China, it is certain that their men are not only here, but also in Hong Kong, the Philippines and other places,' Sumardi said.

'Up to now,' Sumardi said, his organisation has continued to probe and investigate Wong and his men. 'To reveal the case properly, more information needs to be gathered.'

Asked whether the international navigation lane around Malacca Strait and Singapore would be safer since the capture of Mr Wong, Sumardi could not give a guarantee. 'The fact is,' he added, 'that besides Mr Wong there might be other gangs who are in the same class.'

According to Sumardi, his intelligence organisation have been working very hard to uncover this piracy case because Indonesia has always been blamed by the international maritime organisations for the lack of safety of foreign ships.

'We are of course ashamed of being accused of not providing security for this international navigation area. But with the capture of Mr Wong it is hoped that further cases will be uncovered,' said Sumardi.

Meanwhile from the information gathered by *Sijori Pos* in Batam, the MV *Pulau Mas* was frequently stopped in Batam Ampar waters by the Navy. The Navy became suspicious and tried to get close to the ship. But each time they got close, the ship sailed into international water, and then sometimes entered Singaporean water.

But after there was a leak from an ex-crewman (of the pirate gang), the joint operation set up their intelligence network and succeeded in detecting the gang's next victim. At that time the MV *Pulau Mas* was anchored in Batu Ampar water, and ships in this area are under the authority of the LANAL Batam Navy.

Mr Wong himself was only arrested on 1 December 1998 when he was staying at 88 Hotel, room 212. In the meantime there were two foreigners among the suspects who are currently still in the custody of the Navy. The two are Mr See Cheng Yen and Mr Ng Kong Siew. Both are Malaysian citizens. The two were arrested while they were loading logistical supplies onto the MV *Pulau Mas* on 22 November 1998.

Based on the results of the intelligence operation, Mr Wong had a wide network, including contacts in China, the Philippines, Hong Kong and Malaysia. This is corroborated by evidence found on board the *Pulau Mas*.

'The cargo was suspected of being sold in China, like the tankers MT *Suci* and MT *Atlanta*,' which, according to a source, were pirated.

The source even said that on board the ship were ready-made documents including the name of a new ship. 'There are five names of the ship, including all the documents Mr Wong had provided. Once the targeted ship had been taken over, they immediately changed her name and her paintwork,' said the source.

How did Mr Wong get the exact target? According to the source in the Joint Operation, Mr Wong normally planted a crewman as a mole on the ship. The mole would then send Mr Wong all the information regarding the planned route of the ship to be hijacked. Therefore Mr Wong could ambush the ship in the area suggested by the head of the group.

Note: A command of Joint Operation normally consists of the Navy, Police, Immigration and Customs and Excise and is headed by the Navy

Another piece of information prompted my return to Batam – an article on piracy in *The Straits Times*:

Of the 66 piracy incidents worldwide in the first three months of this year [1999] 38 happened in and around South-east Asia: Indonesia, 18; Singapore Strait, 10; Thailand, 3; Malaysia, 2; South China Sea, 2; China/Hong Kong/Macau, 2; Vietnam, 1.

But it was a small, subsidiary piece to the main article that particularly caught my eye. It was titled: 'Mystery pirate: A Nantah econs graduate?', and was about Mr Wong. 'A man carrying a Singapore passport is sitting in a Batam jail awaiting trial for heading what is said to be a major regional piracy syndicate.' So now I knew that Wong was in fact in Batam. When he had been arrested he was carrying a Singapore passport bearing the name Chew Chiang Kiat. But the real Mr Chew was apparently an odd-job labourer in Singapore who had lost his passport and identity card in Malaysia in 1997. Wong was reported to have said that he was a Singaporean and a graduate in economics. He had a wife and two children.

Fortunately, some writing commissions came in just as I was beginning to despair at how I could afford to go back to Indonesia. I booked a cheap flight and knew I could survive for a month. I was excited by the prospect of returning, but also slightly apprehensive. Could I now get the information I wanted to complete the story? Arriving back in Singapore, I booked in at the Sunshine Hotel in Tanjong Pagar, a small family-run hotel in Tras Street, opposite Adam's tea-house office and the fashionable Bisous bar. Adam had written to keep me up to date on how things were progressing with his company, but reading between the lines his optimism, I think, failed to convince even him that things were going well. All the same, I was delighted to be back in S.E. Asia, and spent the first evening sitting outside a café, idly watching the street life.

Nothing ever seemed to stop in Singapore, though I wasn't convinced that it was entirely to do with the rapacious business ethic here. There seemed to be something in the Singaporean psyche, especially the Chinese, which made them constantly active, almost frenetic. Even when relaxing – like the businessmen at a table beside me – they were invariably engaged in some sort of activity (reading a newspaper or book, gossiping, doing business, eating). It struck me as a predominantly 'daily' society, where the concerns of the present, right up to the minute, were what these people thrived on. Perhaps this was because Singapore had nothing of the fettering lethargy of the past (only until recently has its history been officially recognised). And, as a sweeping generalisation, societies that see themselves (as

Singapore does) as the product of a technological miracle, strive to see that miracle maintained – and, as we all know, technology is of the day and changing every day. In such technological societies, people live a day at a time.

I sent a fax to the *Sijori Pos* stating as briefly and clearly as I could that I had read the article on Wong and his pirate gang and would greatly appreciate any assistance in following up the story. I had tried several times to phone their office, but Batam's telephone system was in constant disarray. By late afternoon the following day, I received a reply. Like my own fax, it was brief, handwritten and rather perplexing: 'Dear Sir, if you come to Batam, I will wait for you in the Nagoya Plasa hotel, 14.30 p.m. Juanda.' There was a phone number, so I rang. I was in luck. The person who answered wasn't Juanda, but Mary, one of the reporters on the newspaper. Her English was excellent and she had heard about me.

'Is that Mr Bob?' she asked.

'Yes. I'm trying to get in touch with Juanda. Can you help?'

'Juanda is out at the moment, but I will ask him to ring you.'

He eventually did, and with the help of Socrates, another reporter on the *Pos*, we clarified the arrangements for our meeting the next day. I was excited to hear that Juanda had been covering the case of Wong and had built up a sizeable folder on him.

It was the time of the 1999 'free elections' in Indonesia, and campaigning had already started. Once again, Charlotte disapproved of my intention to go back there. She ranted on at me and once more brought up the matter of how dangerous it was in Indonesia, especially for foreigners. And getting involved with pirates of Wong's ilk was inconceivably stupid. But I was not to be dissuaded. Besides, I now had the relative safeguard of my association with the highly respected *Sijori Pos*. All the same, being barracked by a Chinese woman is a withering experience, and I wasn't at all surprised that many Chinese Singaporean men had concubines, or indulged fantasies of cinematic machismo in the style of Bruce Willis. Or that *ang moh*s like me went in search of pirates.

I left for Batam the next day after booking in at the Mandarin Regency Hotel in Nagoya, where I had arranged to meet Juanda that afternoon. I was unsure what to expect, but at least I now knew Wong was on the island, and if I only spent my time there making representations to the prison authorities to let me interview Wong, that would be a start.

Arriving in Sekupan, I was astonished at the array of banners and flags, the headdresses and T-shirts, all sporting the name of one political party or another. Two were prominent: the National Mandate Party (PAN) and the Indonesian Democracy Party-Struggle (PDI-P). It was like being in the middle of two opposing groups of football team supporters, except in this case it all seemed good-humoured, with the excitement and atmosphere of a carnival. Even the customs and police were sporting political armbands. Outside, all the taxis, cars and bikes alike, were festooned with flags and banners, or flowers and pieces of cloth painted in the chosen party's colours. I didn't want to appear partisan, but I had no choice. Then I noticed a rather forlorn-looking boy sitting on his motorbike a little aside from the rest. He was self-consciously displaying a Partai Buruh Nasional (PBN) banner with its distinctive royal-blue colour, but it was quite apparent that he felt numerically ostracised. I didn't as yet know what PBN stood for, but having a natural sympathy for underdogs, I paid him to take me to Nagoya. I anticipated running the gauntlet of hisses, boos and perhaps a barrage of eggs and chickens' entrails, but instead we were cheered, much to the triumphant delight of my driver. It was, as it turned out, to be a fateful coincidence. I was later to meet the leader of the PBN party.

The Mandarin hotel was impressive, and more Indonesian than the last hotel I'd stayed at. The lounge was cool and sumptuously furnished with capacious leather sofas and chairs and heavy teak coffee tables sequestered behind large potted palms. Waiting by the lift, there was a small sign: 'Massage service available to guests.' I expected another chicken-neck wringer to be tapping on my door within five minutes of getting into my room. I was rather disappointed when not even the faintest tap came. My room had a Buddha-sized bed, a desk and armchairs. It had, like most Indonesian interior design, a sort of utilitarian luxury that invited you to relax but not to be too comfortable. This time, along with my camera, I had brought a small tape-recorder. If I was to be permitted an interview with Wong, I wanted every word recorded.

I had a couple of hours to spare before meeting Juanda, so I decided to figure out some questions to put to Wong and his gang. But the questions that came to mind seemed clichéd or just banal. 'What made you become a pirate?' Had anything *made* him become a pirate? Did he even consider himself to *be* a pirate? 'It's alleged that you have attacked and hijacked over twenty ships: is that true?' Would he be so stupid as to respond to this question before his trial? 'It's reported that you are a syndicate boss and, like the other syndicates operating in this region, you are controlled from China.' Again, I couldn't imagine him even countenancing an answer. I tried to rephrase the questions, but then an awful thought struck me. I was presuming his guilt, and yet his case had still to go to trial. Up till that point, everything (even in Indonesian law) would be *sub judice*. If I got an interview with him, I knew I'd be lucky if I even managed to persuade him to give me his real name. I threw down my notebook and cursed myself.

I bought a beer and told the receptionist that I was expecting Juanda, a reporter from the *Sijori Pos*. The girl knew him.

'And you are Mr Bob, yes?' she politely asked. 'Mr Juanda has telephoned to say he will be a little late. But do not worry. He will come.'

Half an hour later, Juanda arrived. Though I had never seen him before, I instantly recognised him. He walked with a slightly edgy, timid swagger. In his late-twenties, he was wearing a black shirt, black jeans and black leather boots. He smiled at the girl at reception, who pointed towards me. I stood up.

'Juanda?'

'Mr Bob,' he muttered shyly and we shook hands.

I liked Juanda immediately. There was something studious and intelligent about his face, and his manner was genuinely charming. I thanked him for coming and asked if he wanted a coffee. He nodded and we sat down.

'Mr Bob, my English is not very good. I must apologise.' Juanda looked almost upset at having to confess this. 'I would like us to speak in English. Then my English will get better.'

'Fine,' I agreed. 'But please don't call me *Mr*. Just Bob will do.'

He smiled and started to relax. 'Yes. And you must call me Joe.'

He asked me whether this was my first visit to Batam, and when I told him I'd been here twice before, he asked me how I liked it.

'It's certainly *very* different from Singapore,' I said and saw his expression suddenly sadden.

'Batam is not a rich island,' he said, in a tone of apologetic reprimand.

I quietly kicked myself for being ambiguous. 'I mean, I love the place,' I said, and smiled broadly. 'It's *wild*!'

Joe laughed. '*Wild*.'

I'm not sure he understood the word, but I think he knew I was comparing Batam favourably with Singapore.

'And I like the Indonesian people very much.' It sounded very patronising to me, but I meant it. Joe blushed faintly and thanked me.

'Is your hotel comfortable?'

'Very good,' I said, as the waitress arrived with a large pot of coffee and two elegant china cups and saucers.

'The campaigning has started for your elections, I see.'

'Yes,' Joe said as I poured the coffee. 'Are they like your elections in Britain?'

'I wish they were. They would be much more fun.'

I explained as simply as I could how our campaigning and electioneering worked, but Joe grew increasingly bemused, and I think a trifle bored.

'So all your parties' supporters do not wear their colours and have flags and banners, and do not parade in the streets and have rallies?' He looked puzzled.

'The party bosses travel around the country in buses,' I told him, 'and some people place party posters in their windows. Occasionally vans come round the streets calling on us to vote for a particular party.' I made it sound as dull as it is, and then told him that if on the day of elections there happened to be a big football match on the television, nobody bothered to vote.

'That's why we are a democracy – because nobody really cares about politics in Britain.'

Joe shook his head in disbelief. 'Do you know the PBN?'

'My taxi driver was flying their banner. What does "Buruh" mean?'

Joe thought for a moment. 'Labourer . . . Labour. Like your Labour Party. Mr Tony Blair.'

I imagined a world full of replica New Labour parties, and a continental-sized poster of Tony Blair grinning messianically from one horizon to another.

'Dony Douglas, the party's leader, would like to meet you,' Joe said. 'But first, would you like to see our newspaper offices? And I can show you the file on Mr Wong,' he added.

We finished our coffee and left.

The *Sijori Pos* was located in a nondescript concrete building a few miles from my hotel. As part of the Jawa Pos Media Group, I expected their offices to be something on the scale of the offices of a national newspaper in Britain. I was astonished to find that they consisted of just a couple of relatively small rooms, one being the main office with four computers, the other the editor's office. Mary and Socrates were at their desks, hacking out stories for the next edition. It appeared to me like a student rag office, rather than the hard-nosed newsroom the paper's professional finish suggested. I was introduced, and Socrates insisted that I give him an interview about my investigation into piracy on Batam. I found it curious that they assumed that I knew more about it than they did. While I sat with Socrates, Joe went off to collect the file on Wong.

After the interview, which Socrates typed straight into the next edition, I sat down with Joe and the file on Wong. It was substantial, and I asked Joe all the questions I had written out at the hotel, making no mention of the *sub judice* problem. I wanted his speculations, his informed views, his angle. But the material in the file was very disappointing – much of it I already knew, and the rest was just supplementary 'factual' detail. The file might as well have been put together by the military. Joe was hesitant about speculating on anything beyond the information in the file, which overall dealt with nothing more than Wong's detection and arrest by the Guskamla Armabar (the Command of Joint Operation). The newspaper, he pointed out, prided itself on being an organ of news, and nothing else.

'What about Wong's side of the story?' I asked Joe.

'Mr Dahlan, his lawyer, advises Mr Wong to say nothing until his trial.'

As I suspected, the *sub judice* rule had effectively barred reporting of the case.

'Even so,' I said, 'surely Wong has something to say that won't prejudice his trial? Have you interviewed him?'

Joe shook his head. 'I think you must meet Mr Dahlan and ask him your questions.'

'Do you think Mr Dahlan could arrange for me to interview Mr Wong?'

'I will speak to Mr Dahlan . . . I know him well.'

Joe was prepared to do everything to help me, yet I was aware that – like his newspaper – there were certain 'constraints' he was expected to work under. If these were political constraints (censorship, in other words) I would do well to respect them. I couldn't risk jeopardising relations with Joe and his contacts. Under the auspices of his newspaper, and with his reputation and connections, I could operate with a degree of immunity, and safety. And, in the highly volatile atmosphere of the current elections, that struck me as prudent.

Joe's brief for the afternoon was to cover the PDI-P (Megawati Sukarnoputri's party) rally, and he invited me along.

'But first, Bob,' he said, glancing disapprovingly at my clothes, 'you must dress smartly.'

I looked down at myself, and felt embarrassed. He was right. Over the months, the tropics had taken their toll on my clothes: my shoes were falling to bits, my shorts were crumpled and stained, and my favourite cotton shirt was hanging together by no more than a stitch. But that was no excuse, I supposed, for appearing so dishevelled and grubby. On the way to the rally we stopped at my hotel for a change of clothes. As I stepped out of the entrance in a new shirt, long trousers and tidier shoes, Joe smiled and nodded appreciatively. 'You do not look like a tourist now, Bob.' By which he politely meant that I no longer looked like a tramp.

We both rode on PDI-P supporters' motorbikes, their red

headscarves, capes and banners fluttering in the wind, as we headed out of town to a large area of wasteland where the rally was gathering. It was like being on an outrider bike in a presidential cavalcade, except the vehicles we accompanied were clapped-out trucks and cars. On the way, a young motorcyclist came alongside me in a show of support. His pillion passenger was a large eagle, sartorially sporting the party's colours. The bird glared at me, then stretched its wings as if preparing for take-off.

Half a mile or so from the rally, I could see plumes of dust rising into the hot afternoon air kicked up by all the wagons, cars and motorbikes arriving with their supporters. When we arrived, I was astonished by the size of the crowd. There were thousands of people, and their uniformly red dress made the rally appear more like a pagans' convention than a political hustings. And there were people of all ages, many far too young to vote for the party their parents had obviously taken so much trouble to dress them for. Rising out of this biblical mass of people was the speakers' platform, wired up with microphones and mega-size speakers. Perhaps there was to be a pop concert first, just to stir the hearts and minds into a frenzy of excitement. Guarding the platform were the party's security men – louche characters in paramilitary uniforms and dark glasses. I followed Joe into the crowd, snapping photos as I went, and watching out for pickpockets. Then, as the first speaker arrived on the platform with his retinue, a jubilant cheer went up and the air swirled with banners. For the first five minutes before the speeches there were stirring invocations to the crowd, party mantras, all eliciting huge excitement and saluting arms with the index finger and thumb joined in a circle and the other three fingers splayed erect. The surge of the crowd at each call from the platform made me feel increasingly uneasy. They were being purposefully whipped up into a dangerous form of hysteria. Spotting Joe, I pushed my way towards him.

'Are you OK, Joe?' I asked.

He turned to me, and said solemnly: 'They want war.'

The crowd surged again and Joe disappeared. Faces loomed at me grinning and shouting, and I felt my body convulse in sweat. Panicking, I started to push my way out, but only became further entwined in the flux and contortions of the crowd as each deafening cry went up and arms saluted. Then I felt the collar of my shirt being violently tugged from behind, and I spun round with a clenched fist ready to confront my assailant. A policeman stood there smiling at me, his baton raised, and, like the parting of the sea, the crowd moved aside as the policeman led me to the platform and gestured that I had been invited to join the various dignitaries there. I think it was the only time in my life I was glad to see a policeman, however sinister-looking. Another policeman helped me onto the platform and, without interrupting the speech, found a chair for me. A large, shiny-faced woman, highly groomed and sumptuously dressed, smiled at me. For a moment I thought she was Megawati herself, but the banner portraits of Sukarno's daughter bore no resemblance to this woman. But she looked positively like all the others on the platform – portly, rich, and smugly in political favour. These were Megawati's apparatchiks, clapping the speeches, cuddling up to the press, and putting on their best smiles for their rabble subjects - much like everywhere else in the world.

The speeches, on the whole, even though I couldn't understand them, seemed lacklustre and tedious. The point of the rally was principally a show of strength, and Megawati could have little doubt that her party had the largest following in Batam. And, judging by the zeal and temperature of the crowd, there was also little doubt that, given the right signals, these people would violently confront the other contending parties. As the rally ended and the crowd broke up, I noticed a party flag draped over the bonnet of a jeep. In the centre of the red flag was the head of a black bull, its eyes demonically red, its horns sharp and aroused. It reminded me chillingly of fascist insignia.

I was relieved to meet up with Joe, who also felt it was time to go. Quite clearly his allegiances didn't lie with the PDI-P.

'What did you mean when you said they want war, Joe?'

'They are a large party, and many people have an interest in Megawati winning. Many powerful interests.'

I could see that Joe, understandably fearful, was reluctant to elaborate, so I suggested we ride back into town and have a drink. But he had the PAN (National Mandate Party) rally to cover before he stopped work for the day.

'Do you want to come, Bob?' he asked. 'I think you might find it interesting.'

We waited on the side of the road for a couple of PAN motorcyclists to come along, but they were understandably nowhere to be seen. So we returned to town on PDI-P supporters' bikes then flagged down some PAN bikes. I smiled ironically to myself, imagining what it would be like in London if, during an election, all public transport was similarly partisan. The city would come to a standstill.

Like the PDI-P rally, the PAN gathering was being held on wasteground outside the town. It was a much smaller affair, and their blue and white colours blended well with the arid countryside and the bright sky. Musicians were playing on the platform, and above them emblazoned on a large poster was the head of Amien Rais, the party's leader. If it were a true image, I liked the man instantly. He had an engagingly sincere smile, and wore an open-necked shirt and, instead of a salute, held his right arm high as if waving to friends. The atmosphere was certainly less aggressive than the PDI-P rally, maybe because of the calming expression of the ubiquitous Rais.

Amien Rais, a devoted reformer, held a Ph.D. in political science from the University of Chicago. He was no militant – rather a liberal and pluralist, who wanted economic reform but not along ethnic or racial lines, despite being known to have Islamic sympathies. But I suspect his appeal to his followers came from his humble origins as a stallholder (which apparently he still owns) and his sense of humour. He once joked that his stall brought in more money than his prestigious job of Dean of the Faculty of Law at Gadjah Mada University. No doubt there are many university academics in the West who would sympathise with him on that matter.

'He is a great believer in *Pancasila*,' Joe said as we wandered through the crowds snapping pictures.

'*Pancasila*? What's that?'

Joe struggled. 'It means the Five Pillars. When Indonesia was founded in 1945, Sukarno said that our country should have no one religion or ideology. The Five Pillars are a belief in one God . . . a civilised and just society . . . unity . . . wise democracy . . . and social justice for all Indonesian people.'

These were admirable tenets, but from what I had seen so far in Batam, *Pancasila* was not on anyone's political agenda, in practical terms anyway. When an economy is in ruins, virtuous humanitarianism is usually found at the back of the queue . . .

We weren't invited onto the platform, but the speeches seemed quieter and more earnest, without the rhetorical hype and feverish incitement. And all the time, the face of Rais smiled down with brotherly beneficence like a pastor at a Southern Baptist meeting in America. I expected the proceedings to be wound up with some solemn collective gesture of allegiance, with everyone joining hands and singing the party anthem, but instead a band came on and a lively rock song played the rally out. At the foot of the platform, and under the boots of heavily uniformed policemen, young children looked on with bemused and happy faces. It wouldn't matter to them who won the election, even though they made up a significant part of the crowd.

It was late afternoon before we arrived back in Nagoya. I was ready for a beer, but Joe had to get back to the office to write his report. I reminded him about Mr Dahlan and asked Joe to phone him as soon as possible to see whether an interview with Wong would be possible. Attending political rallies, however interesting, was not why I was in Batam. Joe promised to phone Dahlan as soon as he got back to his office, but he insisted I had to be patient.

'Mr Dahlan is a busy man, Bob. And things happen slowly here.'

I agreed to be patient and wait for Dahlan's response. However, I suggested to Joe that perhaps he could arrange a meeting with Dahlan just to reassure him that my interest in Wong was purely journalistic and that I was prepared to guarantee non-disclosure of sources, also that I wouldn't inaccurately attribute anything to Wong . . .

Joe smiled and waved his hand to stop me. 'Be patient, Bob, and I will have an answer for you soon.'

I apologised for my impetuosity but stressed that I couldn't leave Batam until I'd met Wong.

'Tomorrow, Bob, Mr Dony and I will come to your hotel and collect you. As for Mr Dahlan . . .'

'I know. I must be patient.'

We shook hands and Joe hopped on a bike and went back to his office.

Streams of supporters were arriving back in town on trucks, motorbikes, jeeps and cars. Rather than plunge myself into a shower (which I badly needed) I decided to get some photographs. After all, it was a historic occasion. It wasn't just an election that was occurring, but the testing of Indonesia's commitment to democracy. As far as I could make out, I was the only foreigner on the streets. In Jakarta, no doubt, the international press would be besieging the place and probably outnumbering the party supporters. But here on this small island the politics were, like its legislature, provincial – and who in the world (apart from perhaps Singapore) was interested? Multiply this lack of interest by the number of islands which made up Indonesia, and the so-called democratic aspirations for this country looked decidedly frail, if not perilous.

After shooting a roll of film, I walked down a backstreet to get away from the dust and mayhem. Sitting under a palm tree and loading another film, something further down the street caught my attention. An army truck had just pulled up and soldiers were climbing out, dressed in grey riot gear and armed with batons and rifles. They mustered at the side of the truck for a brief inspection by their officer. Pretending to be a tourist, I approached them with respectful politeness and smiled at them. The officer nodded officiously at me, then turned back to his men and continued giving his orders. Were they expecting trouble? As the excited party supporters converged on the town and confronted each other, it was likely a flashpoint could occur at some point during the evening. At a discreet distance, and seeing that the soldiers were distracted by their various duties, I started taking photographs of them. There is a kind of telescoping illusion about photography in such circumstances especially while using a tele-photo lens – for while you think you are safely and discreetly concealed by distance, in fact you're often very conspicuous. Then, through the viewfinder, I suddenly saw one of the soldiers pointing in my direction. Quickly pushing the camera round my back to hide it, I started to walk away, but the officer called out to me and, wielding his baton, beckoned me over. Tremulously I approached him, assuming that at the very least he would demand the film. He didn't. Instead, he ordered his men to present themselves for a company photograph! Those on the ground dutifully lined up while the others in the trucks straightened their caps and uniforms.

'Ready!' he called to me, and the Indonesian Army's unofficial foreign photographer started snapping away. It was a bizarre experience, but very little surprised me about Indonesia now.

I walked back to the main boulevard to catch the last stragglers returning from their rallies. Still ecstatic from their day's campaigning, they waved and saluted as they tore past, all the colourful paraphernalia and party bunting flying above them like the triumphant ending of a fashion show. Then another thing, equally extraordinary, caught my eye: with each different cavalcade of supporters, the policemen lining the route surreptitiously changed their party armbands accordingly. The military, I knew, were banned from showing any political allegiance, but this apparently didn't apply to the police. An inspirationally simple means of crowd control.

I expected the campaigning to go on throughout the evening and into the night, but by around nine o'clock there was hardly a banner or flag to be seen. Batam had resumed normal life: the bars and restaurants were full of animated conversation, the shoe-shine gangs were out, the taxi drivers once more were cruising the streets blowing their horns, the shops were open, the sewers ran pungently, and rubbish was bunging up holes in the cracked pavements. And at the food court where I sat eating my satay and drinking beer, a group of giggling prostitutes pulled up their satin mini-skirts to show me more of their thighs.

Modern democracy was as foreign to these people as the classical language from which the word derived. Witnessing the campaigns and rallies, the huge turnouts and fervency of the supporters, I had at first been immensely impressed by the 'political consciousness' of the ordinary people here. But I wasn't so sure now. The real 'politics' that seemed to turn them on was the hedonistic pleasure of it all – the flag-waving, the gaiety, the day off work, the carnival atmosphere. And whatever party they supported was because of custom and tradition –

not ideology. Here ideology belonged to the party bosses and commissars, and the 'democracy' they were now committed to (in the first place, electoral) came with a monitored blessing from the West. If democracy meant anything to these people, it wasn't about enfranchisement, free and fair elections, sealed ballot boxes, majority or plural victories – it was about living their own life, and the way they lived not being demeaned or censured by others, including myself.

After more than a few beers, and avoiding the temptation of taking one of the girls back with me, I stepped in the shower in my hotel room and soaked myself thoroughly. A pool of reddish mud gathered round my feet, and the harsh spray sobered me up. Drying myself off, I flicked through the various cuttings I had on the MV *Pulau Mas* and Wong's case. I had no idea what Wong looked like, but I had an image of him that preoccupied my imagination. Throughout the day I had been thinking about him, languishing in his cell, a man of fifty-six with an economics degree from Singapore, a wife and two children. I also had a degree, a wife and two children, and I suppose it was this similarity that made me curious about him as a person. Why had he turned pirate? Why had he assumed another name and identity? Why had he abandoned his wife and kids? Wong had all the advantages and could have prospered in Singapore, perhaps going into merchant banking, or telecommunications, or the financial services. His salary would have been substantial and he and his family could have lived the affluent Chinese middle-class life with the prospect of a fat pension and comfortable retirement. Yet Wong had chosen piracy! Had he had a sudden crisis in his life and just walked out? Perhaps he had been tempted by a business deal that had inadvertently got him embroiled in organised crime and he hadn't been able to extricate himself from it. Wong was already an enigma before I had even met him (if in fact I ever was to meet him). I was investigating the enormity of modern piracy in S.E. Asia, yet here was a man who fulfilled the romantic myth of historical piracy.

Next morning I woke early. The usual hubbub of traffic and horns was being unusually swelled by shouting and someone speaking through a megaphone. For a moment I wondered if, as Joe had feared, some form of civil disorder had broken out. Grabbing my camera I hurried down to the hotel entrance, but the lobby was empty and quiet. The night porter, going off duty, wished me good morning, and the receptionist smiled. I walked out on to the boulevard and saw a dazzling, tumultuous waving and swirling of orange under the dawn sky. The Partai Republik (PR) was assembling for its rally. There were lorries full of supporters, some whistling, some blowing horns, and the air of excitement was palpable. One group waved at me ecstatically, inviting me to go with them. Another group posed ridiculously for a photograph. An astonishingly beautiful girl, her features and dusky skin radiantly enhanced by her headdress and robes, smiled at me demurely. As the vehicles revved their engines in readiness to go, the air bulged and plumed with smoke, and the whole boulevard was momentarily turned into a primitive *mise en scène*. I watched them head out of town, another carnival on the road. As the air cleared, a barrage of horns blew and the flags and banners unfurled to reveal the party's insignia – a clenched fist.

I found a restaurant that served buttered toast and raw, black coffee and settled down to watch Batam come alive. Batam had one considerable advantage over the rest of Indonesia – its proximity to Singapore and Malaysia. Its future fortunes (if it had any) lay inextricably with these two countries, more so with Singapore. Batam was desperately trying to sell itself as a tourist centre (as Yulius had explained to me), but instead of creating a better infrastructure of communications – repairing and extending its roads, for example – and generally tidying the place up, as well as fixing the drains and pavements, it seemed any financial investment it had received had been frittered away on half-baked or misconceived projects, or just pocketed by unscrupulous developers. As far as I could see, the island's political fathers had little interest (beyond their own personal interests) in realising any potential for Batam. Then, of course, there was the plurality of its politics, all of its forty-odd parties contending to set up a government hundreds of miles away, for which in due course Batam would be granted some nominal, parochial legislature that would inevitably be controlled by the same old clique of businessmen and military. It struck me that it urgently needed some form of autonomy (which it was gradually getting), and an identity that aligned its interests with its own particular geography and ambitions, also a decent set of serving – not self-serving – politicians.

By ten o'clock I was beginning to worry. Dony was meant to have arrived with Joe at nine thirty. But I had to remind myself once again that this was Indonesia, and arranged times of meetings happened within the hour, not ten minutes or so either side of the appointed time. I noticed the pile of magazines on the table in front of me had been thumbed almost to the point of being shredded by other impatient visitors; also the ashtrays, which were scarred by long lines of nicotine, probably the result of cigarettes being abandoned by incensed businessmen who assumed they had been let down. Then I saw Joe walk into the hotel, his nervous swagger slightly more pronounced as, behind him, entered Dony Douglas, the leader of the Partai Buruh Nasional. I got up, and Joe introduced us.

Dony was in his thirties, smartly dressed and pulsating with energy. With a quick shake of my hand he dispensed with the niceties of introduction and ordered coffee for us. He had a slim efficiency and astuteness about him. He didn't speak to you, he addressed you. Dony was every bit the politician – incisive, alert, confident, self-aggrandising. Business trained, he had, I gathered, also studied law. His friendly demeanour had a rehearsed conscious sincerity, as if at any moment he could be called upon to press the flesh of the world's leading statesmen. He had a steady eye for his own ambitions, and he revered Tony Blair. And Dony, I think, saw me as a potential go-between, delivering his party's manifesto and profile to Downing Street with an invitation to the Blairs to join the Douglas's for a brief informal summit over dinner at his home in Batam. I wished I could have arranged such a meeting – Dony would have left Tony breathless.

He leant towards me, his hand raised beseechingly: 'We must have reform – reform of health and education, of our fiscal and parliamentary systems, our judiciary . . . and we must find ways of distributing wealth more equitably. Corruption must be stamped out completely . . .' He was ticking off in his mind the major points in his manifesto, which to me, a hardened political cynic, sounded like earnest soundbites. Joe meanwhile was scribbling away in his notebook, taking down every word Dony uttered. The *Sijori Pos*, I presumed, was backing his campaign.

Dony drank his coffee fiercely, as if it was an irritating distraction from his schedule. He straightened his tie, pinched his cuffs, smoothed his moustache, and announced that we had to be at the Courts for a meeting with PBN delegates. On cue, Joe flipped his notebook shut and beckoned me to follow. Dony was already trooping out of the hotel.

I stopped Joe. 'Have you heard from Mr Dahlan?'

'Yes, Bob. We will meet him tomorrow.'

'And do you think there's any likelihood of an interview with Wong?'

'Perhaps. But Mr Dahlan will tell you tomorrow.'

I would rather have gone to see Dahlan than to the PBN meeting, but my impatience to get to Wong wouldn't have been served by annoying Joe, or for that matter Dony. I was not just their guest; I was now Dony's unofficial head of PBN's international PR apparatus.

Batam's Court House reminded me of a small English county court in leafy suburbia. And it had that same air of sanctified aloofness and musty professionalism. The delegates were already assembled when we arrived. There were six of them, all seated round a large polished table with their papers and agendas at the ready. As Dony briskly marched in, they all shuffled with slight uneasiness. Equally brisk were the greetings. Then I was introduced.

'This is Mr Bob Stuart, a journalist from England.' We all shook hands. 'He is going to help give our party international publicity.'

Dony made me feel very privileged, though whether I could carry out this onerous duty was quite another matter. But I had no wish to disappoint anybody and duly sat down beside Dony. The meeting was conducted in Indonesian, with Dony occasionally summarising their discussions in English for my benefit. Unlike the rallies of the other parties I'd attended, this was a very subdued and earnest affair. Once the delegates had reported on how their own contribution to the campaign was going, Dony expressed his thanks and the meeting was adjourned for lunch.

'After lunch, Bob,' Dony announced, 'I shall be speaking at a rally and I would be pleased if you would come.' I looked forward to seeing Dony in action.

Lunch was at a small restaurant outside Nagoya, where other delegates joined us. This was, I presumed, Dony's cabinet-in-waiting. They struck me as a very ordinary lot, more blue-collar than white. And surprisingly, there wasn't a woman among them. I considered mentioning this to Dony, since gender in Western politics was a vote-winning issue. I thought I could do it subtly by quoting Margaret Thatcher: 'In politics, if you want anything said, ask a man. If you want anything done, ask a woman.' But Dony would not have appreciated the quote. Blair was his man, not Thatcher.

When the meal arrived – an endless succession of small dishes – I was invited to try each one. As before, it was apparent that the food had been reheated and I could already hear myself groaning in agony on the toilet that night. But in the role of my new office, I felt obliged to set an example and show my appreciation of our leader. Each mouthful, I knew, was simply racking up the pain I would experience later. If I'd had to pay for the meal, it would have compounded my distress.

One of the delegates sitting next to me spoke a little English. 'Do you think you will be able to tell Mr Blair about our party?'

I was being put on the spot again. 'I can certainly write to him and send your party's . . .' I was going to say 'literature' but I had none. 'Do you have any information on your party?' Upon which the delegate delightedly opened his briefcase and handed me a leaflet.

He looked pleased with it. 'It tells you everything about our party's manifesto.'

It was very unimpressive – like the sort of promotional leaflet you might be handed in the street by some pushy marketing girl and immediately chuck in the nearest bin. Nevertheless, I thanked him and tucked it carefully in my wallet.

Lunch over, Dony glanced at his watch and told me that we had to catch a ferry. Belakang Padang island, on which Dony was due to meet his supporters, was about half an hour's ride off the north-west coast. Climbing into Dony's smart Japanese four-wheel drive, we sped off on the next leg of the PBN's campaign trail. Joe hadn't stopped writing since we had met that morning. Wearily he turned the pages of his notebook as Dony reeled off more of his plans. I stared out of the window and thought of Mr Wong. If all else failed, I thought, I would break into the prison to get to see Wong. But I was full of beer from lunch, and feeling stupefied by politics.

The ferry ride was very pleasant, and while I dozed in the sun, Dony silently, but with theatrical animation, rehearsed his speech, and Joe stretched his writing hand. The ferryman seemed asleep. He was an old man and had probably made this journey so many times that he now steered his boat on autopilot. A cigarette hung from his lips and his naked stomach lay in a heap above his wasted legs. I trailed my hand in the sea and thought about my family back in Britain. I was thousands of miles away from them, and at this moment, equally distant in my thoughts of them.

Arriving at the village, I saw that it was a traditional *kampong* of bamboo-stilted huts built out into the sea. As we motored slowly in between the huts I noticed the water had turned the colour of molasses. It was stagnant and full of all sorts of detritus and domestic waste. I drew my hand in quickly when I touched something oily and hard. Dony, now composed and rehearsed, rolled up his shirt-sleeves and fiddled with his tie. A few of the villagers, kids and mothers with babies in arms, watched us as we approached. There was no bunting or cheering or flag-waving. Just curiosity. The PBN, like the other parties who had occasional flags here, was just another visiting circus.

Where were the taxis and cars? The island was the quietest place I had ever been to. There were only trishaws and motorcycles. Cars had either been banned from the island years ago, or they had not managed to reach the island. How this had happened, I was too amazed to ask. As Joe, Dony and I climbed into our trishaw, a small boy ran up to us waving a PKP (Justice and Unity Party) flag. Dony scowled at the flag, but smiled sympathetically at the boy when he realised, on seeing Dony's party card, that he had made a ghastly error. The boy dropped his flag and winsomely held out his hand to me for money. Impressed by his cheekiness, I gave him a bunch of almost valueless rupiahs. Forgetting to pick up his flag, he ran off. Now I had bought off an opponent's supporter (albeit ineligible to vote), I felt marginally better in my new 'job'.

The village where Dony was to hold his rally was a small hamlet of a few buildings, all of them wooden with faded white paint, and there were very few people about. The population could not have been more than a few hundred. The trishaw driver delivered us to the village hall. The whole place was reminiscent of a genteel, small American backwoods town, steeped in civic pride and gossipy Puritanism. I almost expected the local pastor, or perhaps the mayor, to meet us with ebullient greetings. But we were just stared at by old men and women, and cats scratching themselves on shady porches. There were few, if any, party banners or flags to be seen (I certainly can't remember even seeing a PBN one), and I began to grow apprehensive about Dony's chances of drumming up a round of applause, let alone a vote for his party.

Dony too, I think, was disappointed when we entered the hall to find fewer than fifty people all politely and silently seated on rows of old wooden chairs. A metal table by the door had a spread of drinks and confectionery for the visiting delegation. If this had been a Women's Institute meeting back in Britain, I would have expressed my delight to Dony at the turnout. Despite the small attendance, calculated against the population of the island, Dony hadn't really done so badly. As the local delegate officially greeted Dony once he had sprung onto the stage, there was a tremor of applause. Not at all despondent, Dony smiled rapturously at his audience and, after adjusting the microphone, welcomed everyone. Joe and I sat discreetly at the back of the hall taking photographs of Dony and his ensemble.

He began his address with endearing humility and restraint. He introduced both Joe and I, and informed the audience that he would occasionally speak in English for my benefit. A few of the old folk looked my way and grinned and waved at me, while a little girl on her mother's knee sucked her thumb and peacefully drifted off to sleep. Dony elaborated his manifesto, adroitly tailoring it to the aspirations and ambitions of the island's inhabitants. He was a man who identified with the working people – people like themselves – fishermen, farmers, labourers, the old and young alike, irrespective of ethnic or religious background. He wanted to reform all the major institutions to improve their chances in life, to bring about a fairer and more just society. The first part of his address completed, he paused and wiped his brow with a handkerchief. A somniferous round of applause followed.

When Dony launched into his second and, I guessed, more polemical part of his address, his voice hit a new rhetorical note. He was starting to get into his stride, and his audience from now on was not just this village gathering of incurious folk, but the whole Indonesian nation. He threw up his hands as his voice rattled with almost supplicating entreaty. Dony, all at once, had transformed into an incandescent orator. At one point, he became so animated that he nearly lost his balance on the stage and had to grab the microphone to stop himself falling. Finally exhausted, and nearing the end of his speech, Dony beseeched his audience to vote for *themselves* – 'vote for PBN!' The applause woke up, and Dony stepped down from the stage with a smile of missionary zeal.

Wiping his heavily sweating forehead, he asked: 'How was that, Bob?'

'You were very impressive.'

As an unofficial apparatchik, I felt obliged to offer praise and reassurance, though I had the unsure feeling that Dony had made little or no impression here. At best they had reacted with bemused interest. Obviously, these were people not inclined to get worked up about matters of national political importance. A large catch of fish, perhaps, or a good crop, or a repaired bicycle – but not politics. Being told their vote counted, that the right party would ensure a better future for them, provoked barely more than a shrug of polite indifference.

Dony hardly spoke on the journey back to Batam. Like most politicians, I suspect, he had resigned himself to the fact that winning elections would be considerably easier if it weren't for the necessity of an electorate. For all his passionate commitment, he was beginning to realise how unrewarding a job politics could be. He stared out across the sea, not with a vision of Indonesia, but with (it seemed to me) troubled self-regard. His nascent party appeared doomed to be marginalised by the bigger, politically higher-octane parties that I had seen play so successfully – and dangerously – on the tribal ticket. Dony talked a good deal of sense, and convinced me of the integrity of his beliefs, but what he had accomplished in terms of political acuity, he lacked in professional guile.

Dony dropped us off at the *Sijori Pos* offices. Joe had his column to write and I wanted to know if Wong's lawyer, Mr Dahlan, had left a message. Mary was on duty, and as soon as we walked into the office she told us that Dahlan would meet us tomorrow and furthermore he was sure that, with conditions, an interview with Wong was possible at the prison. It was a great relief. But I wondered what the 'conditions' would be. As Joe set about writing his column, I sat with Mary and chatted about the day's events, and more especially about Wong and piracy.

'Have you met Wong?' I asked Mary as she poured coffee.

'No. But I believe he is a very dangerous man.'

'Where have you heard that from?'

'Mr Dahlan.'

'So what exactly has he told you about Wong?'

She became vague and her English grew worse. It was an evasive ploy. I suspected that she knew more about Wong and piracy in Indonesia than she was prepared to say, certainly to a foreigner. Indeed, I suspected there was more information at the newspaper's office on Wong and the Indonesian military's involvement in his capture than they were willing to admit. Censorship of the newspaper was the principal reason. Of all the information I had seen in the newspaper's files about Wong, there was not an iota of criticism or questioning of the military's role. Yet my intuition, and Mary's coyness, suggested otherwise.

As I had anticipated, my lunch turned into an evening of agony. By the time I had got back to my hotel and opened the whisky I was feeling decidedly nauseous and weak. My stomach began to gurgle and my bowels emitted the foulest smells. The worst indignity of the shits is how quickly it reduces one to a whimpering coward. In a tormenting moment, I wanted to get out of Batam, out of Indonesia, away from S.E. Asia, and forget the whole damn business of piracy. I wanted to go home. Yet in the midst of my agony Wong's imaginary face kept appearing to me. With a kind of miasmic, apparitional terror, yet coldly self-possessed, his face quivered semi-opaquely in my mind, like a diabolical talisman. In a ghastly waking nightmare I saw the mutilated and skewered bodies of the slaughtered crew of the *Cheung Son*, and Wong standing among them, proudly having his photograph taken, his sandals and rolled-up trousers meaty with blood.

'You don't look well, Bob,' Joe said with concern as we organised a couple of bikes outside the hotel to take us to meet Dahlan next morning.

'Lousy stomach, that's all,' I replied, trying to play it down.

Joe suggested a visit to a doctor first, but I had no intention of being late for our meeting with Dahlan. Besides, I'd decided the best cure was simply to ignore it.

The day was stiflingly hot, and as we sped off on our taxi bikes I could already feel my skin bristling with the sun's heat, even with the cooling breeze of the bike ride. Joe had arranged for us to meet Dahlan at a coffee shop near his office somewhere in town. It felt as if I was on another trip to a secret rendezvous, like the one I had been on with Yulius the night I had met the two men I had supposed were either pirates or military personnel. But on this occasion, I felt much safer. My real luck in Batam was meeting Joe, who looked out for me with almost brotherly consideration. The coffee shop was on an anonymous arterial road leading out of Nagoya, and certainly didn't look the sort of place a well-heeled lawyer would choose to drink at. But perhaps Dahlan had chosen it specifically for its ordinariness.

Dahlan, accompanied by his daughter (also a lawyer), was there when we arrived. He was in his fifties, opulently large in stature and with a heavily jowled face. His daughter, rather on the stout side, had attempted to Westernise her appearance and had partially disguised her Indonesian good looks with excessive make-up and jewellery. She said nothing throughout our meeting. Dahlan genially shook my hand, but I detected a nervousness in his eyes that was slightly unsettling. In front of Dahlan, Joe was a model of deference and, like Dahlan's daughter, said nothing. He sat awkwardly to the side of us, and neither took notes nor asked questions. This surprised me, since what Dahlan had to say about his involvement in Wong's case would have made good copy for his newspaper. Dahlan spoke through the side of his bulbous mouth in a rushed and truncated way that exacerbated the problem of understanding him.

'I am very anxious about this case,' he confessed. 'It could damage my reputation and my law firm.'

I asked him why.

'Mr Wong is accusing the Indonesian Navy of an act of piracy when, as he claimed, they boarded his ship. It is his only defence.'

Naïvely, I asked him why this should pose a problem. After all, I said, the Indonesian Navy had long been suspected of being involved in piracy.

Mr Dahlan smiled. 'But there is no proof, you see? Even in your country there must be evidence.'

'So if this is Mr Wong's only defence, I take it you will have to allege in court that the Navy itself committed an act of piracy?'

'Yes. But I do not have any proof – only the word of Mr Wong and his fellows.'

I was beginning to appreciate his problem. By making this allegation against such an illustrious part of the Indonesian establishment, Dahlan could be committing professional suicide.

'Do you have any other witnesses that might corroborate Wong's story?'

Dahlan shook his head. He mentioned that one of Wong's gang had turned informer and had helped the joint intelligence operation in uncovering Wong. But he had since 'disappeared'.

'Mr Juanda tells me that you would like to interview Mr Wong,' Dahlan said.

'Would that be possible?'

'Yes. But you must understand that I will have to be present and that your questions will be restricted.'

I agreed on the terms of the interview, and Dahlan phoned the governor of Batam Prison. There was a very amiable discussion between the two and Mr Dahlan gave me an encouraging smile.

Then Dahlan said to me: 'You must be at the prison at 10 a.m. tomorrow.'

Before Joe and I left, I asked Mr Dahlan if he believed Wong's story. 'Mr Wong is a very clever man,' he smiled cryptically.

Joe returned to his office, and I spent the rest of the day aimlessly wandering around Batam centre, drinking at bars, gazing into shops and sitting on the roadside watching the traffic. For all Dahlan's misgivings about representing Wong, I was sure that it would be no more than a show trial and that the outcome had already been decided: a *res judica*. Since Wong was the first high-profile 'syndicate leader' in the world to go on trial for piracy, his trial would inevitably have considerable political ramifications for Indonesia. They needed his conviction for an international PR coup, which would convince the world maritime authorities that they were 'cracking down' on piracy in their waters. But, as Batam's military intelligence had admitted to me, there were two other pirate gangs operating from the island. Why had they not been arrested along with Wong? If it was because of lack of evidence, the evidence against Wong was, as I later discovered, circumstantial. In fact, the story Wong was to tell the next day in Batam Prison left considerable doubt in my mind about the Indonesian military's probity.

– CHAPTER TEN –

I was livid with Joe. By 9.45 a.m. he had not arrived and we were due at Batam Prison at ten. I asked the receptionist to phone his home, his office and his mobile phone, but there was no answer anywhere. In desperation, I phoned Dahlan's office, but his secretary told me he was not there. Of course, he was at the prison waiting for us. When Joe eventually arrived, he looked sheepish, and was apologetic. Apparently he had been delayed by some crisis at the newspaper. I wasn't prepared to listen to him.

'How long will it take us to get to the prison?' I asked.

'Half an hour,' he replied, apologising again for the delay.

'I don't suppose you have the phone number of the prison?'

Joe shook his head. 'I can asked them at reception.'

I told him we were wasting time and that we should set off immediately. 'Would it be quicker by bike or taxi?'

'Bike.'

Hopping on a couple of bikes outside the hotel I told Joe to offer the boys more money to drive as fast as they could. It was a near-fatal mistake. That morning the traffic was unusually busy, and though our riders manoeuvred skilfully among the traffic, at a junction my driver almost lost control as he tried to beat an on-coming lorry. The lorry was going faster than he had anticipated, and to avoid a collision he swerved perilously in front of the vehicle, just missing its fender, and we skidded into a shallow ditch. Astonishingly, the bike didn't go over, and, shaken as I was, we returned to the road in a cloud of dust. Joe and his rider had disappeared.

I had expected Batam Prison to be a grim and austere place, but as we arrived outside its gates I was surprised to see how small and, as a building, how architecturally attractive it was. There were no high walls laced with barbed-wire or razors, no watch towers, no searchlights, no CCTV. In fact, had it not been for the prison sign and the heavy steel gate, I could have mistaken it for a monastery of an enclosed order. Adjacent to the prison was a rundown garage where three surly mechanics sat smoking among piles of oily engine parts. Joe was waiting for me. I paid the riders, who, grateful for the tip, sped off gleefully. Joe threw up his hands.

'Mr Dahlan has gone,' he said abjectly.

I approached the door to the prison and banged hard on it. The observation hatch slid open and a guard's face appeared. He glared at me momentarily then asked what I wanted. I signalled to Joe to translate.

'We have come to interview Mr Wong. It has been arranged through Mr Dahlan, Mr Wong's lawyer. Can we speak to the governor?'

The hatch slid shut. For the next ten minutes we paced up and down, but the guard did not return.

'We've fucked it!' I said, and Joe looked crestfallen.

'I will go back to the city and speak with Mr Dahlan.'

'If it'll do any good . . .'

Joe walked to the road and flagged down a bike. I suspected he was relieved to get away from my glowering anger. After he had gone, I felt guilty for the way I'd treated him that morning. Joe had been magnanimous with me, and I had not considered just how much help he had given me so far. Angrily I kicked at the dust. The bemused mechanics scowled at me. I looked despairingly at the prison. Mr Wong and his gang of pirates were only a matter of a few metres away, and now it seemed that the likelihood of my interviewing them had all but gone. I doubted very much if Mr Dahlan would bother to return to the prison today; and I certainly couldn't imagine him agreeing to an alternative arrangement, not after our failure to arrive on time.

I went back to the gate and knocked again. Once more the observation hatch slid open and the glaring eyes of the guard fixed me.

'Huh?' he grunted. With resigned pleading, I told the guard that I had come all the way from England to interview Mr Wong, and that I could not return home without finishing my story. I beseeched him to let me see the governor. He squinted at me in utter confusion, and slid the hatch shut. I glanced at my watch, and decided to give myself ten more minutes before I finally called it a day and left. The mechanics, still on their extended tea break, shook their heads in my direction. What was this madman doing, trying to get *into* prison?

Just as I was about to leave, I heard a sharp wrench of metal and within seconds the prison gate slowly opened. I waited with heart-stopping anticipation. The guard appeared halfway round the door and beckoned me. I walked over to him unsure as to what was to happen next. He opened the door a little wider and nodded his head for me to enter. The first thing I saw was a pretty landscaped garden with flowers and decorative stone. Beyond was the prison rectangle, also landscaped and shaded by small flowering trees. And this was a place of detention and punishment! I was escorted to the guardroom, where I was asked to wait. I expected at the very least to be searched and asked to fill in some official form. But I was just left there waiting, watching an ancient fax machine sporadically spew out reams of blank paper. The guard glanced at it contemptuously and went on reading his newspaper. A fan burred above us swirling the pungent smoke of the guard's Indonesian cigarette.

I felt tired, and with the gentle whirring of the fan and a peaceful view of the garden beyond the door in the courtyard, and the heat, I began to drift off to sleep. Then I heard footsteps and two guards in olive-green uniforms strolled into the room. They waved at me to follow them. I was escorted along a narrow cloister into the anteroom of the governor's office. The guard announced my presence to the governor, who immediately came out and shook my hand. This was Dr Frandono.

'Mr Bob?' he smiled. 'Ah, there seems to have been some confusion. Mr Dahlan has had to return to his office.'

'My fault, I'm afraid.'

He gave me a forgiving smile and invited me into his office.

Dr Frandono spoke impeccable English. His pronunciation was

elegant and precise, and his phrasing had a relaxed intelligence about it. He was taller than the average Indonesian, and his features were slim and patrician. He looked Caucasian. Rather than a uniform, he wore a dark casual suit and tie.

'Would you like a drink? Tea? Coffee? Water?' he asked.

His office was plainly decorated with bookshelves and two large leather sofas. There were no bars on the windows, and no visible security systems.

'Coffee, please.' Within minutes it was brought to me, with a glass of water, on a small tray with a napkin.

Relaxing behind his desk, Frandono wanted to talk about England. 'Do you know Pete Townsend?' he asked.

I nearly choked on my coffee. 'You mean *the* Pete Townsend, from the band The Who?'

'Yes,' he smiled. 'We are related.'

There are weirdly surreal moments in life, and this for me was one of them. I was sitting in an Indonesian prison, drinking coffee, waiting to interview a syndicate pirate boss, and here we were, the governor and I, talking about an ageing British rock star!

'My mother was originally from England – a Townsend,' he said. 'My father was Dutch. When they married they came to Indonesia around the time of independence and decided finally to take resident status here. Then my father changed his name to Frandono. I am Pete Townsend's cousin, on my mother's side.' I almost expected Frandono, in celebration of this famous connection, to bring out a hi-fi system and start playing 'My Generation'.

I think it was the fact that I was English, and therefore bound to know of Pete Townsend, that finally got me into the prison. I couldn't imagine any of his staff being impressed by his famous relative, or even knowing who Pete Townsend was. And Frandono was evidently eager to tell someone.

Dr Frandono then produced a small orange pamphlet and handed it to me. It was titled: 'Peristilahan Pemasyarakatan (Terms of Correction)', with the subtitle 'Indonesian – Inggris'. It was a glossary of Indonesian legal words and terms with the English translation alongside. Frandono was very proud of it.

'I have written it. It is unique,' he smiled.

I flipped through it. It was arranged in alphabetical order. To practise piracy was 'merompak, membajak (laut)', and pirate was 'pembajakan (laut)'. And if you are ever unfortunate enough to face the death sentence in Indonesia, the word for hangman is 'algojo'. He gave me a copy and asked me to send it to the London Law Society when I returned to Britain. As I was reading it, Frandono phoned Dahlan and conveyed my apologies for being late, explaining that I was at the prison and wished to interview Wong as soon as possible. Dahlan told him that he and Joe were on their way and that I could start the interview without him. Frandono asked one of the guards to fetch Mr Wong and one of the other pirates – his chief officer.

I congratulated Frandono on running a very humane prison. 'It is very different from some of our prisons in Britain,' I said. 'Many of them were built in the last century when there wasn't any form of enlightened policy towards prisoners. Generally it's as harsh now as it was then, especially in the top security jails.'

'In my prison,' Frandono said, 'I insist that the prisoners are treated decently and that their dignity as human beings is respected.' At the time he was working on installing air-conditioning in the cells (paid for by the prisoners themselves, as I later discovered).

When Mr Wong and his chief were brought in, I immediately stood up. Even in his slacks, short-sleeved shirt and sandals (no prison uniform), Wong had a commanding presence. His chief, dressed similarly, was slightly less impressive. We shook hands and Frandono arranged more seats for us. What instantly struck me about Wong was his cool impassiveness, as well as his harsh, unyielding eyes that held me almost at a physical distance from him as he sat down. Uncannily, there was something almost avuncular about his expression, especially when he smiled. He is a very clever man . . . I recalled Dahlan's description of him, and I could clearly see what he meant. Wong did look 'clever' – intimidatingly so. He told me politely that he would prefer Dahlan to be present during the interview.

Dahlan and Joe arrived in due course. Once the seating had been rearranged, I began to interview Wong and his chief. I wanted to be clear first of all about the background to the events leading up to Wong's arrest.

'I was contracted as the shipping agent,' said Wong, 'to sail the ship – MV *Pulau Mas* – to Johor in Malaysia and deliver it to the owner there. While we were anchored, a small boat came alongside us. There were six men in the boat, three dressed in Indonesian Navy uniforms and three civilians.'

I asked him if he knew any of the men.

'I knew one of them. Frangky.'

'Who was Frangky?'

'He was the Navy's informant. He told them that I had hijacked the ship.'

'Was Frangky formerly one of your gang?'

Wong smirked and said nothing.

'Were these men armed?' I asked.

'Yes. They had guns and knives.'

I asked Wong to continue describing the events.

'They separated me from the rest of the crew and took me to a small room for interrogation. Frangky said that if I gave him $S50,000 I could have the ship. The Indonesian Navy men urged me to pay. I told them that I did not have that kind of money. One of them then pointed a gun at me and asked me if I wanted to be shot in the head or the stomach. I was very frightened. I told them again that I did not have that amount of money.'

'They obviously believed you. So what did they do next?'

Wong continued: 'They stole everything from the ship. My very expensive Rolex watch . . . even my shoes!' he laughed. His chief held up his wedding finger. 'They stole my wedding ring,' he said. I could see a slight indentation mark where the ring had been on his finger.

'So what happened to the ship and its crew?'

'We were ordered to sail the *Pulau Mas* back to Batam.'

'And that's when you were arrested and charged with piracy?' I asked.

'No. They took us to the police station where we were questioned. Then they let us go.'

'When they questioned you at the police station, did you mention that you had been threatened with a gun and held to ransom?'

'Yes. But they said I should have paid!' he laughed.

Several days after being questioned at the police station Wong, his chief and the crew of the *Pulau Mas* were picked up by the police and charged with pirating the ship.

Wong's clear recollection of the events certainly convinced me that the Indonesian Navy had, with menaces, colluded with Wong over the hijacking of the *Pulau Mas*. But then there was the matter of the incriminating evidence found by the Navy on the ship – evidence that surely suggested, as they later claimed in court, that the *Pulau Mas* was Wong's pirate HQ.

'On board the ship, or so Admiral Sumardi claims, the Navy discovered various articles usually associated with piracy: handcuffs, masks, bayonets, paint, even a speedboat. What d'you say to that?'

Wong looked at me with an unflinching stare. 'It is not unusual for a ship to have these things. The handcuffs may have to be used to restrain an unruly crewman; in severe cases of disorderliness, the threat of a bayonet might be needed; as for the masks, they are used to keep the sun off the crew's faces.'

'And the speedboat?'

'When you are at anchor, off a port for instance, it is quicker to use a speedboat if you need supplies. Or in the event of an emergency.'

I decided not to question him further about the inventory. It was obvious he could justify everything that was discovered on the ship.

'Your name is not Mr Wong, is it? Apparently you have two passports. Why?'

A mischievous smile crossed his face. 'For operational reasons.'

'What *operational* reasons?'

He laughed. 'I told you!'

'Are you a pirate, Mr Wong?' I hoped the directness of the question might surprise him into betraying himself. But he simply laughed again.

I couldn't catch him out. Wong had masterfully conducted the interview himself. I asked if I could take a photograph of him. He refused, but I took it anyway. Whatever the truth was behind his arrest, I was certain of two things: first, he was a member of a syndicate of pirates; and second, the Indonesian Navy had committed an act of piracy or 'sea robbery'. Both their stories – Sumardi's operation published in the *Sijori Pos* and Wong's own account – seemed too close in the context of 'mutual interests' to be at total variance with one another. Disturbingly too, Frandono (who should have been entirely impartial throughout the interview) seemed unusually sympathetic to Wong. Dahlan, however, looked on with subdued resignation, knowing that Wong could cost him both his practice and his reputation.

'Shall we have coffee?' Dahlan asked Joe and I once outside the prison. I sensed that Dahlan wanted to tell me more about Wong. In any case, a ride back into town in Dahlan's comfortable car was far preferable to a motorbike ride.

We found a café, rather noisy, and Dahlan ordered coffee.

'I cannot talk about Mr Wong's case,' Dahlan began, 'but I can tell you that he is a member of a syndicate of pirates.' Since Dahlan was Wong's lawyer, this struck me as an astonishing admission. 'His boss is in Hong Kong.'

'How many members of the syndicate are there?' I asked.

'Perhaps three or four; one is in Malacca, I think. Another is in Jakarta. Mr Wong was based in Singapore.'

'Do you believe that Wong intended to hijack the *Pulau Mas*?'

'I think that was the case. They intended to sail it to the Philippines.'

'Do you believe Wong's accusation that the Indonesian Navy attempted to hijack the ship?'

Dahlan smiled. 'I cannot say at this time.'

I was keen to find out about Wong's modus operandi, how he and his associates set about hijacking ships.

'As a shipping agent,' Dahlan said, 'Mr Wong knows all the ships passing through the Strait of Malacca and into the South China Sea. He knows their names, their cargoes, their inventory, the crews and where they have come from and their destinations. Everything. So . . .' He paused to sip his coffee. 'Mr Wong pays one of the crew to inform him exactly of the position of the ship during its passage.'

'How does the crewman do that? Surely not over the ship's radio!'

Dahlan laughed. 'Simple. Mr Wong gives him a hand phone.' Simple indeed!

'So the crewman tells Mr Wong – or one of the other syndicate pirates – where and when it would be best to attack the ship?'

'Yes.'

'Are the gangs who attack the ships local people? Fishermen perhaps?' I was thinking of the fishermen on Sendora island.

'Yes, they are local people. Indonesians.'

I had almost forgotten Joe was with us. He was quietly taking notes.

'So who alerts the gangs? The crewman on the boat, or the syndicate boss?'

'The crewman always keeps in touch with the pirate boss. If the boss thinks it is the right place and time to attack, he alerts the gang. The crewman then waits to help the gang board the ship.'

Dahlan's knowledge of piracy and how it operated seemed extraordinarily good, and I could only imagine that his information had come from Wong. But why was Dahlan telling me all this? He had earlier asked me not to publish anything about what we had discussed until Wong's trial was over. But could he trust me? Or did he perhaps wish me to publish it? It would have been quite easy for me to get a column in *The Straits Times* back in Singapore, and in that event the integrity of his defence would have been totally impugned. He would undoubtedly have been taken off the case. Perhaps this was his ploy. All the same, I kept my promise.

As we left, Dahlan said: 'Mr Wong's name is not Chew Cheng Kiat. I think it is Chow Kah Pong.' How could Dahlan properly defend a man whose name he didn't really know?

Wong himself was a complete mystery. He had apparently assumed two names for 'operational reasons'. Dahlan thought that 'Wong' was his syndicate name, and that his other pseudonym, 'Chew Cheng Kiat', was the name he used for falsifying shipping documents. The two passports Wong possessed were in those names, the latter of course being that of the labourer in Singapore. So where was his official passport? Or had Wong disposed of this and assumed a totally different (dual) identity? When I offered to visit his wife and children in Singapore, Wong smiled and shook his head vigorously. Wong had all but severed himself from his past life. He had become a doppelganger, on the one hand operating as a successful and respected shipping agent, and on the other setting ships up for attack and hijacking. But with over twenty attacks allegedly attributed to Wong, why hadn't the ship-owners and agents with whom he had dealt become suspicious of him? Or were some of them – as has been suggested – actually colluding with Wong in order either to claim insurance or a slice of the profit? Wong, as far as I could discover, had been operating in his dual role for over seven years, and yet it was only on the word of an informer (Frangky) that Wong and his gang had finally been caught. And yet for several months, so the Indonesian Navy claimed, they had been playing a cat-and-mouse game with Wong and the *Pulau Mas*, attempting to board it while it was anchored in Indonesian waters, only then frustratingly to see it escape into international waters. Was someone in the Navy informing Wong and his gang each time the Navy approached them? The *Pulau Mas* was a lumbering ship and no match for the Navy's high-powered boats. And why had Frangky, a self-confessed pirate who knew Wong, turned informer? Perhaps they had fallen out and Frangky wanted revenge. Dahlan intended to call Frangky as his chief witness, but not long before Wong's trial Frangky, as Dahlan mentioned, went missing (there was a rumour that the Indonesian Navy had aided his disappearance). Not that Frangky's testimony would have made much difference to Dahlan's case, since the Navy would have dismissed it as fiction.

Listening to the recording in my hotel later, I came back to my earlier conclusion: that the Indonesian Navy – perhaps the Malay and Singapore Navies also – were implicated to a greater or lesser degree in piracy. It also struck me that the ethno-economic structure and hierarchy of piracy here (unless I was mistaken) was the perfect arrangement: the Chinese, with their obsessive passion for money and their renowned business acumen, formed the syndicate operation; while the Indonesians and Malays, with their more, easy-going laissez-faire 'Third World' attitude, plus their maritime skills, provided the crews and logistics. Nor was I convinced that Wong, like the other syndicate members, acted alone. Wong would have cultivated a fiefdom of influential people, fawning acolytes, cronies, corrupt officials, and, doubtless, a few unscrupulous politicians. His 'gang' extended well beyond those merely hired to attack ships or assist in running his HQ. It simply had to be the case, given the sophisticated and complex business of selling off stolen cargoes, and disposing of or 'phantoming' whole ships. And, however covert the operation, the huge profits involved were as unmissable as a lavish Chinese banquet.

I left Batam the next day and a week later flew back to Britain. Until Wong's trial was over, there was little hope of getting any more substantial information on his syndicate operation, or on how deeply the Indonesian authorities (and perhaps other countries) were involved in piracy. I had heard so many rumours, allegations and stories, and witnessed enough myself to draw some tentative conclusions – but Wong, I knew, held the conclusive evidence . . .

Before I left for Britain Adam and I met for a last drink to discuss what ideas I might try and sell once back home. But I knew he was asking for a salvage operation. Within weeks of returning, I heard that his business had folded. It had ended, predictably, in acrimony and bad debts.

Joe faxed me on 18 June 1999 regarding the progress of Wong's trial (it began on 16 June). His information was brief and stated that the Navy had called two witnesses against Wong, and a further two after a month's adjournment. Wong, and his crew of seven, denied the witnesses' evidence. Dahlan, unsurprisingly, had no witnesses to call and the conviction was a foregone conclusion. Understandably, Dahlan, with or without witnesses, had no enthusiasm for accusing the Navy of piracy. Wong was duly sentenced to eight years in prison – six years for being a 'chief of piracy', and two years for immigration violations. His crew, also found guilty, got lesser sentences.

Dahlan might well have given up Wong's case at this point. Instead he took his sentence to appeal at Province Riau's law court (a higher court). There his sentence was reduced to three years for piracy and two for immigration violations. Dissatisfied, Wong insisted on going to a further appeal, this time to the high court in Jakarta. In the meantime, a dramatic turn of events occurred. Wong escaped from his cell in Batam, apparently with the help of Dr Frandono, the governor of the prison. According to Joe's information, Frandono and Wong had apparently come to a deal: Wong would sell the MV *Pulau Mas* and share the profit with Frandono. The ship was worth around $300,000. But Wong was caught in Jakarta. Was he trying to make contact with his syndicate colleague there to arrange the sale? The court inevitably took a dim view of Wong's escapades, and reinstated the original sentence of eight years. They also recommended that he be moved to another prison, a less 'enlightened' one in the Province of Riau Pekanbaru, in Sumatra, some distance from Batam.

Wong had obviously lied to me about the MV *Pulau Mas* when he maintained that he didn't own the ship and was returning it to its owner in Johor, Malaysia. I suspected it was stolen and was in fact Wong's piracy HQ – his 'mother' ship, as the Indonesian Navy had maintained. I also believed Wong and his gang had been responsible, as the Indonesian Navy had claimed, for hijackings and attacks on more than twenty ships. I was inclined, however, to believe Wong's story that the Navy (with their informer Frangky) had committed an act of piracy, not only by boarding the ship, but also by demanding with menaces $50,000 for the release of the ship into Wong's hands. Intelligence operations, in any country, are notoriously murky.

And, as far as Dr Frandono was concerned, I wasn't entirely surprised to hear that he was complicit in Wong's 'escape'. It only further proved how susceptible this country was to corruption.

I felt compelled to return. Now that Wong and his gang had been convicted, perhaps he would be more forthcoming about the whole background and organisation of piracy, even about his own part in it. Effectively, his imprisonment meant the end of his career as a syndicate pirate – unless, with his skills of disguise and connivance, he could start pirating ships again in another part of the world. And what of the Indonesian Navy's contentious part in the affair of the *Pulau Mas*'s seizure and the arrest of Wong? Had their 'intelligence operation' other ulterior motives? And what further light could Dahlan now shed on the Wong trial and piracy operations in general in the area? For all my investigations, this part of S.E. Asia seemed to remain as mysterious and unavailing of its piratical secrets as ever . . . But I had to return.

– CHAPTER ELEVEN –

'YOU like nice fresh girl? We go and see mama san. You like KTV? I take you . . . You want a beer? Where are you staying? I fix you up with good hotel . . . How long you staying?' I was back in Batam, 'bandit country', and the first bandit I met was my taxi driver, who drove me down from Sekupang port to Nagoya. His old Nissan jalopy rattled and bumped along the road as if running on a combustible recollection of how the car once performed millions of miles and years before. Resting his elbow on the open window, he smoked a foul-smelling Gudang Garam cigarette and glanced at me occasionally, as if trying to figure out what other seductive offers he could make to empty my wallet. Outside, the huge jungle lining the road on either side hung with languorous beauty, above it a darkening crimson sky. At dusk Indonesia is at its best, almost romantic. Watching it as we drove lulled me away from the prattling solicitations of my driver, who, finally accepting that I had no interest in anything he had to offer, fell into a surly silence.

In the two years since I'd last met Joe we had corresponded infrequently, but he hadn't told me that in the meantime he had married and had a small daughter, nor that his mother had died. I met Rini, his wife, at the *Sijori Pos* office the following day and, as arranged, went back to their house to meet Joe. Rini was in her twenties, with characteristic Indonesian features. She had the good looks of a woman in early maturity, and would never lose them. Her manner was typical of Muslim women, reserved, excruciatingly shy, with an unfortunate servility. As we arrived outside their small house on a modern complex, Joe appeared with his mother-in-law holding his daughter Anna. We greeted each other as we had left each other those two years before, with a huge embrace.

Joe had put on weight, but he had the same indefatigable and engaging smile, and those dark, penetrating eyes. I took Anna and held her.

'Why didn't you tell me you had married and had a daughter?'

Joe shrugged. 'Many things have happened since you were last here, Bob.'

Joe and I took a taxi to Nagoya and the hotel Joe had arranged for me, the Bukit Nagoya. Despite it being cheap, I was very dismayed when I saw the room. The bed comprised a couple of mattresses, the furniture was falling apart, and the bathroom was filthy. 'Pretty good, Bob . . . for the price,' Joe remarked. I opened my bottle of whisky and poured some drinks, sniffing the foul air of all the room's previous occupants. A lizard ran across the ceiling, and a group of mosquitoes spun around the light shade. The view from the window was of an old rusted corrugated shed and a pile of garbage. In the surrounding hills were the *rumah liar*, the slums of the immigrant workers.

'So, Bob,' Joe began. 'We must plan our strategy.'

'Have you been in touch with Dahlan about what happened at Wong's trial?'

'You want to interview him? I'll phone his office now.'

Dahlan was busy in court but promised to phone when he was available. 'We may have trouble with Dahlan,' Joe said. 'He lost the case and that means for him a loss of face. He may feel embarrassed to talk to you.'

'If necessary,' I said, 'we'll go round to his office and sit there until Dahlan agrees to see us!'

Joe laughed. 'You've not changed, have you? Still as impatient as ever!'

I had three weeks to complete my research on piracy, and this time I fully intended to get all the information I wanted, and more. I gave Joe a list of my requirements: apart from Dahlan, I wanted to interview the Guskamla Armabar, Navy Intelligence, specifically about the capture of Wong and the smashing of his pirate operation, and how in general they were tackling the problem of piracy in the region. I also wanted first-hand detailed information about how piracy operated, from the syndicates down to how the actual attacks on ships took place. And I wanted to meet, if possible, an active pirate. Lastly, I wanted to see Wong again. As I went through the list, Joe looked increasingly daunted and I wondered if I was asking too much of him.

Draining his glass, he nodded his head and smiled thoughtfully. 'We will do it, Bob!' he exclaimed with his usual enthusiasm. 'Now let's go for lunch. I have many things to tell you . . .'

Joe had become a district official in the Partai Buruh Socialist Democratik (Democratic Socialist Labour Party, PBSD). The party, despite having a small electorate, was gradually becoming a recognised force in Indonesian politics. One of its priorities was to raise wages (the minimum wage in Indonesia is 550,000Rp per month), and by doing so reduce the rampant corruption in the country. Health, welfare and education were also priorities. Joe had the ideological optimism of a young Muslim sworn to martyrdom, yet everywhere about us were the harsh, implacable realities of an urgent need for change – fetid, open sewers, collapsing roads and pavements, abject poverty, pollution, rats. Joe was embarrassed by the state of his country and its poor infrastructure. He gazed at a complex of shabby, concrete buildings where we were eating. 'We must paint them. We must make it beautiful – like Switzerland.' Like many of his contemporaries (the young intelligentsia of Indonesia who desired change), Joe's grasp of *real politik* was naïvely endearing. 'When I am president of Indonesia, Bob, you will see how beautiful and rich this country will become.' In the meantime he and his party had to fight the entrenched cynicism and corruption of the Megawatti regime and all her unsavoury predecessors. Their task was to rebuild Indonesia's self-perception and restore its national integrity. But, as Joe said, it would take several generations to accomplish it, and (he admitted) the probability of considerable civil strife. As Joe and I got drunker we planned to become gunrunners and revolutionaries and fight alongside the Aceh people of northern Sumatra against the Indonesian central government. Our nights were full of comradeship and dreams.

Next morning I was brought my breakfast by one of the hotel's staff:

a cup of sweet black coffee and a plate of sliced bread adorned with coloured chocolate chips. I had just been in the bathroom, where belatedly I had discovered there was no toilet paper. To top it all, my legs were covered in mosquito bites. 'Morning, Mr Bob,' the receptionist brightly called to me as I walked out. 'Shit-hole,' I mumbled under my breath.

I was due to meet Joe at ten to plan our day and try to get an interview with the elusive Mr Dahlan. At an Indian coffee shop I met Krishna and his Chinese Singaporean friend Mr Chew. Krishna was in his early sixties and suffered from diabetes. He had been a very successful oil engineer and had travelled throughout the world with his job. And his English was excellent. When I told Krishna my reason for being in Batam, he became concerned.

'There are many bad people here in Batam, and those involved in piracy are very dangerous people. They are Mafia. You must be very careful,' Krishna said, almost in a whisper.

Krishna had lived in Batam with one of his daughters for many years, and I took heed of his warning. When I told him about my hotel and how much it cost, he shook his head. 'You see, Bob? They are all crooks here!' After we finished our coffees he took me round to his apartment. 'If ever you are in trouble, or are in need of somewhere to stay, you may come here any time.' I thanked him for his kindness, and truly felt I could trust the man. As I left, he called to me.

'Bob, trust no one in Batam.'

'Not even you, Krishna?'

He smiled sadly. 'Not even me.'

Joe and I had arranged to meet at the Valhollo, a modern coffee and cake shop. It became our regular venue, and a few days later it was here that I was to get my best lead. Infuriatingly, Joe never kept to arranged times, and always ambled in half an hour or more late. 'Rubber time,' he would grin.

'Phone Dahlan's office, Joe. We need to speak with him today.'

Joe phoned him and Dahlan once again seemed rather non-committal. As Joe talked I asked him to tell Dahlan that it was urgent we meet, since I was due back in Britain soon. Dahlan said that he would be in his office after twelve o'clock and would phone us then.

I shook my head. 'That's not good enough, Joe. He's being evasive. Why?'

'Perhaps, as I said before, the loss of face . . .'

I ordered a beer and brooded on the matter. Meanwhile, Joe perused the papers and phoned some friends. Irritated by sitting around, I told Joe that at twelve we would go round to Dahlan's office and sit there until he saw us. I was beginning to resent the Indonesian's procrastinating attitude.

'Another thing, Joe. We need to make arrangements to interview Navy Intelligence. Where are they based?'

'Tanjong Pinang, on Bintan Island. It's about an hour by ferry. I'll have to phone the *Sijori Pos* there to ask them to make contact with the Navy.' Joe went back to his newspaper.

'Do it now, Joe,' I insisted.

Joe laughed. 'No more rubber time, eh, Bob?'

At twelve we walked round to Dahlan's office. It was on a tree-lined street with a large open sewer running down the middle of it. The foul stench mingled with the fumes of motorbikes and the smell of lunchtime. Dahlan's office, compared to the adjacent shops, was chic and modern, with smoked-glass windows. As soon as we stepped in, Dahlan's assistant, Robert, introduced himself. He seemed uneasy and politely asked us to wait while he went to talk with Dahlan. Ten minutes later he returned, and told us that Dahlan would see us. I was shocked to see how Dahlan had aged in the two years since we'd last met. He had become greyer and his face had a sallow, sunken appearance. He greeted me warmly, and when we shook hands I could feel the bones in his fingers. I had brought a tape-recorder, and while I set it up, Joe and Dahlan talked amicably. Joe was excellent at putting people at ease and, as I was to find out, considerably adept at getting information. He was a superb journalist, and I couldn't believe that he had walked out of his job at the *Sijori Pos* after (as he put it) 'an irreconcilable difference with the owner over policy'.

We started the interview by talking generally about Mr Wong. Wong had admitted to Dahlan that he had originally planned his pirate operations from Singapore, and then came to Batam to recruit pirates. His boss was in Hong Kong and he had two syndicate associates, one in Jakarta, the other in Johor Bahru, Malaysia. I was keen to know about the circumstances of Wong's arrest. Had Wong been arrested at sea and held to ransom by the Indonesian Navy?

'Yes,' Dahlan said. 'They arrested him and his gang of eight in international waters.'

'Do you believe Wong's story that he was returning the ship to its owner in Johor?'

Dahlan laughed. 'Mr Wong and his gang were on an operation to hijack a ship. The Navy knew this because the informer (Frangky) had information about the operation.'

'Wong claimed that the Navy held him at gunpoint and demanded $(S)50,000 for the release of the ship into his hands. He accused them of piracy.'

'It was a trick,' Dahlan said.

'A trick?'

'Yes. Once Wong started to negotiate with them, they then had the evidence that the ship wasn't his, as he had claimed, and that he had pirated it.'

'The Navy found several incriminating articles on the *Pulau Mas*, including bayonets and masks. How did Wong explain these in court?' I asked.

'The knives?' Dahlan grinned. 'Wong said they were for the kitchen!'

'And the masks?'

'Wong claimed they were used for painting!'

Basically, Wong had no defence at all. His court case had been little more than a farce. Wong had made enemies – he had cheated his gang out of money, he had tried to set one gang against another by 'talking too much', and, I think, the Navy hated him because he was a foreigner, a Singaporean, and had become too 'greedy'.

'What was the deal between the informer and the Navy?' I asked.

Dahlan shrugged. 'I think they must have offered him money, security, perhaps a job. But he never appeared in court as a witness. He disappeared.'

We discussed the Frandono affair. 'Ah, yes,' said Dahlan. 'Mr Frandono! Wong offered him 25 million rupiah to take him to Jakarta so he could sell his stake in the *Pulau Mas* to his syndicate associate.'

'And what had he intended to do with the money once he had sold his stake in the ship?'

Dahlan smiled conspiratorially at Joe. 'I think he might have paid Frandono to release him.'

I had heard that this was not uncommon in Indonesia. If you had sufficient money you could literally buy your release, no matter what the crime. I had also heard that prisoners in Batam jail paid to go out on weekends to clubs and KTV bars! I smiled ironically to myself when I remembered remarking to Frandono that he had a very 'enlightened' penal code at his prison.

I was not convinced by Dahlan, nor did I entirely trust him. Wong was undoubtedly what Dahlan had said he was – a syndicate boss who had operated gangs on Batam. Yet Wong's, and his colleague's, description of their arrest, the ransom demand, and the stealing of their personal belongings and valuables from the ship by the Navy seemed altogether more plausible than the Navy's entrapment operation. However, in court, it would have been a very effective rebuttal of Wong's *laughable* claim that the Navy itself had committed an act of piracy!

Over lunch, Joe and I discussed the interview and I confessed my doubts to him.

'While you were packing your recorder away,' Joe said, 'Dahlan told me that the case had been very successful.'

'What did he mean?' I asked, intrigued.

'He told me that he had managed to convince the court that the rightful owner of the *Pulau Mas* lived in Johor Bahru and that it should be returned to him.'

I was confused. 'But Dahlan said the ship was owned by Wong and two other syndicate bosses, one of whom lived in Johor.'

'Yes,' Joe smiled. 'But he didn't tell the court that.'

'So?'

Joe hesitated and then drew closer to me. 'I think Dahlan and Wong have struck a deal to sell the ship and then to split the money between themselves.' Joe leant back and watched me for a moment. 'Corruption, Bob!'

'Do you really believe that the Navy tricked Wong – or do you believe Wong's version, that they tried to extort money from him, but he couldn't pay?'

'What do you believe?' he asked.

'Wong's story,' I said resolutely.

Joe smiled and nodded.

'Christ, Joe! Your whole damn country's corrupt,' I said.

'Not all our fingers are the same length, Bob,' Joe replied, looking at me with a kind of inconsolable helplessness.

I spent much of the evening reviewing the recording, trying to detect in Dahlan's voice and Joe's translations anything I had misheard or not heard at all that might confirm our suspicions that Dahlan was in fact in league with Wong (as Frandono had been) and, furthermore, that the 'success' of the case could just as likely involve the judiciary in Wong's trial. How did Dahlan manage to convince the judges that the *Pulau Mas*'s legitimate owner lived in Malaysia when the Navy Intelligence already knew via their informer that the ship was Wong's pirate HQ and was share-owned between himself and two other syndicate pirates? Dahlan's impressively duplicitous manner, combined with Wong's potentially very profitable 'estate' and the judiciary's apparent openness to negotiation, strongly suggested a conspiracy.

As I lay on my bed a lizard suddenly appeared on the ceiling, and I watched it dart with a kind of rapid, furtive precision from one corner of the room to another. Then, as if by magic, it disappeared down some almost invisible crevice in the wall. It seemed to epitomise the character of Indonesia – stealthy, opportunistic, mesmeric.

I made another friend in Nagoya – Taman. He was twenty-seven years old and owned a small kiosk opposite a massage parlour. His kiosk sold beer and spirits, soft drinks, cigarettes, toothbrushes, snacks, mosquito-repellent candles, coffee and soap. The kiosk was also Taman's home. He earned approximately 400,000Rp each week out of which he had to buy his stock. He, his sister and brother were originally from Jakarta, but family circumstances had changed and their education had been abruptly curtailed (their parents could no longer afford to send them to school). Like so many others, they had come to Batam to find work. Comparatively, they had been successful – his brother ran a taxi, his sister worked in a factory, and Taman owned his kiosk. But Taman, for all his irrepressible cheeriness, was a deeply disenchanted and melancholy figure.

'Do you know, Mr Bob,' he said one morning as he ate his breakfast of noodles and water, 'I always used to come top in English at school. My teacher was very proud of me,' he added with a rueful smile.

I asked him if he had a girlfriend.

'Oh, yes. But she lives on another island. When I can afford to speak to her I phone. We would like to get married, but . . .' He shrugged his shoulders. 'I cannot earn enough money to pay for a house for us.'

'What do you reckon your future is, Taman?' I asked, almost anticipating the answer.

'I live from day to day, Mr Bob. I eat, I wash, I run my kiosk, and I am happy to sit with you and talk and practise my English. Have you heard of Ratu Adil?'

I said I hadn't.

'Ratu Adil is a god – neither male nor female. You hear of this god in Java. Some say Ratu Adil will save Indonesia. Then all the people will be happy again.'

'Do you think the Indonesian people are sad?'

'Yes, I think they are sad, Mr Bob. The little people like myself. And we are so many in Indonesia.'

I would wake Taman every morning at seven o'clock and help him prepare his kiosk. Some mornings he found it difficult to get up. His kiosk was near a busy crossroads and the traffic never stopped. Then there were the rats and the mosquitoes. He had already contracted malaria. Some mornings I wondered if I would find him dead, wrapped in his thin blanket, clutching his crossword puzzle book that he loved so much.

Joe arrived early at the Valhollo that morning and we ate pastries and coffee. I told him how impressed I was by his punctuality.

'Rini told me I must not be late any more,' Joe smiled with a cowed look. He paused. 'What do you think marriage is about, Bob?'

'You've only been married a couple of years. Why are you asking that?'

'I am a Muslim; you are a Christian. But we are both men married to women.'

I laughed. 'Perhaps marriage is about always having an alibi!'

At that point, his mobile phone rang. It was his contact at the *Sijori Pos* office in Tanjung Pinang. They were phoning to confirm that Navy Intelligence would see us tomorrow afternoon.

'Things are moving ahead quickly for us. This is good news,' Joe said. 'But I think we should draft some questions on paper first. Then we can give them to the Navy so they can prepare for us.'

I accepted Joe's suggestion and together we wrote a list of very anodyne questions, none of which I was particularly interested in asking. The Navy Intelligence, I assumed, knew about the Wong case, and I wanted to put to them some potentially embarrassing questions about their role in his capture, as well as general allegations that the Navy colluded in piracy. However, I kept this to myself. I had no intention of compromising or endangering Joe. He had come to trust in my integrity and I think this alone had convinced him that he could reveal information to me without fear of my being indiscreet with its use.

As we figured the questions out, Joe suddenly looked up and called to a friend. 'Goman!' I looked round to see a rather suave man dressed in slacks and a cotton jacket with a white V-neck jumper. He had a small, well-trimmed moustache and his physique was lithe and athletic. He carried a briefcase. Joe whispered to me, 'Goman will tell you everything about piracy!'

I was introduced and suggested Goman joined us for coffee. He said that he had several meetings to go to, but could spend half an hour with us. Goman was the headman of Belakang Padang island, off the north-west coast of Batam, where Dony, Joe and I had gone two years before on Dony's fateful PBN election campaign (Dony lost his deposit when the PBN collected only 2 per cent of the votes). Goman was a self-taught surveyor for sunken treasure ships, and he was currently negotiating with the various government agencies and a Swedish diving firm to explore a wreck. Initial exploratory dives and research suggested that the wreck's cargo – bullion and Ming vases – was worth conservatively $6million (US). He was intrigued by my own story and told me that his island had been the place from where one of Wong's gangs had operated.

'Are there still active pirates on the island?'

Goman smiled coyly. 'I do not know . . . Perhaps. But I have heard nothing.'

'Do you know any pirates, active or otherwise?'

'Yes,' Goman said. 'I know two.'

'Would it be possible for me to speak with them?' My excitement was barely containable.

'Perhaps. But I must phone them first. He punched in the number on the mobile phone of one of the pirates, but there was no answer. Nor was there an answer from the second.

'I think the second guy will phone back when he has a chance. His name is Kelin; it's his codename. It means "black".'

'Codename?'

'Yes. All pirates have codenames. For security, you understand?'

Joe laughed. 'Goman is *his* codename!' Goman gave Joe a surreptitious smile.

'Do you know Wong?' I asked.

'Yes,' Goman nodded. 'He operated a gang from my village. A bad man, and very dangerous.'

'Then you'll know,' I continued, 'that Wong was convicted of being a syndicate boss and he and one of his gangs were sent to prison. What happened? There was an informer . . .'

Joe was listening intently, and I switched on my tape-recorder.

'Wong got greedy. He cheated one of the gangs out of a lot of money. And he talked too much. He became arrogant and boastful about his successes and taunted the police and Navy. He made enemies.'

'So what is the structure – if there is one – of a pirate syndicate?'

Goman took my notebook and pen and turned to a clean page. In one circle he entered the words 'Mafia boss.'

'This is the man who buys ships and cargoes from the pirates' syndicate boss, like Wong. Wong's boss was in Hong Kong. There are others in Malaysia, Jakarta and the Philippines. They never come to Batam but [here Goman drew another circle and entered 'representative'] they send a representative to negotiate with the syndicate boss in the country of operation, in this case Batam. When they meet, in a hotel perhaps, they have already targeted a ship to be hijacked. They will know its flag, route, cargo, crew. They may even at this point have a mole on board to keep them in touch with the ship's passage. The basis of the deal is then negotiated. If a ship and its cargo are worth, say, $10 million (US) on the open market, on the black market it will fetch half that amount. The $5 million (US) would be split three-fifths to the syndicate boss and two-fifths to the gang. Some money is then put up front by the representative, and the balance paid when the ship and cargo are delivered to the Mafia.'

'And before the ship's delivered to the Mafia, it has already been reflagged, re-registered and repainted. An entirely new ship. A phantom ship.'

'Yes,' said Goman. 'The Mafia either sell it on the open market or use it as a phantom ship to steal more cargo from unsuspecting shipping firms.'

'What about the pirate gangs themselves? How are they structured?'

Goman drew fives lines emanating from the circle representing the syndicate boss – the Mr Wong. 'There are usually five gangs, consisting of five to eight pirates. Each gang will be in a different village and each will be unknown to the other . . .'

'Why is that?' I asked.

'Security. If one gang is busted, they won't be able to name the other gangs in the syndicate.'

With the illustration of the pirate syndicate's structure in my notebook, I was keen to find out from Goman how the pirates actually attacked a ship.

'They use a *pancung*, a traditional fishing boat. Have you seen one?' he asked, preparing to draw one in my book.

'Yes. I know the type of boat.'

'They attack at night, around seven or eight in a *pancung*. They are masked and carry *parangs* – long knives.'

'Do they use guns, Goman?' I asked. 'I've heard that they occasionally do.'

'Not the pirates I know. They tell me that the *parang* is a more frightening weapon. Besides, the sentence for carrying a gun here is twenty years in prison.'

'So do they attack the boat from the stern or the side?'

'The boat has two engines, 40 or 60hp. They drive the boat into the side of the ship, and a vacuum is created. The *pancung* sticks to the side of the vessel. This is the most dangerous time. If the ship rolls heavily, it can turn the *pancung* over. They have to be quick, stealthy.'

'So how do they get on board?'

'They use a *satang*, a pole with a hook on the end. If the pole doesn't reach, they tie another pole to it. Once the pole is hooked on to the side of the ship, the gang climbs up. Two men stay in the boat.'

'As easy as that?' I smiled with astonishment.

'Yes,' said Goman. 'But you must remember that they are out at sea, and not only do they have the waves to contend with but also the turbulence from the ship.'

'So once they're on board, they attack the crew and steal the money from the safe, even sometimes, the ship itself.'

'Yes. It's a fast operation. They will know where the safe is and how much money is in it. Within half an hour or so, they're back in the *pancung* and gone.'

Goman looked at his watch and politely excused himself. He assured me that he would phone Kelin and try to arrange a meeting for me. Before he left, he gave Joe Kelin's number.

After Goman had gone, I turned to Joe. 'I was watching his face while he was talking to us – he was talking from experience.'

'Maybe you're right, Bob,' Joe smiled enigmatically.

I had another awful night at my hotel and barely slept. The air-conditioning unit started to malfunction and spat cold water over my bed. This in turn enlivened the mosquitoes. I dosed myself with the last of my duty-free whisky and poured some over my legs in the hope it would either repel the mosquitoes or send them whizzing off in a drunken stupor. By 5 a.m. I decided to pack and check out. I had a shower (only cold water) and the shower-rose fell off and hit my foot.

The toilet seat broke as I tried to ease my bilious stomach. Then, taking my clothes from the wardrobe, the doors fell off their hinges. In a rage I kicked over the chair, threw all my belongings into my bag and marched down to reception and thumped the desk. In a back room, the boy on night duty rose from his mattress on the floor and looked bleary-eyed at me.

'Mr Bob?' he said, looking sleepy and apprehensive.

'I'm checking out,' I told him. 'Can you make my bill out?'

He immediately rang his boss, the woman I had met when I first arrived at the hotel. He explained to her that I was checking out, but he was plainly unsure how much I still owed. He handed me the phone.

'Is there something the matter, Bob?' the woman asked.

I listed all the problems with the room and politely told her I was extremely unhappy with the situation.

'Oh,' she said, 'these Indonesian workers are very bad. That is the trouble.'

'It's your hotel,' I said angrily. 'It's your responsibility. Don't blame the workers.'

Within ten minutes she was at the desk, fawning over me with sycophantic apologies. Feeling utter contempt for her, I nearly walked out without paying the account, but I knew that might cause trouble for me. So reluctantly I settled the outstanding amount and left.

Slinging my bags over my shoulder I walked over to Krishna's café. It was six o'clock and they had just opened. I asked for a Kopi cosun, a rich black Indonesian coffee. It was a fillip to my spirits after the Bukit Nagoya Hotel. I had two hours before Joe and I were due to meet and catch the ferry to Tanjung Pinang, so I decided to read through my notes from the meeting with Goman. What puzzled me was why Goman revealed so much information to me, and without a request for anonymity; nor had he asked me to invent a fictitious name for his village, Belakang Padang, which, I had told him, I intended to visit again. Perhaps now that Goman had found 'respectability' in his new career as a surveyor for shipwrecks, plundering antiquity was a less dangerous and much more rewarding occupation than robbing ships. He also had a wife and two young daughters. And now with

Wong in prison, the stranglehold Wong had obviously had over Goman's village had gone. If piracy still operated from there (and I was sure it did) it was now just part of the 'village economy', and not Mafia-organised.

By eleven o'clock Joe and I were on the ferry from Telaga Punggur to Tanjung Pinang. The boat was small and cramped, and the seating frayed and damaged. But once out into the main channel, the ferry lifted its speed and a fresh sea breeze filled the cabin. It was an hour's journey, and I spent most of the time gazing at the islands we passed. If the continental shelf of Indonesia were raised out of the water, as a continuous land mass it would stretch from north Malaysia almost to Australia. It was vast, even as an archipelago. And it was a country of extraordinary contrasts and diversities. We had left Batam with its industrial park of small hi-tech industries and its modern complex housing estates, and here on the islands I could see ancient ways of life – the *kampongs* and *kelangs*, the fishing methods that had not changed in centuries, the boats hand-crafted from local wood, the villages built in traditional style, the evolving coral reefs, and a sky that seemed to have neither weather nor seasons, but to lie in a timeless zone across an equatorial stasis.

When we landed at Tanjung Pinang, Joe phoned his friend at the *Sijori Pos* office. I can't remember her name, but she arrived on a motorbike and had lunch with us. She was unattractively thin, with a sharp stare, and had powdered her face white. She spent much of lunchtime arguing with her boyfriend on her phone. Had it not been for Joe's amiableness towards her, I felt sure she would have left us in the lurch. As it was, he persisted in encouraging her to confirm the arrangements with the Navy, and finally we got a definite time for our meeting – three o'clock. Joe decided we should go to the newspaper's office and wait there. We took a small minibus (public transport) to the office, a rather unprepossessing concrete building with a large sign outside. Tanjung Pinang was like Batam centre – chaotic, dilapidated, impoverished. Its residential complexes reminded me of the dourness of Eastern European 'collectivist' architecture. But the sunshine and warmth always seemed to redeem the worst of it, even the slums.

While Joe sat in reception and read the newspapers, I went out to take some photographs. After taking some general shots of the main street, I walked up an alley. I had heard someone playing a guitar and the sound of children laughing. In a small, dusty square of depressing slums, I discovered them. The children, their mother and the young man with the guitar giggled with delight as they posed for me. Then I heard a yelping, but I could see no animal. The yelping occurred again, this time more distressed and pathetic. It came from a basket pannier on a motorbike, the sort used for carrying durian fruit. I walked over to it and saw something struggling in a sack.

'Dog,' said a man who suddenly appeared at my side holding a sharp knife. His son stood beside him. They lifted the sack from the pannier and dropped it on the ground. Tying a piece of rope firmly round its neck they then threaded the rope through a chain and tied the dog to a pole. Before cutting away the sack, the man kicked it repeatedly to ensure that there was as little life as possible left in the animal. He then started cutting the sacking away, first off its body, next from its head. The dog lay exhausted on the ground, only once lifting its head slowly in the direction of its persecutors. Its eyes were almost lifeless, with that expressionless, serene horror that is often seen at the point of death. The man kicked it again, and its head sank unprotestingly to the ground.

'It's suffering,' I implored the boy. 'It needs water.'

The boy smiled at me and nodded. 'We eat it.'

I offered to kill the dog myself, just to put it out of its misery. But the man shook his head. He kicked the dog again, and I watched the white of its eyes effloresce, like sticky white petals enclosing the pupils. The man knelt down, lifted the dog's head and started slowly carving at its neck as if slicing an uncooperative loaf of bread. The dog tried to yelp and squirm, but the knife had already penetrated the main artery, and a vomit of blood cascaded from its neck. Lifting the dog up by its hind-legs, the man shook the blood out of it. His son beamed at me. Tonight they would eat *nasi anjing* – dog rice.

When I got back to the *Sijori Pos* office, there was a flurry of activity. Joe had organised bikes to take us to the Navy Headquarters. Two journalists were coming with us. I went with Hussein, while Joe rode with the girl we'd met for lunch and who was still arguing with her boyfriend on her phone. It was a ten-minute ride, and as we rode into the compound our identities were cursorily checked. I offered my bag with the recording equipment for inspection, but they were not in the least bit interested.

The headquarters was an impressive building, and had obviously not been built by the Indonesians. It was colonial in style, with a large airy entrance hall adorned with photographs and paintings of ships and a large portrait of Britannia. We were politely shown into a spacious waiting-room, where I whispered to Joe, 'Who are we meant to be meeting?'

Joe looked earnestly at me. 'All the chiefs – the Head of Intelligence, Colonel Sutanto . . . By the way, Bob, have you got the questions we wrote out? I think we should give them to the Navy now.'

'Sorry, Joe. I left them at the hotel.' I had no intention of allowing them to prepare their answers, nor did I wish to give them any indication as to the precise matters I wanted to discuss. Goman had told me that he knew of incidences of the Navy being corrupted by pirates for 'protection', and I wanted to put this to them in the context of larger allegations of the Indonesian Navy's collusion in piracy. I didn't expect to receive an understanding or cooperative response.

Half an hour later we were invited into another office where our identities were scrupulously checked. They took a photocopy of the receipt I had for my passport that was at the hotel, then phoned the hotel to check that I was resident there and my room number. It disturbed me. I understood that they had to verify my identity, but all the same it made me feel very vulnerable. Finally we were shown into a large meeting room with a video projector and screen. Five senior Navy officers, including Sutanto, sat opposite us. It struck me immediately that this meeting was going to be conducted by them – not an interview, but a PR exercise. The *Pos* journalists sat humbly and respectfully at the end of the table. Lieutenant Commander Edwin was the Navy's chief spokesman and he opened the meeting by welcoming me and the other journalists and introducing his fellow officers. The proceeding started with a video show to illustrate their anti-piracy techniques and strategy. It opened with a lengthy and inaudible interview with a Singaporean Navy officer who talked about Singaporean–Indonesian joint patrols in the Phillip Strait and how together they combated sea piracy. In front of me was the Navy's own list of pirate attacks on ships in the year 2000 – over seventy of them! As the video progressed with a simulated pirate attack on a ship (in broad daylight with the pirates yelling and shouting as they approached their target!), we saw the pirates shimmy up the ship's side and overwhelm the crew. Hadn't the crew seen or heard them coming? But rescue was near at hand – the Navy's anti-piracy unit (their version of the Seals) had apparently got wind of the attack (how?) and looking more like pirates themselves than the pirates they confronted, had the situation quickly under control once on board the beleaguered ship. Like Joe, I found the whole thing totally implausible. After that, I was invited to put questions to the Navy.

'Consistently over the past ten years there have been more pirate attacks in Indonesian waters than anywhere else in the world. Do you have an explanation as to why this is so?' I asked Edwin.

He smiled and nodded, as if he had anticipated this question and had a ready answer. 'The International Maritime Bureau put these figures out, but there's a degree of exaggeration . . .'

'Exaggeration? I don't think they've invented their data.'

'Of course not. But you must distinguish between sea robbery and the wholesale pirating of ships. In the latter case, the incidents have declined considerably.' He seemed rather smug about this.

'But over seventy attacks on ships in the year 2000 isn't by any standards a good track record,' I said.

'Most of those attacks were just cases of sea robbery,' he shrugged almost complacently. 'Now more ships are using ship-loc – at least most tankers are these days – and as a result our detection of pirated ships has improved considerably.' He referred me to an illustration of how the Navy had intercepted pirates on the MT *Seylang* last year that had been tracked on ship-loc.

(Ship-loc, an easily-fitted onboard radar system, emits signals to a central monitoring unit in Kuala Lumpur and elsewhere and enables ships' courses to be continuously tracked throughout their voyage.)

Two weeks later, on my return to Singapore, I happened to meet two Malay engineers who had been advising the Indonesian Navy on how ship-loc worked. According to them, a recently hijacked ship carrying this equipment was 'lost' by the Navy even though they were given the exact coordinates of the ship's position. The Malay's explanation? 'Either total incompetence, or the Navy was in league with the pirates.'

I was eager to broach the subject of Wong's arrest and to see whether *their* description of his arrest corroborated the 'sting' story that Dahlan had told me. But as I began to put Wong's side of the story to the Navy (the ransom demand for $50,000 for the ship and the stealing of the crew's personal effects), Joe interrupted me.

'Bob, they know nothing of the Wong case!'

Of course they do, I thought to myself. They're the Intelligence section of the Navy! There was an uneasy silence, and I looked at Joe curiously. He was warning me to get off the subject of Wong and the controversy of his arrest. Reluctantly I resisted pursuing the question, but I thought I might be able to ask it in a slightly different context.

'I'm told that piracy in this region is organised by the Mafia. Is this true and if so how are you dealing with it?'

Erwin again had a pat answer – but this time it was rather more revealing of the Navy's attitude towards piracy. 'Yes, it's true. Ships are stolen by organised crime – by the Mafia – people like Mr Wong. They're very smart people. But,' he added with a note of contempt, 'they're not Indonesians. They're from China, Malaysia, Singapore, the Philippines. We don't want them here.'

I deduced from this that while to a degree they tolerated sea robbery (because it was committed by local people), they excoriated the 'foreigners' who were simply exploiting Indonesia's poverty, high unemployment and strategic geography. Furthermore, I suspected, the big money from pirating entire ships was ending up in the Mafia's coffers, and not in the collective rice bowl for all to share.

We ended the interview by talking about the vast area of sea that the Indonesian Navy had to police – an impossible task, and I was sympathetic.

'Bob,' Erwin implored, pointing at a wall-sized map of Indonesia behind me, 'we don't have the resources to cope with the amount of water around the many thousands of islands that make up our country. I hope you appreciate this and will tell the West.'

I rather liked Erwin. In subtle ways he had indicated to me that while the Navy accepted that sea robbery (*pencurian laut*) was endemic in Indonesia, ship piracy (*pembajakan laut*) was an embarrassment to them. And yet, as I had heard, there were at least two other syndicate gangs operating with impunity from Batam. This, Erwin emphatically told me, was a matter for the police, not the Navy.

A young subaltern served us sweet tea and we all gathered around for a group photograph. Erwin, I could tell, was pleased with how the PR exercise had gone, and he assured me that any further information I needed, I only had to call him.

I wanted to ask him in private about the widespread allegations that the Indonesian Navy were involved in piracy; also I wanted to know about their part in the Wong case. But Joe's earlier interruption suggested that I would be wise to leave these controversial matters alone – unless I was prepared to take the possible consequences. In Indonesia there are not just politics – there are the *politics* of politics, and it was for my own good that I understood this.

'That was very disappointing,' I said to Joe, as we left the building. 'It was just a PR exercise for the Navy. They don't imagine I'm that gullible, do they?'

'What did you expect?' Joe grinned. 'Anyway, you had your photo taken with Indonesian Navy Intelligence!'

'Why did you interrupt me when I started asking about the controversy over Wong's arrest? They knew about it.'

'Bob,' Joe smiled. 'Sometimes you walk on dangerous ground with your head in the sky.'

As we climbed on our bikes to return to the *Sijori Pos* offices, Joe told me that we had missed the five o'clock ferry back to Batam and would have to stay the night. I thought it an amusing irony that it had been the Navy of all people who had made us miss our boat. We found a reasonably priced hotel in the centre of town, cavernous and rather scruffy. Deciding to share a room, Joe threw one of the mattresses on the floor.

'That's your bed, Bob. I like to stretch out . . . and I snore heavily.'

Joe switched on the TV and found the MTV channel, which featured a Jakartan Blues band. He lit a cigarette, lay on the bed, and began to sing along with the band. His mercurial whining sounded like a muezzin's call to prayer. Within minutes he was spread-eagled across the bed and snoring heavily. The room had a balcony that overlooked a squalid array of Komplek housing and a few grim shops. It was dusk and timid lights were beginning to flicker on in doorways and houses. The smell of the day's garbage in the streets was beginning to ferment into a humid, heady cocktail, and scrawny, wild dogs were sniffing it with interest.

Joe suddenly woke and bellowed, 'My wife's not here, Bob. I think we must drink much beer tonight!'

We showered, went to a nearby food court and ordered several bottles of Tiger beer and some satay. A pretty girl was waiting on us and, as was customary, sat with us quietly filling our glasses as we drank. Joe was in buoyant mood and began discoursing on the essential qualities of smartness. He had mistaken a remark I'd made earlier about my having to look smarter when I went to meetings, and construed smartness to mean 'intelligence'. I put it down to the beer as he gabbled away incoherently in rhetorical flourishes that seemed as disconnected as his alcohol-fuelled brain. Finally I stopped him and told him I was referring to my clothes, not intelligence.

Joe shook his head. 'Your language is very strange – one word has two meanings. "Smart." Very strange!'

Joe began to hum and then slowly broke into song. It was an Indonesian love song and the girl at the table began to swoon.

'It is a song of unrequited love, Bob,' Joe smiled. 'A young man and a young woman fall in love, but are eventually separated. Years later, both married with children, they meet again and their love is rekindled. They want each other, but know it is too late. Their parting is sorrowful and full of tears . . .'

'Recollection of love past . . . ever was romance!' I said, trying to remember who I was quoting – or misquoting.

'I have loved many women, Bob. And I remember them all as I loved them,' Joe said, savouring his sense of romantic melancholy.

'You're just an old romantic bastard, aren't you?' We laughed.

'You have a saying in the West, don't you, that money can't buy everything – it cannot buy love,' Joe said. 'But here we say, money can't buy everything, but everything can be bought with money.'

'Does that include love as well?'

He hesitated. 'Yes.'

But there was a sadness in his reply that I understood as a kind of regret, that money had corrupted everything in this country, where even love was a purchasable commodity.

Corruption profaned Joe's romantic sensibilities; likewise it strengthened his political conviction. Yet the reality of money in Indonesia, and the belief that it could buy everything, had more visible credence in the pinched, destitute and yearning faces of his fellow countrymen than it had in Joe's principled, but naïve aspirations.

Next morning we caught an early ferry back to Batam. Joe went home to his family, and promised to phone Goman about meeting his pirate friend Kelin. We agreed that we should make a trip to Belakang Padang Island as soon as possible; Goman had told us about a café there where the pirates used to meet. Perhaps some still did. In any case, I wanted photographs of the village. On my way back to the hotel I stopped at Taman's kiosk for a chat and a beer. He had just phoned his girlfriend and was feeling ecstatically happy. As I listened to him talking about her, a man approached and bought some cigarettes. Instead of moving off, he sat down, took out a cigarette and gazed at me. He had a dour, almost malevolent face, and he seemed to be listening intently to our discussion. Irritated, I stared back at him until, embarrassed, he got up and left.

'Who was he?' I asked Taman.

'I don't know.'

'Why was he staring at me?'

'Indonesian people sometimes do that to foreigners. They mean no offence.'

I was not convinced by Taman's explanation. Another wave of paranoia swept through me, and for the rest of the afternoon I felt as if I was being watched. Taman had told me that he believed there were no secret police in Indonesia, but I found that inconceivable. Every country has its internal security. So was I being followed? I didn't care to put that question to the next man I found staring at me across some tables in a café. I went back to my hotel, packed and checked out. That evening I booked into the Sentosa Hotel in the backstreets of Nagoya. A little way down the drive to the hotel was Megawatti's PDI-P Headquarters with its distinctive red-and-black bull ensign crossed with spears dripping with blood. Opposite was a meat-packaging factory where, every morning, I saw hundreds of dead chickens laid out on the street wrapped in cellophane. It struck me as an oddly apt metaphor for Indonesia: a political tyranny overseeing its plucked and trussed subjects.

That evening I walked for a mile or two to find a restaurant, well away from my normal area of dining. If anyone was following me, I was sure they would give up after the first mile. The restaurant I decided upon was well lit and on a main street, and there were plenty of people eating there. I felt less conspicuous.

After the dog incident on Bintan Island I had vowed to become a committed vegan, if only for the rest of my stay in Indonesia.

While I was eating mixed vegetables and rice, Jasmine joined me. She was in her twenties, attractive and dressed in Western-style clothes. Jasmine introduced herself by placing a white leather handbag and mobile phone on my table. I was glad of her company. She was a welcome distraction from my paranoia.

'Have you no girlfriend?' she asked.

'As you can see, I'm on my own.'

She laughed with a gaucheness that reduced her to about twelve years old. I could sense that she was embarrassed, not least because – though I knew she was a prostitute – I responded to her awkward seductiveness with polite indifference.

'Do you want a drink?' I asked.

'Lemon tea,' she said, now looking somewhat agitated since I wasn't immediately booking her for the night.

When the lemon tea came, she was already glancing at her phone to see if there were any messages for her.

'Do you want a woman tonight?' she asked, curling her mouth up into a confidential whisper.

'I don't like sharing my bed with a stranger. Besides, I don't sleep well and I snore.'

She laughed again, perhaps thinking that I would succumb eventually. But I wanted to talk to her. 'Do you come from Batam?' I asked.

'From Jakarta. I went to university there, but . . .' she shrugged and smiled with that familiar defeated smile, 'my father had a stroke, and my mother is just a washerwoman.'

'So they couldn't afford to keep you at university. Is that right?'

'Yes. Now I have to look after my family and pay my father's hospital bills.'

Jasmine had been in her first year of university studying English when her father had fallen sick. Now she was a prostitute in Batam.

'How much money do you send back to your parents?'

'It depends on how much I can earn. Sometimes half a million rupiah a week, but usually less.'

Jasmine's mobile began to ring. Answering it, she spoke in perfect English to 'Mike', presumably one of her punters. He wanted her at his hotel – now. Jasmine seemed in a dilemma. I could sense that she didn't like Mike and that she hoped I would have her instead. My pity for her left me amorously flaccid. I gave her some money because I enjoyed talking with her. As she hopped on a motorbike taxi to go to Mike, I saw a good woman, possessed of her own mind, but not of her own body. Most tragically, not of her own life.

I had forgotten just how impoverished the island of Belakang Padang was. As Joe and I walked along the stilted boardwalk, I looked across at the shacks that verged on the sea. A woman was putting clothes out to dry on a veranda, and directly below was a huge pile of garbage. This was the village's refuse tip, a breeding ground for rats, mosquitoes and God knows what else. Raw sewage lay in sour, thick puddles around the stilted buildings. There could be no real life expectancy here, only the certainty of sickness and disease. We walked through a myriad of dark, narrow alleyways, taking care not to step on one of the countless broken planks. We were searching for the Café Eni, the place where pirates met to drink coffee and plan their attacks.

A girl's face smiling through a glass food-stand caught my attention. Above her was a sign: 'Eni, Belakang Padang.' It was dimly lit, scruffy with Formica tables and plastic chairs. The walls were adorned with old posters advertising coffee and cigarettes.

I ordered drinks and Joe and I sat down. An old, gnarled man was sitting opposite us, smoking a cigarette and drinking tea. He smiled, his decayed teeth appearing oddly white against his black, windburnt face. When the girl brought our drinks, I scribbled *'pembajakan laut'* (sea pirate) in my notebook and discreetly showed it to her. She giggled nervously, shook her head and went off to tell her mother. The old man was craning his neck to see what I was writing.

'Why don't we ask the old man?' I said to Joe.

'I think you must be careful, Bob.'

I persuaded Joe to translate for me. Did the old man know of any pirates in the village?

'I am only the ferryman to Sambu island,' he grinned, and flicked his cigarette ash on the floor. 'Only the ferryman . . .'

But I could detect in his face that he knew precisely what I was asking.

'I'm told pirates meet – or used to meet – in this café,' I said to him.

'Maybe,' he replied.

'You know about piracy here, don't you?'

He grinned at Joe. 'The night work!'

'The night work?'

Joe looked at me and smiled conspiratorially. 'The night work – piracy.'

'Are there any pirates in the village we could talk to?'

'I know nothing,' he said. 'I am only the ferryman to Sambu.'

At a table near us, two young men sat, obviously interested in our conversation. I decided to go and talk to them. *'Selamat sore,'* I said, and watched them laugh at my mispronunciation of 'Good afternoon.' After correcting me, I sat down with them and opened my notebook and began to draw a pirate attack on a ship. I was becoming quite practised at it and they immediately cottoned on.

'Pembajak!'

'Yes,' I said. 'Pirate!'

'Here? Belakang Padang?'

Like the old man they smiled shiftily and declared they didn't know. I drew more detail on the picture, this time including a *satang*. '*Satang*?' I mimicked the motion of hooking the *satang* onto the side of a ship. They looked at it with instant recognition.

'*Satang*.' One of them said. Then he shrugged his shoulders doubtfully. 'No, no – anchor . . . *jangkar*!'

He drew an illustration of a homemade anchor, a shaft of wood to which was strapped a stone, and at its point three curved metal hooks. It was an improvised grappling hook. Then he mimicked hurling the 'anchor' tied to a rope onto the side of a ship. Like Goman, this man, I felt, was almost reliving the experience, and I knew I was talking with someone who had been involved in piracy. He seemed fascinated that I had the detail right, especially regarding the modus operandi of attack.

'That is how it is done,' he said, almost jubilantly.

'And the *pancung*?'

'Yes. Maybe two, three *pancungs*,' he answered, numbering the boats with his fingers.

'*Parang*?'

'Yes,' he said again. '*Parang*.' And he imitated putting the knife to the throat of the ship's captain, then laughed.

But I could sense that he felt he was revealing too much and was becoming nervous. 'I must go back to work now,' he said.

As he stood up, he whispered: 'MT *Paula*. Off Sumatra last month.' I figured out that he was telling me this ship had been pirated. I thought it curious that the Indonesian Navy had claimed no knowledge of any attacks on ships this year.

Thanking him, Joe and I left.

'This place is still active with pirates. I'm sure of it,' I said to Joe as we walked back to the ferry. Coincidentally, Goman was returning from Batam with his daughter. We chatted for a few moments, and I took a photograph of them. Goman told me that he had been in touch with Kelin, and he was prepared to talk. He would phone Joe soon.

As we boarded the ferry, Joe turned to me, and whispered: 'I think Goman's the representative of the pirates here.' I was certain of it too.

Leaving Belakang Padang I could see Singapore in the hazy distance, only about three miles away. Between this island and Singapore lay the Phillip Strait, where hundreds of ships were passing through. *Night work*! The island was ideally located for running piracy operations. Why hadn't I investigated this island the last time I had been in Batam? I wondered if Kelin could tell me more . . .

Until Kelin phoned there was little I could do, and it was frustrating. I went back to my hotel room at the Sentosa to listen to the tape recordings I had made. But the room was depressing. Cigarette burns on the carpet and furniture, torn chairs, and a view of the shantytown on the hill – this was hardly the class of hotel it claimed to be in its brochure. Its only luxury was a swimming-pool. I went out to chat with Taman at his kiosk. It was past ten o'clock, and Taman had his tilly lamp burning brightly on a hook. The mosquitoes were as frenetic as ever and a family of rats were playing on the wasteground behind the kiosk. Mr Ramal, who owned the 'traditional' Thai massage parlour opposite the kiosk, was there; also Sulayman, a motorbike taxi driver. A game of dominoes was in progress, and the pieces were being furiously slammed down on the board as the game reached its climax. I watched as Sulayman jubilantly threw down a matching six and swept up the stake money.

'Heh, Mr Bob! Let me steal some money from you!' he said, his beaming eyes flashing in the gaslight. He did – 100,000 Rp.

'You want to go anywhere tomorrow?' he asked. 'I take you.'

I had thought of having a day off while Joe and I waited for Kelin to get in touch, and had heard of a small fishing village, Nongsa, on the north-east coast, near *kampong* Melayu.

'Very peaceful there,' Taman said. Sulayman agreed to take me.

I gave Taman some money to make up for his losses and went off to meet Mr Hanafi, who owned a small 'tented' café near the Sari Jaya hotel. He was in his fifties and constantly complained of lack of sleep. His bed was in a corner of the café, which closed at 4 a.m. 'I think I must take one night at a hotel . . . I am so tired.' His watery, pale eyes drooped listlessly, and his body seemed racked with cramps and tiredness. He talked in an endless, incomprehensible, patois drawl, but I nodded and smiled all the same. The irony was that Hanafi was such excellent soporific company, especially since I hadn't been sleeping particularly well recently. After a couple of beers and an hour of Hanafi's droning, I felt very comfortably mellow.

As I walked back past the luxury Nagoya hotel, out of the darkness appeared an attractive woman in a long, silken dress. 'Hello, Mister,' she said in *basso profundo* as I caught her eye. 'She' was a transvestite. A few metres away, a group of workmen, on scaffolding, were watching. 'Chicky-chicky! Cockledoodle-doo!' they laughed.

The ride to Nongsa was wonderful, and it was good to be out in the country again. Arriving at the village, three-quarters of an hour later, I could understand what Taman had said about it being peaceful. The village was on the beach surrounded by tall palm trees. There were just a few motley wooden houses, a couple of cafés, both with shaded dining areas on stilted promontories, and ducks waddling among the surf and naked kids leaping into the waves. A little way out to sea was Lady Island, festooned with radar antennae for the shipping in the Phillip Strait. It was lunchtime and I had a beer and *udang* (prawns) cooked in oil and garlic. They were delicious, and for the first time in almost three weeks I began to relax and enjoy Batam. As I sat there enjoying the cool sea breeze, I was joined by two young men who had stopped for a drink while sailing back to the marina, where they worked, a mile or so further up the coast. They were curious to know what I was doing in Batam since, as one said, I didn't look like a 'typical' tourist (I think he was being polite about my now terminally scruffy appearance).

'I'm investigating sea piracy,' I told them, feeling safely far enough away from the town.

'I go with the Navy sometimes on their patrols,' one said. 'They use me for information.'

Yet again, almost by pure chance, I had met someone who I thought could help me. 'Information?' I asked. 'What kind of information?'

'Where and when ships are most likely to be attacked. You see,' he continued, 'I know the water very well in the Strait, and my hearing at night is very good.'

He could see that I was puzzled by his mention of his hearing.

'I can hear the *pancung*, and know by its engine sound what it is doing – if it is approaching a ship, or is not where it should be.'

'You mean if the *pancung* and its crew are acting suspiciously?'

'Yes.'

He told me how once he had helped the Navy foil an attack by three *pancungs*. 'They were hiding in the darkness, their engines running very low, and they were waiting for our boat to pass. But I heard the ticking and the sound of the hulls in the waves. I told the captain and he steered our boat towards the *pancungs*, with the searchlight scanning the sea. But as we approached, they roared off at great speed, and I could just make out that the boats were full of men, all wearing masks . . .'

'Tell me,' I asked, 'do the Navy ever take bribes from the pirates?'

He was slightly taken aback by my question, and the direct way I had asked it.

'No, but it has happened,' he replied. 'You see, so much is corrupt in Indonesia.'

I regretted this question immediately, since I could see that his answer (almost a confession) embarrassed him.

'There is corruption in my country too,' I said.

'But here,' he replied, 'it is everywhere.' He looked out mournfully to sea. 'You are right – the Navy are sometimes involved.'

Nongsa was beautiful, and it seemed to me a shame to be discussing Indonesia's endemic corruption here. I bought them drinks and changed the subject. We talked about their lives, their friends and families, and how they hoped one day they could go to 'England'.

I wanted a ride in a *pancung*. In fact, I wanted to go out into the shipping lanes. I had to convince myself that these boats were indeed the very ones used by pirates. So I wandered along the beach to where I'd noticed a fisherman working on his boat.

'*Pancung?*'

He looked up and smiled. '*Pancung.*'

I offered him a sizeable amount of money to take me out to sea, and before I could count out the notes, the boat was launched and his son was sitting in the bow. The *pancung* had a 60hp engine, and at first it measured the swell admirably, careening over the shore waves and wallowing in the pitching sea. There was a sharp breeze and, as we approached the shipping lanes, a combination of the ships' turbulence and large rogue waves started to make the *pancung* roll uncomfortably. With a twist of his wrist, the boatman opened the throttle and the boat leapt into its own masterful seaworthiness. We approached the stern of a large tanker, and though I was soaked with the bow spray, the *pancung* kept leaping forward, its stability now balanced in its sharp V-shaped keel. I realised that it would take immense daring and courage to approach the ship nearer than we were, but I was certain that the *pancung* could have gripped the ship's wake and – powered with another engine – locked itself into the ship's stern. The *pancung* is made from meranti, a hardwood that not only carves well, it is also immensely durable and, as I was later told, has a 'natural sense of buoyancy'. It was the perfect pirate boat. On our return we picked up the only two inhabitants of Lady Island, an old married couple.

Sulayman arrived early to collect me, so we sat in one of the cafés and had a drink. I told him about my adventure in the *pancung*, and how impressed I was by its manoeuvrability and robustness. Sulayman's father had been a fisherman in Java, and Sulayman could remember going out to sea with him as a small boy in the *pancung* and how it 'danced on the waves'. Sulayman told me he and his father had once seen the sea goddess Ny I-Roro-Kidul. She had warned them of an impending storm, and sure enough that evening a torrential wind blew up and the sea, as Sulayman said, 'seemed to climb into the sky'. Back in Nagoya, I gave him a large tip, and as he rode off, I heard him cry out: 'Sulayman!'

Opposite the Nagoya Hotel was a large Chinese café that made the best coffee in Batam. As I sat at a table writing up some notes, a woman joined me. She was rather rotund and had a chubby, angelic face. Spreading a newspaper over the table, she exclaimed, pointing at a picture: 'See this?' I looked up. She turned the newspaper round so I could see the picture. 'I was there . . . I saw the murder happen!'

I examined the picture which showed a group of policemen apparently examining the scene of the crime.

'Do you know how they killed the man?'

Bemused, I shook my head.

'He was throttled . . . and tickled!'

'Pardon? Did you say *tickled?*'

'Yes. As he was being throttled by one man, the other one tickled him!'

I burst out laughing. 'I've never heard of anyone being tickled to death!'

She didn't share my ghoulish sense of humour.

'When the police found him, his tongue was hanging down to his stomach!' She illustrated with her hand a two-foot-long tongue.

I wanted to roar with laughter, but the woman had obviously been deeply shocked by the murder.

'I'm Elizabeth,' she said. 'I'm a preacher.' She was also, she claimed, a faith healer.

'I had a friend come to me who was dying of cancer. Her stomach was riddled with it. The doctors said they could do nothing more for her. She was not a religious woman, but I told her to have faith – faith that she would get well. And do you know? She is alive to this day!'

'Where are you staying?' Elizabeth abruptly changed the subject.

'The Sentosa.'

She grimaced. 'A dirty place, full of criminals and prostitutes.' I rather shared her opinion. 'You must check out of it immediately and come and stay at my hotel. It is just over there.' I had in fact noticed it already, with it colourful Dutch-style façade. 'I have a nice clean room, with a window, if you wish.'

Elizabeth conveyed an autocratic maternalism, and perhaps had seen in me a soul in need of her guidance and succour. I agreed to take the room that afternoon. 'Good,' she said, and went back to her newspaper, mumbling at the picture, 'Terrible . . . terrible . . .'

I walked back to the Sentosa, packed and checked out. 'There is a message for you. Mr Juanda called.' The receptionist handed me a scribbled note from Joe. 'Bob – Urgent. Phone me.' I suspected it had something to do with our meeting with Kelin. At the phone shop opposite Taman's kiosk, I rang Joe on his mobile.

'Bob. Good news. Kelin is willing to talk to us. Ten o'clock tonight at Hotel 81. Let us meet beforehand.'

When I put the phone down, my forehead was dripping with sweat.

Suddenly I felt a huge surge of elation and exhaustion. For over two years I had been waiting for this moment – to come face to face with a pirate. Meeting Wong had set me on the trail to discover the truth behind piracy in the South China Sea, and now it appeared likely I was to hear it first-hand. His nickname was Kelin, but his real name was Ishmael. *Ishmael*!

I went to Krishna's restaurant for a beer. Krishna was there and greeted me with a flourish of smiles and handshaking.

'Bob, where have you been? I have not seen you for several days.'

He could see my excitement, and that I was sweating profusely. 'Are you not well? Have you a fever?' he enquired with troubled concern.

'Have you ever read Melville's *Moby Dick*, Krishna?'

He seemed convinced by the oddness of this question that I had indeed come down with a fever. 'Malaria!'

'No, no, Krishna,' I said. 'I'm not sick.'

He looked confused, but thought better of making me any more agitated than I appeared. 'Yes, I have read *Moby Dick*.'

'Can you remember the opening line?'

He thought for a moment. 'Call me Ishmael . . .'

'Yes! And guess what? I'm meeting a pirate tonight called Ishmael!'

Krishna shook his head despairingly. 'I tell you, Bob, this is all very dangerous. You must be careful . . . you must trust no one.'

I met Joe at the Valhollo at six and we went for dinner. Joe was as excited as I was. 'He said he wants to tell his story.'

'Do you believe him? I mean, do you believe he is a real pirate?'

'Yes, Bob,' Joe said emphatically. 'Ishmael is *real*.'

'Why couldn't we meet him earlier?' I asked Joe.

'He doesn't finish work until nine. He works on an oil platform.'

'So he's no longer a pirate?'

'He was a pirate for many years, but someone betrayed him and he was sent to prison. But he knows everything, Bob – *everything*!'

Joe's journalistic instincts were, in the event, to be proved absolutely correct. Ishmael did know everything . . .

Later we went round to Hotel 81 and sat in the restaurant drinking endless cups of coffee. Neither of us spoke, but we kept looking out of the panel window for sign of Ishmael.

'Will you recognise him?' I asked Joe.

He nodded his head. 'I will know him. Don't worry.'

In the lobby I could see two old Chinese men who had hired a couple of girls for the night. One of the girls was hugging a teddy bear. She could not have been older than sixteen. Tonight she would earn 200,000Rp for sleeping with a man old enough to be her grandfather. Two months ago (so it was reported in one of the local newspapers) a similar old Chinese man, on Viagra, died on top of a young girl.

Just after ten, a short, stocky man in an overcoat walked into the hotel. His face was black and grizzled, and his eyes hunted round the lobby. He stood there for a moment, then Joe sprang up. 'That's him!'

Joe went to meet him and I watched them shake hands. Ishmael smiled, but I could see that he looked tense. I was introduced to him. He had a fiercely engaging face, and a smile that lurked in the blackness of his complexion. His presence was compelling, and even as we sat down I could scarcely take my eyes off him. Ishmael was the *night work* – even his voice seemed to echo out of the darkness. I was transfixed, but also frightened by him.

Joe spoke with him for a while and I could see Ishmael relaxing gradually, although he never let his guard down once with me. Occasionally he glanced my way, and I could see that he did not trust me.

Eventually, Joe turned to me. 'Kelin wants to speak with me first, alone. We will go to a café.'

This disconcerted me, but I had no choice but to agree. There was still a chance, I thought, that Joe could persuade him to talk with me and that I could record our conversation. I was reassured by the fact that Kelin had earlier told Joe that he wanted to 'tell his story'. Whatever his reason for wishing to do this, I hoped it would make him finally reconsider our arrangement regarding the interview. But needless to say, I wasn't very happy with how things were turning out.

Joe and 'Kelin' Ishmael left, and I sat down on a large leather sofa and wished I had a whisky of equal size. They were away for over an hour and a half, and I eventually began to imagine all sorts of unfavourable outcomes. A man walked into the hotel, looking pathetic and disreputable.

'I have a doctor's note here,' he said, producing an illegible prescription, 'but I cannot afford the medicines. Please can you help me? I am sick.' This was a cleverer ruse than some of the other begging tactics I had come across, so I gave him some money. But he insisted I gave him more – his prescription would have to be repeated. I lost my patience with him and told him to go. Then a couple of Singaporean businessmen joined me and wanted to know my opinion of Singapore.

'You can't make Singapore any larger just by pursuing reclamation schemes,' I said, thinking about the Singaporean government's sand excavation schemes around the Indonesian islands, but failing to make myself clear.

They looked baffled. 'Please can you explain?' one asked.

'You're taking millions of tons of sand from around these islands and it's irreparably damaging the coral. Did you know that?'

Still puzzled, one asked: 'Perhaps you would like to join us for a drink at the KTV bar?'

I thanked them, but refused and walked outside to sit on a wall with an ornamental fountain and pond. I was beginning to despise the rich Singaporean men for their arrogance and naïvety. They liked Indonesia for one reason – it was cheap and easy to exploit. And they liked to form 'relationships' with the KTV girls because they couldn't tolerate their own wives.

Joe finally appeared with Ishmael. I noticed that Joe was looking concerned, and a little apprehensive. 'Let us sit down and talk,' Joe said quietly. And we went into the restaurant again. I looked at Ishmael. There was something uncompromising about his expression, and I suspected he was about to make some kind of demand. I was right.

'Ishmael says to me that since he is giving you something, he would like something in return . . .' said Joe, cagily.

Quid pro quo – money! 'How much is he asking for?'

Joe continued. 'He suggests you make him an offer.'

'But he's got to give me some indication of what he would be willing to accept.'

'You make an offer, Bob.'

'Tell him that whatever his wages are for one hour I will double it.'

Joe translated my offer; but it simply provoked a derisory smile from Ishmael.

'I take it he's asking for more money, Joe. Ask him how much.'

'He wants $500 (US) – and a guarantee of confidentiality.'

I was being held to ransom, and I didn't like it. If Ishmael wanted to tell his story, then I expected him to negotiate reasonably.

I turned to Joe. 'I haven't got that sort of money.'

'Then I will tell him that we will think about his demand.' And so he did. After which Ishmael got up and left on his motorbike.

Back at my hotel, Joe and I sat down to decide what to do about Ishmael. I respected Ishmael's request for confidentiality, and I wasn't averse to paying him a nominal amount. But I wasn't willing to be intimidated by him, nor, I felt, could I entirely trust him to give me the full story of his life as a pirate once I'd paid him. On the whole, I felt angry and let down. But Joe had a surprise for me.

'Bob? Why do you think I was away for so long with Ishmael?' He smiled.

'What are you not telling me, Joe?'

Joe helped himself to a bottle of beer with an almost self-congratulatory flourish.

'He told me his story – he told me everything! Remember,' he grinned, 'I am a good journalist.'

Ever since I had first met Joe, his journalistic guile and shrewdness had appealed to me. Behind his casual bonhomie was, in the best sense, a calculating artfulness. I could understand now why he had turned his interests to politics.

I set up my tape-recorder, and over the next hour Joe told me Ishmael's story.

Ishmael had been a pirate for more than ten years and his gang's area of operation had been the Phillip Strait, the narrow water between the island of Belakang Padang (where they lived and operated from) and Singapore. Sometimes he and his gang had worked with Mr Wong, stealing money from ships that Wong had targeted, or helping to set up the hijacking of a ship. More often, though, they operated alone. It was easy for them to attack the ships since every night over a hundred of them would pass through the

Strait, and the ones flying flags that suggested they had large sums of money on them (Ishmael preferred US dollars) were the ones targeted – Panamanian, Japanese, Russian, Chinese. Russian ships were especially favoured since they usually carried heroin or guns and had a great deal of money on board. Rarely did they attack Indonesian ships – 'the rupiah is worthless!'. The date of the ship's sailing was also important. Apparently, towards the end of the month most ships had large sums of money aboard, possibly because they were coming to the end of their voyage and the crew had to be paid.

Ishmael had been a seaman on merchant ships for over five years, and the knowledge that he had gained during that time was of immense value during attacks. He knew, for instance, precisely where the captain's room (which contained the safe) was. More generally, he could ascertain almost exactly the number of crew on any particular ship, and the times when it would be most vulnerable, usually when the guard was changing, which was every four hours.

Disguised in masks and carrying *parangs* (they never used guns), the pirate gang numbered seven – five climbing on board the ship, two steering the *pancung*. Their boat would always have two high-powered engines, one to steer the boat, the other to maintain its stability in the rough wake of a ship during an attack. For every attack, Ishmael bought new engines.

To board a ship they used the *satang*, or sometimes an improvised grappling hook. It was a highly dangerous manoeuvre, more so if, as sometimes happened, hot water was shot from the stern of the ship as a deterrent against pirate attack. Occasionally the *satang* – which could have three pirates climbing it at one time – would slide with the rolling of the ship and lose its grip, throwing the pirates into the sea. Rescued by the remaining gang in the *pancung*, the pirates would then make another attempt.

Once on board ship, they attacked the captain first by putting two *parangs* to his neck, one on either side. The attack would last for approximately twenty minutes. Sometimes the captain would be so frightened that he forgot the combination of the safe, in which case the pirates stole the safe and broke into it later.

Occasionally, however, no money was found on a ship. Then they would return to the *pancung* and attack another ship. In one night alone, Ishmael and his gang had attacked three ships. This was the maximum number of ships they ever attacked on a single night. Weather conditions were crucial to the attack – a rough sea on a moonless night was ideal.

During ten years of piracy, Ishmael and his gang had stolen a considerable amount of money (he wouldn't divulge exactly how much). After they divided a haul amongst themselves, a proportion was donated to the village. Effectively, this was bribe money to ensure the villagers' silence, though Ishmael liked to think of himself as a latter-day Robin Hood!

He had been a resourceful pirate. Once, while attacking a Russian ship, he had discovered infra-red night-sights. These he used on subsequent raids. 'Everything was green,' he said, describing what it looked like through the sights. 'The sea, the sky, the ships, all green.' They were invaluable also in spotting Navy patrol ships. Ishmael was contemptuous of the Navy – he thought them incompetent, even stupid. And they didn't have infra-red sights! The pirates' knowledge and experience of the sea was vastly superior. As well as knowing the configuration of the coral reefs in the Strait (where the ships were forced to slow down in the channel), they knew the geography of the coastlines, and every island where they could hide or escape from a pursuing Navy patrol.

Once, Ishmael and his gang came near to being caught when the alarm on a ship they were attacking was set off. Seizing the money, they made a hasty departure before the Navy patrol arrived to investigate. Next morning, while sitting in the Eni café having a coffee, and looking out across the sea to Singapore, Ishmael chuckled to himself when he read in *The Straits Times* that a ship the previous night had been attacked in the Phillip Strait and $20,000 (US) had been stolen! His amusement was short-lived, however. Ishmael soon received a phone call from Mr Wong in Singapore demanding to know where the other half of the money was. He had told Wong that only $10,000 was on the ship. Wong, who had set up the attack, knew precisely how much money had been on the ship – $20,000! After that, Ishmael went freelance.

And what did he do with all the money he stole? He enjoyed himself with his friends, spent it on women, sat in the café all day drinking, and shared it with the villagers . . .

As a chief pirate, Ishmael had become an important man in Belakang Padang. However, his notoriety soon attracted the attention of the police, notably after a series of complaints from Singapore about the rise in piracy in the Phillip Strait. Several times the Indonesian police tried to arrest Ishmael, but he was always too vigilant, either escaping down the trapdoor in his house and into his boat, or being given a 'safe-house' on another island. Or he and his gang changed their area of operation, usually to the Malacca Strait, where they had 'friends' to hide them.

But Ishmael's ten years of piracy were to end when one of his gang informed on him. The police had tortured him (by pulling his fingernails out!). Ishmael was arrested one morning at the Eni café, and would have faced the same treatment had he not paid the police 'not to hurt him'. Convicted on this 'witness's' testimony, Ishmael went to prison for one year. The court had hoped to send him to prison for nine years, but there was insufficient evidence to prove that Ishmael was a 'chief pirate'.

Why had Ishmael become a pirate? The prospect of making money. Ill-educated, poor, and unemployed, Ishmael, like the others in his gang, was an easy recruit into piracy. His only skill was seafaring – but combined with a good deal of daring and courage, he had the opportunity to make more money from one night's work than he could in a year as a ferryman or labourer. The economics of his situation, like that of the other pirates, were unarguable: he had the choice of a lifetime of abject poverty, or wealth through crime. As Ishmael had poignantly said, 'Is it a crime to wish not to be poor?' The distressing sight of Belakang Padang made me sympathetic.

Ishmael was now in his fifties, and felt he only had a few years left to him. By telling his story, he told Joe, he hoped it would discourage others from becoming pirates. Mostly he regretted the dissolute lifestyle he had had as a pirate, and the fact that for ten years he was nearly always on the run from the police. For all the money he had made, missing from his life was security, home life and peace. And he never made enough money to buy a decent house. But his wish to discourage others was naïve, as he must surely have known. There were other pirates actively operating from Belakang Padang, as well as from the numerous other islands off Batam and Bintan. And they were motivated by exactly the same reasons. Ishmael had at last found himself a good job – but for the many others, in his village and other villages, the two cruel options that had faced him when he had become a pirate, poverty or crime, were still inescapably there.

I had intended to take a flight to Sumatra to visit Mr Wong again, but I decided against it in the end. Would Wong tell me any more than he had already said at our first meeting? I doubted it. All that I would have asked him was who his Mafia contacts were in China – and it was highly unlikely that he would have divulged this information. In any case, I now knew how the syndicate operated, and about Wong's downfall. Besides, I secretly wanted Wong to remain in my imagination, as he had done over the two years I'd been investigating the story, as a mystery. The mystery of Mr Wong was the fascination I had with piracy.

I saw Joe once more before I left Batam. By now I was feeling very uneasy about staying any longer. Joe understood and sensitively encouraged me to think about going home. He knew the risks we had taken to get the story – but he was Indonesian, and as he had perceptively said to me: 'We Indonesians can read each other's faces – but your face is foreign to us.'

Our last day together was spent on the island, Belakang Padang. I had wanted to go back there because it gave me a true sense of what piracy in the South China Sea meant. Joe left me to sit on my own, looking out across the sea to Singapore and the Phillip Strait, where the majority of attacks happened. I sat where so many pirates from this village had probably also sat, gazing at the ships and the unattainable affluence of Singapore's skyline.

The sky was as I remembered it on my first visit to Indonesia – heavy and tropical, with a heat-haze shimmering across the sea, and the breeze almost temperate. Three miles or so separated me from a culture of wealth that relegated what was behind me almost into the

Stone Age. Between these two worlds, hundreds of ships sailed, oblivious to this huge disparity. Beside me a young girl washed her family's clothes in a tin bucket – the water was cold and the suds were a day or more old. In Singapore, her counterpart would be in school, neatly dressed in school uniform, learning English and technology. Someone had left a cart of eggs on the walkway – chickens' eggs, but they were small, and the shells were frail. Below me, fishermen were repairing an engine on a *pancung*. If it had been Ishmael, perhaps he would have been fitting a new engine in preparation for another attack. The village's poverty upset me, and I was angry with the Indonesian government for having no regard for the welfare and self-respect of its people. Piracy was a manifestation of this neglect, a wilful oversight – also by the various government agencies (police, Navy, Customs) who themselves stood to profit by it. Piracy summed up the culture of this country, where corruption was a sanctioned expedient of endemic crime, and to live beyond poverty required a sacrifice.

When I said goodbye to Joe at Sekupang on my return to Singapore, he took me aside. 'Bob, piracy is not a big story in Indonesia. It is just a way of life.'